Bev:

I hear that you
agree with me:
Sport rules!

Enjoy.

Alan

# A-Plus In *Disconnect*

*

## How Canadian Universities
## Dropped The Ball

Alan Watson

ISBN 978-1-4357-0950-8

# *Acknowledgments*

I was fortified by the support and assistance of a great many people. From the very get-go were a pair of curators, Jason Beck of the B.C. Sports Hall of Fame and Museum, and Ron Wellwood of the Roman Catholic Diocese in Nelson. Both opened up the files in their archives unflinchingly, in tune with my intent. Dozens and dozens of people gave me freely of their time, thoughts, views and news, when they had no need to, much less knew for certain who or what I was about, or what I might make of their contribution. My editors, Tony Allison, Darron Hargreaves and Steve Bareham, were a dream team for spit and polish. And at the end of the process, the people at Lulu couldn't have been more accommodating or professional. Only I am accountable for any missteps.

On a personal note, huge thanks must be given to the faction on the sidelines, comprised of understanding employers, and supportive friends and family. If not that big, no matter, still easily the most important group of all.

AW

# *Foreword*

*"The mastering of one's body is a training in the disciplining of self; the drive for excellence in athletic achievement carries over into the intellectual sphere. It is almost embarrassing to set down such truisms, were they not so foreign to the way in which our schools approach fitness training and athletic participation."*

- Report of the 1969 Task Force on Sport For Canadians

**scholarship** n. 1. The methods, discipline, and achievements of a scholar. 2. Knowledge resulting from study and research in a field. 3. Financial aid awarded to a student.

"Einstein defined insanity as doing the same thing over and over and expecting different results, and that's the Canadian university system. They're doing the same thing they've always done."

– Sports scientist Istvan Balyi, August 2007

# Chapter One
## Painting the Canvas

Everyone's got their own take on things. Here's mine.

Mid-morning on the eve of Canadian failure at the 2004 Athens Olympic Summer Games, I settled down on the deck with a cup of coffee and the day's papers, Noodles, the dog, content at my feet. I found the story I sought and started to read. Suddenly, a welling up and out of my throat …

"Nooooooooooooooooo!"

Noodles took off in a flash, barking furiously, determined to protect me, but I couldn't see a soul, just the leaves waving gently in the trees. It couldn't have been more peaceful, private or beautiful that morning, in Deep Cove, British Columbia. "It's OK, Noodles," I sputtered as I continued to read, "it's only the federal sports minister."

The day before, speaking at a news conference in Athens, Stephen Owen said this: "I think at the end of the day, if we didn't win a medal but we found that the quality of life measured by the amount of physical activity and health of the Canadian public, was increased, that would be a real good thing."

If we didn't win a medal? Winning, I think all agree, isn't everything but, a single medal? Owen went on to say: "I think we've got to be really careful about a fixation on medal numbers. We're all interested in it but it's not really indicative of sport health in our country."

What is indicative then, Mr. Minister? The D grades on our youths' physical fitness report cards?

Canada has never had a senior cabinet member as sports minister, just a junior minister since 1977 when Iona Campagnolo was sworn into a Trudeau government. Ever since, despite its best intentions, the federal government has had little positive effect on Canadian sport. Now, to read the spouting of such pabulum made me blow mine.

Sorry for disturbing your snooze, Noodles. Here we are in the 3rd Millennium, 33 million proud and strong and on guard for thee, on top of the world in so many ways, and Mr. Minister just attached a diaper to our entire team. Our sports system is healthy, we can half-heartedly shout to the multinational crowd as they clamber up and over our backs en route to the medal podium, which, as was painfully performed and documented, is precisely what happened. After finishing the Sydney 2000 Summer Games with what was described as a "humiliating" medals total of 14, we sunk lower in Athens, down to a dozen.

Yet, on the day the Canadian team was officially welcomed to Greece, by our government, on behalf of our people, Owen let it be known that it didn't really matter if our athletes won or lost. At least, tactfully, Owen stated this part of his government's policy approach to athletic achievement before the media rather than in front of our Olympians when he addressed them later in the day at the official welcoming function. There he lauded them as heroes, and with a rah-rah pep talk, Owen urged them to compete with heads held high on behalf of us all. Go Team Go.

Not a word about winning.

Speaking notes for The Honourable Stephen Owen, Minister of State (Sport) on the occasion of the 2004 Olympic Team Reception Athens, Greece
August 11, 2004
*Olympians, Partners, Fellow sport fans,*

*I am very pleased to be here — so soon after having been appointed Minister of State for Sport — to meet some of our country's finest athletes.*

*Canadians are proud people.*

*We are intensely proud of who we are and the values we stand for.*

*Nous sommes fiers de faire partie d'un pays qui défend la liberté, la diversité et la dignité humaine. Nous croyons au courage, à la détermination et à l'intégrité.*

*I am proud to be part of a Government that is the largest investor in Canadian sport. We have a great sport system in Canada, and you are at the heart of it. We plan to build on your success.*

*With the cooperation and support of all the provinces and territories, we have built a common vision for building a leading sport nation.*

*It is our roadmap to success. And with their support and that of all our other valuable partners — sport organizations, the private sector, communities, and individuals — we will achieve our goal.*

*Of course, our country's sport system is centred around athletes at all levels. And you, our high-performance coaches and athletes have a major role to play in Canada as a leading sport nation.*

*Sport brings out our pride and encourages us to express it. At Olympic events, in particular, we see Canadians waving the Canadian flag wildly and cheering our athletes at the top of their voice.*

*You are about to represent Canada on the biggest sport stage in the world.*

*You will share our Canadian values and way of life with people from around the world. You carry all our dreams. Watching you live your Olympic dreams will inspire us to achieve our own.*

*Of course, I know you have not been alone in your quest for excellence. I would like to acknowledge and thank the coaches, volunteers, parents, and friends whose tremendous guidance and support have been essential in your journey.*

*As you face the significant contest ahead of you now, you carry with you the admiration, the love, and the confidence of all Canadians.*

*We are proud to be Canadian. We are all proud of you, our athletes!*

*Best of luck at the Games!*

It's amazing how vapid government speak can be. This, to some of our country's most highly-tuned specimens, internally-driven athletes who have striven for years pretty much on their own to reach this point. Go out there and … go? In the process of their getting there, I rather suspect they have a fixation on winning as opposed to a fixation on temporizing defeat before even toeing the starting line. Nothing personal Mr. Ex-Minister (ahhhh, the vagaries of politics), you were actually productive for Canadian sport during your short time at the helm, and the sanitized speeches go with the territory.

This strange rationalization for taking or leaving winning is not new to our elected representatives. But when Campagnolo began her tour of duty she took a look at the lay of the land and, in enquiring about the sports health of the country, heard one main theme, which she distilled as thus in her 1977 Green Paper: "Do something about the sorry performance of most Canadians in international competitions." In some prominent quarters, Campagnolo was ripped to shreds, perhaps for having the temerity to admit it publicly, perhaps for other reasons. With no disrespect for Canada's actual Olympians since, current or future, nothing has changed — and the summer of 2004 was nearly three decades since the sorry theme emerged in the Green Paper.

In Athens, we bombed, again, worse than we bombed four years earlier. Nine athletes won medals and four of Canada's five reigning world champions never even made it to the podium in their event: hurdler Perdita Felicien, divers Alexandre Despatie and Emily Heymans, and the men's eight rowing crew. Meanwhile, back home, our sporting health, if reflected in our health care costs — wait until you see what Campagnolo has to say on that subject — suggests our sorry performances aren't restricted to within the white lines wherein our international athletes compete.

There is no other way to put it other than I was honoured when, six weeks after the Athens Summer Games, Campagnolo, then B.C.'s Lieutenant-Governor, agreed to sit for a fireside-type chat about sports at her official Government House in Victoria. The embodiment of charm, style, eminence, grace, wit, you name it, all rolled up in one, Her Honour oh so humanly epitomizes the provincial saying: Beautiful B.C.

"First, I should tell you that when Mr. Trudeau asked me to be sports minister, that famous day, I burst out laughing. I laughed because I said, "Oh sir, I've always been a hothouse flower. Why would you choose me to do this?" Imagine the twinkle in her eyes as B.C.'s most famous daughter relates this. "He said that sport was totally dominated by men and as I was a feminist, perhaps I could do something to balance the scales. Although I don't think I did anything spectacular in that regard, the scales are much better balanced than they were. I was almost delirious with joy when the Canadian women won the gold in ice hockey at the last Winter Olympics Games. It was just a wonderful time because I noticed following the win by the men, the men and women were equally honoured by all the public, the way such things are recognized. It was a great joy from coast to coast. In those days, they were pretty well condemned to ringette. That they have come so far is one of the great things I see in sport."

Campagnolo's preferred sport is figure skating, a sport in which we haven't had a women's world champion since Karen Magnussen in 1973, or won a medal at the Olympics since Elizabeth Manley earned silver in 1988 (see men for relief).

Sport has always evolved but Canada has mostly spun its collective wheels. Try one medal in the 1960 Rome Summer Olympics, and many other dispiriting single-digit Olympic Games medals totals. In Lake Placid in 1980, Canada won two medals, the minor miracle of those Winter Games. Campagnolo's appointment, and the very creation of her office, came on the heels of the ignominious 1976 Montreal Summer Olympic Games in which we became the first host nation in the history of the Games to not win a single gold medal. To prove it was no fluke, we did it again 12 years later in Calgary. Duplicate that, any and all challengers.

In the mid '70s it's safe to say that Participaction and other federal sports initiatives and programs had faded in and out of the collective consciousness. It's also safe to say Canadian sport has long been in non-productive disarray, aside from that glorious, chockablock-full pipeline of our young men into the National Hockey League — and now women on the world stage. In Campagnolo, Trudeau tapped into qualities of character and courage and opted for a fresh approach to a troubling situation, recognizing, as was his knack, that there's two trillion sides to everything. If you're your country's first sports minister, it's much more specific.

"The idea was that if we were going to have a healthy populous, we had to have mass sport as well as elite sport and we should not cut one off from the other and that there should be resources for both. And that's still being argued!" says an exasperated Lieutenant-Governor. "If we want a fit population they have to move, they just can't go on the Atkins Diet. It's easier [the diet], but walking 40 minutes a day will change your body. It seems to me that we've come a long way down that road to bring people to a greater consciousness of their own fitness. The fact is that it is a citizen's duty to keep off the health care system unless they need it — it's my conviction in my own personal life."

Walk 40 minutes a day and change your body. Keep off the health care system, as a national duty. Now that is truly beautiful.

One of Her Honour's most cherished moments in her voluminous portfolio was when Canada won the Commonwealth Games in 1978 in Edmonton. Near the end of our visit, she directed my attention to the commemorative photos in her office: a pope now on track to sainthood, a certain Caribbean revolutionary leader, "Mr. Trudeau," of course, and several other recognizable figures, but her favourite this day was a picture of her being tossed in the air by the Canadian team at the closing ceremonies in Edmonton, a la Japanese baseball managers after major victories; there she is mostly horizontal, legs akimbo but absolute joy emanating from the faces, all the many,

many young faces holding her up for the world to see. Was ever a sports minister so feted by a national team? "That was a great one in '78 when we won, after 40 years of losing. We were terribly proud, it was a high point. They [the British] wanted me to apologize for winning - and the Australians. If you think I'm going to apologize for winning, you're wrong."

Right you are: Medals mean never having to say you're sorry. So sayeth Her Honour, even if Ottawa would not or could not pre-Athens.

In 1987, in the lead-up to the 1988 Calgary Winter Games, Ottawa native Currie Chapman, then head coach of the women's alpine ski team, wrote in his book (co-authored by The Toronto Star's Randy Starkman), *On The Edge*:

Chapter Twelve
The Road to the Olympics

"How many medals are you going to win at the Olympics?" If the team had a dollar for every time it was asked that question, we wouldn't need a cent of government funding. I think in the past, Canadians somehow accepted losing and being a good ambassador was considered enough. But that attitude has changed. People don't want to know how many of our skiers could place in the top fifteen or top ten. They don't want to hear whether we've developed as an alpine nation since the last Olympics. They aren't interested in the progress made by our skiers in certain events. They just want to know who's going to reach the podium. When we talk to the Canadian Olympic Association (COA) about our program, that's what they want to be told. Now that we've enjoyed some success and some victories, people want and expect more. Getting the message from the public, getting the message from Sport Canada, getting the message from the media, the number one thing is to win." Too bad, so sad, Currie, things went astray.

A week or so after meeting Her Honour, I managed to reacquaint, after some 25 years, with Chapman in Sydney, B.C., a province he has more or less made home since he joined the National Ski Team in 1964. His bio from the Canadian Ski Museum's Hall of Fame:

"Currie Chapman was responsible for the Canadian National Women's Alpine Skiing Program from 1978-1988, leading the team to international prominence with 11-World Cup victories, 2-World Championship Medals and an Olympic Medal. Some of the skiers who became internationally prominent under his coaching include, Kathy Kreiner, Gerry Sorensen, Liisa Savijarvi, Laurie Graham and Karen Percy. He was a member of the Canadian National Alpine Ski Team for 5-years from 1964-1968 and became the first Canadian to graduate from a university through an athletic scholarship; Notre Dame University, Nelson, British Columbia, B.A. degree (majoring in psychology and counselling)."

After the handshakes and backslaps, the coffees and ice waters poured, and we noted that he actually wasn't the first student-athlete in Canada to graduate from a university having benefited from an athletic scholarship (see one Murray Owens of Kamloops, B.C., in that regard), we got down to business. "Our system? It isn't very productive," was his first comment as the tape started to roll. "We have pockets, we don't have a very consistent system. We can't fool ourselves into thinking that we are the same as the Australians, because their culture is different. We can't go out there and just say 'Well, they can do it. Why can't we do it?' As much as we, at least some of us, might like to."

As for the new funding via the 2010 Own The Podium Program? "I really have to say that's a band-aid solution. You throw some money at it and sure, that means you get a few more training days, and you get that extra assistant coach you needed and you get a few things like that, but there is much more wrong with our system. Those are things, yes, you can throw money at. And [2010] is five years out, we're just about there, and yes, maybe, maybe you can make a slight difference. But, I'll tell you what, it won't fix our system." Currie, me thinks thou did expect too much, and doth not protest enough, given the constrictions strangling the system. Hindsight.

A few months later I've got the ear of Dale Henwood, president of the Canadian Sports Centre at the University of Calgary, arguably the most important legacy of the '88 Winter Games. (It certainly wasn't our gold medal anti-bonanza.) Henwood spoke in his office, a hundred or so steps from the speed skating oval, which should — must — be re-named the Le May Doan/Klassen Oval. "First of all, I'm not sure as Canadians we value sport," said Henwood, agreeing to except hockey. "We don't value sport, we certainly don't value excellence, I don't think in any endeavour. I've tried to do a lot of work on excellence and I can't find anywhere, and I hope someone will prove me wrong on this, but I can't find anywhere where as a government we've said we wanted to be the best in anything. The closest I can find is something [former federal cabinet minister] Alan Rock said about five years ago about innovation where we wanted to be in the top four or something. At least we had a number there. I think it's important we have a target and we try to be the best. I don't know why we wouldn't want to value excellence in every endeavour. I think it is noble. We're not going to be the best in everything, but to try to be the best, there's nothing wrong with that. As Canadians, I think we are known for just being part of the game. We pride ourselves on being in the G8 [Group of Eight], in the United Nations, in NATO [North Atlantic Treaty Organization], but we're just there, we buy the pizza at the party. We're not leading. We like to be in the middle and we've got to change that, our whole culture. Is sport important? We've got to say that. If it's important, and excellence is important, it's a long-term process and it's expensive."

Henwood made his comments one year before our grand performance in Torino, where an unprecedented investment in our elite athletes in the run-up to those Games raised only one question: Why did we ever wait so long? I mention Minister Owen's soothing message that medals are not important. "And what was his audience when he said that? I think it was in Athens! You know, here I am, I just spent 10 years of my life to represent the country and you tell me it's not that important — ouch! Because, I think sport is important, I think striving for excellence is important, not because of the medal, it's what the medal does. The medal inspires others, whether it's kids or adults or older people, to get active, to set targets, to stretch themselves; it changes attitudes, it changes behaviours, and it unifies the country. I think they are important for that reason — but we don't value that," says Henwood.

Soon after the Athens Games, he and John Bales, president of the Coaching Association of Canada, delivered a 10-page analysis of Canada's results in the Association's official publication, Coaches Report, in which they rang the alarm: "Based on totals for the last three Olympic Games and Canada's tumble down the country rankings from 11th to 19th over that same time frame, there is every reason to be concerned about the health of our sport development and our ability to compete internationally."

One ouch, then another. Henwood: "You can debate this I guess, but I am going to suggest the best indication of the health of a sports system is the medal count, no different than the balance sheet is the best indication of the health of a business. In the sports system, the way we get evaluated, internationally, is on medal performances. We pride ourselves in being in the G8. In Athens, we were last of all the G8 countries and they were all in the top ten. There is a 250 per cent decrease in medals from the 10th country, which was Great Britain [30 medals], down to us. If we pride ourselves in being there, then we should be there on the medal side also, and in terms of the investment that we require. We were happy to be last in the G8."

To make matters worse, it eventually came out that the powers-that-be in Ottawa had been preparing Canadians for a harsh landing on their expectations well before the Olympic Torch was actually lit, given their first-hand knowledge and all. Recall Owen's soothing balm? In a Toronto Sun story a month after the Athens Games, we learned what they knew when they knew:

*By Maria McClintock*

*The federal government went into panic mode about Canada's prospects at the Athens Olympics a year before the Games and after being publicly slammed by athletes for a lack of funding. Documents obtained by the Sun under Access to Information show that in the months leading up to Athens, there was a flurry of activity within Sport Canada to shoot down perceptions the government wasn't supporting Canada's high-performance athletes — including a last-minute $30-million funding boost to the organization.*

*In September 2003, e-mails between Sport Canada's Athletic Assistance Program manager Bob Price and his colleagues note the feds were concerned about "our chances in Athens."*

*"Attached is a summary of the financial information found in the 2002-2003 annual report of UK sport," wrote Price in a Sept. 22, 2003 e-mail.*

*"This is factual information which shows the extent of the gap between our funding for HP (high-performance) sport. How the #*!! can we expect to compete in some of these sports when the HP programming in other countries is 10-20 times more than what we provide?"*

*The e-mail came on the heels of a scathing letter written by Canadian International Olympic Committee member and former Olympic sailor Paul Henderson to a Toronto newspaper accusing the feds of not adequately funding their elite athletes.*

*Henderson's letter prompted a special briefing note to the sports minister. It was one of several special briefing notes to the minister that kept track of public criticism of funding for elite athletes.*

*The feds announced in their February 2004 budget that Sport Canada would get a $10-million boost. But further pressure was applied in April during a series of "round-table" discussions on the future of high-performance sport funding.*

*"In order to achieve Canada's high performance funding, future investments in high-performance sport must be targeted," said a discussion paper on the meetings.*

*"It is recognized that in order to meet Canada's high-performance goals, a significant additional investment is required and for this investment to bear fruit it must be targeted to all sports with the greatest demonstrated potential."*

*In May 2004, the feds announced an additional $20 million for Sport Canada. But it wasn't until September that newly appointed Sports Minister Stephen Owen announced the athletic assistance monthly stipend would be increased, even though the feds were urged to announce it before the Athens Games.*

*Canadian Olympic Committee president Chris Rudge was surprised by what was going on behind the scenes. "This is the first time I've heard the government finally say this ... I'm encouraged that it seems to be a call to arms within the government to say, 'We've been ignoring this challenge and we're going to pay the price publicly for that,'" Rudge said. "One of the reasons we didn't do well in Athens and Sydney is the falloff of funding through the '90s."*

*Tom Jones, a spokesman for Athletes CAN, an organization that represents thousands of Canadian athletes, said the documents show the athletes who spoke out had an impact.*

*"What I see on the outside is that there was certainly a flurry of activity prior to Athens which is typical of government when the prospects are not very strong."*

*Owen's spokesman, Alastair Mullin, said the minister is committed to improving conditions for athletes. "Minister Owen's first announcements were around investing that (extra) $30 million in areas which will make a difference to Canada's performance in the future — notably coaching and increasing the athletes' stipend," Mullin said. "And that's where we will continue to make investments so that Canada can succeed in Olympics."*

*A month before the federal government announced it was boosting Sport Canada's budget by an additional $20 million, it did an internal survey of athletes, sport organization officials and coaches on funding for high-performance athletes.*

*Here are some of the key results:*
*- 36% of the 65 respondents surveyed said annual funding of between $70 million and $90 million is needed to ensure the success of Canadian athletes.*
*- 78% agreed the best way to ensure athletes succeed is to target funding; and 49% said that cash should be funnelled to sports rather than individual athletes.*
*- As part of the announcement, the federal government said the funding would be used to enhance the results of high-performance athletes, coaching and supporting sports organizations."*

So, in the summer of 2004, we knew going in it wasn't going to be a pretty picture, but it was the way we painted the canvas with our chins in Athens that was the worst part. IOC President Jacques Rogge, at the opening ceremonies: "Athletes, through your conduct, give us reasons to believe in sport that is increasingly credible and pure by refusing doping and respecting fair play. Our world is in need of peace, tolerance and brotherhood." But apparently not a Canadian medal haul. Our 134 women and 132 men is our smallest Summer Games team in 24 years due to tougher Canadian Olympic Committee qualifying standards. Chris Rudge, COC CEO: "It has, if nothing else, sent a message that athletes are going to compete, not participate. There is a focus on not just wanting to get a personal best but on winning," showing a rather forceful difference of opinion from his Minister's bleatings. "I'd like to see 16-20 medals. Realistically, we're going to do 14 to 18." David Bedford, Chef de Mission: "I don't think there's any correlation between team size and success. We think we have a very strong team." We didn't.

We had pockets of performance, once again. Our baseball team came within a wind gust of perhaps winning gold before coming home empty-handed, reminding us you're never going to win them all and exposing us to Canada - as an Olympic gold medal baseball country? On the eve of the Games, shortstop Kevin Nicholson of Surrey: "Larry Walker somewhat paved the way for us. Now you see Canadians in professional baseball all over the place. I think the success the national team has had is also an indication of the type of player we're turning out. Hopefully, we can have some success here and it will help kids realize there is an opportunity here. Maybe they'll decide there's other sports besides hockey where they have a chance to do something." If the opportunities aren't there, they should be. It was mostly opportunity lost in Athens.

**DAY ONE: Saturday, August 14, medal-less**

Swimmer Morgan Knabe of Calgary set the tone. Four years earlier in Sydney, he finished sixth in the 100-metre breaststroke; this day he failed to even qualify for the semi-final round of 16. "I don't know where I went wrong, what I did wrong," said Knabe, who spoke with his head hung, his voice barely a whisper.

**DAY TWO: Sunday August 15, medal-less**

Nine months before the Games, fencer Sherraine MacKay of Brooks, Alta., became the first Canadian to win even a medal (bronze) at the world championships. Nine months after the Games, she achieved the number one ranking in the world. Clearly a rising world power, and this day ranked eighth in the world, she was upset in her first bout by world No. 39 Jeanne Hristou of Greece. MacKay, who lives and trains supported by her musician husband in Paris, and is a quote-lover's dream, had this to say afterward, courtesy French philosopher Blaise Pascal: "Misery reflects the glory that can be, I guess."

**DAY THREE: Monday, August 16, bronze**

"After nearly three full days of plucky Canadian effort, the nation finally has its first Olympic medal in Athens — a bronze in synchronized diving. Our new favourite sport," is how one wag put it after divers Emilie Heymans of St.-Lambert, Que., and Blythe Hartley of North Vancouver, captured the bronze in the women's synchronized 10-metre event. It neatly captured the euphoria felt back home, judging by the coast-to-coast front page coverage. "I hope it's inspiring," Hartley said. "I know all the athletes feel a lot of pressure and they want to perform to the best of their abilities. The key is to just relax and believe in yourself. I hope this motivates people and inspires them, and if I did anything to help them at all, I'll be thrilled." Said Bedford of the meagre three-day haul, "These are the early days. There has been a lot of team stuff going on and preliminaries. There were really no expectations over the first few days." No expectations?

**DAY FOUR, Tuesday, August 17, medal-less**

Another shutout, but we were treated to a nasty outburst from swimmer Rick Say of Victoria, after the 4X200-metre freestyle relay team finished fifth in the final. "I was trying to make up for the mistakes our team made earlier in the race," said Say on national television after swimming anchor. "I'm pissed off, I wanted a medal in this race and I take full responsibility. I couldn't get these guys up and get myself up to win a medal. That's what happens, you come fifth.

Obviously, I let them down. It's unacceptable. I'm pissed off. This is crap." And cue our swimming team's meltdown; zero soles on the medal podium these Games. Knabe, after finishing 8th in his 200 metres breaststroke heat, six seconds behind the leader: "This is the hardest thing I've ever had to say, but I guess I wasn't meant to be an Olympic contender or medalist."

**DAY FIVE, Wednesday, August 18, medal-less**

Rowers Dave Calder of Victoria and Chris Jarvis of St. Catharines were disqualified from their men's pair rowing semi-final for leaving their lane just before the finish line. Naturally, they also lost the appeal. One bronze in five days, and counting.

**DAY SIX, Thursday, August 19, medal-less**

Stretched the shutout streak, which is a good thing in hockey. Guess that "no expectations" comment was more accurate than first thought. Perdita Felicien, of Pickering, Ontario, from the perspective of those who do as opposed to those who watch and want to cheer their guts out: "To most athletes, it's probably crushing when the public doesn't really appreciate your accomplishments, because, for a lot of us, they're huge. It's not only about medals. People need to understand that. Everyone looks at how many medals Canadians have won versus whoever else. That really is not the point. There's so many personal achievements, there's so many great stories. Someone might be sixth but to them that might really be a big breakthrough. Who knows? They were probably ranked 30th or whatever. Those are some big stories as well." Three days later, Myriam Boileau of Montreal delivered her international best finish of seventh coming off career-threatening back surgery. Expressing her teammate's sentiments perfectly, this platform diver exclaimed, "For me, this is like winning five gold medals."

**DAY SEVEN, Friday, August 20, silver**

We discover our second new favourite sport as reigning trampoline world champion Karen Cockburn of Toronto gave Canadian medal addicts a fix in a discipline that prepares you for trick sky-diving. "People are always saying, 'Oh, we don't have any medals,' and when you're in a place where you're expected to win, you feel it. Then you put even more pressure on yourself. I was obviously feeling it. That's why I was really nervous today," said Cockburn. Her routine was a delight to watch as well, unlike our swimmers, often a source of past pride but who in these Games are providing buckets of mud-slinging. Victoria's Ron Jacks, a three-time Olympian swimmer and coach since 1976: "We have nothing coming up below our national team and a lot of veterans are retiring — that's a scary thought. We have no domestic program of any value. A good leader has followers and [head coach] Dave [Johnson] has no followers. Our club system has been killed in favour of eight national training centres. I agree we don't have money or support. But almost all of what we have has gone to national centres. We need to put more money in development and beat the bushes looking for fresh new talent and that only comes out of the club level." That was nothing, there was much more verbal finger-pointing yet to come.

**DAY EIGHT, Saturday, August 21, silver**

To open a Summer Olympics Games by going gold medal-less over the first eight days is a telling sign and a fatiguing watch. Unfortunately, that completely overshadowed one of Canada's finest sporting moments on the international stage. Ask any average Joe today what event occurred and then bet the house he wouldn't know. You're guaranteed to win more houses than you lose. A silver for the ages gave us our third Olympic medal by a rowing four, after a bronze in 1924 and a gold in 1956. That part about the ages? "There have been some wonderfully great moments in sport — England winning the World Cup in 1966, Lennox Lewis knocking out Mike Tyson, Frankie Dettori riding all seven winners on one race card and Sir Steven Redgrave winning his fifth successive Olympic gold medal in Sydney — and this one can stand alongside any of them." — James Mossop, The Sunday Telegraph

The world over witnessed the embodiment of the original Hail Olympia. A more valiant losing effort would be hard to find compared to the one put forth by Cam Baerg, Tom Herschmiller, Jake Wetzel and Barney Williams, who went stroke for powerful stroke with England's Matthew Pinsent, Steve Williams, James Cracknell and Ed Coode in a race in which there were so many lead changes approaching the finish line it was like watching a zipper being done up. After 2,000 metres, the English crossed the finish line in 6:06.98, Canada in 6:07.06. Rowing might just be the most physically demanding endurance sport so you knew you were going to see fatigue at the end, but this was of the ultra-fatigue variety.

"After what felt like two or three minutes, I kind of realized that it was all Union Jacks waving and not Canadian flags," said Williams, who hails from Salt Spring Island, B.C. The team slumped as if collectively drugged, disoriented looks of bewilderment on their faces, not yet having enough time for the fact to register: After dedicating a sporting lifetime, and racing in an Olympic final, they'd been eight one-hundredths of a second short of a share of gold.

"There was no sense of disappointment. It was a little bit of amazement that we were that close to a gold medal, but at that point we were completely soaking in that we put in 100 per cent of our effort for it." As Williams describes the finish: "All of a sudden, 100 metres away, there's a tiger, and he's going to kill you and you start running like the wind. That's what basically happens in the last bit of the race. You dig within and you find something extra."

Britain's Pinsent, who won his fourth gold medal of the Games, said he'd initially thought they'd lost, which would have counted as a complete disaster back home as the British team had dismantled other combinations to stock this boat. Saskatoon's Wetzel on that: "I think when you're in that type of situation you don't look at them as anything else but peers. If you build your opponents up to be the greats then you're not going to stand a chance of beating them. They beat us but we brought them down to earth." And, on the photo finish: "It's about the smallest of margins, it's about the best performances. I think that's what really makes the Olympics special, there's four years of preparation for each country. They put their best out there. And Britain put their best out there … they put all their eggs into this. They're one of the great rowing nations and to be able to be in a race like that is special."

**DAY NINE, Sunday, August 22, gold**

Kyle Shewfelt to the rescue, as the Calgary gymnast ended our golden drought. Talk about coming out of the blue: Canada had never won a medal in traditional Olympic gymnastics. Yes, that is as in never. Until Shewfelt, who performed to his peak with a polished presence of character the judges were only too happy to reward, with a delivery akin to watching the best fireworks of the night explode.

If Shewfelt's virtuoso performance in the floor routine came from out of the blue, Canada's other frontline Olympians that day stayed stuck in the blue. And, to make matters worse, they were counted among our biggest hopes, as reigning world champions.

Ladies, first.

Heymans stands second before her last dive in the 10-metre platform final. But somehow, inexplicably, she chunked it so emphatically as to effectively nuke any medal chances. One commentator described the degree of difficulty as something she could do in her sleep, but this was living a nightmare. If the spectators needed to be stunned, Heymans couldn't have done any better. As Heymans described it, she "kind of landed on my back," not a good position except if you're attempting the heretofore unknown reverse belly-flop. Caught on camera while clearly consumed with grief in the dressing room, she said of that moment, "I knew I'd screwed my chance. There's nothing you can do about it, that's the worst thing."

She also felt compelled to apologize to us. Added her coach Michel Larouche, "She just missed it. She was ready to go, to fire. We don't know what happened. It's a mistake. I feel sorry for Canada, because I know that things haven't been great for us and it's just another opportunity to talk badly about us." Head coach Mitch Geller: "Emilie is one tough cookie. We'd expect when it comes right down to the last dive that she can tough it out with the best of them. It was a minute mistake, with just terrible consequences. I'd rank this with every Olympics I've seen. They all uncover every fissure in people's diving."

Fissure away as we return to the rowing regatta to watch the men's eights, lauded before the Games as one of our "sure-thing" gold-medal favourites. World champions, undefeated internationally since teaming up, but on this day the crack in their shell which had appeared in the semi-final broke wide open for all to see. As goes sport: a day after a rowing moment ne'er to be forgot we watch with slack jaws a Titanicesque melt-down by our blue chip entry on the water. The eights wobbled right from the start, then relentlessly if unmercilessly faded from medal contention. The U.S. won with a crew built for the final following the replacement of half their team. Any of this starting to sound familiar?

Coach Mike Spracklen said, "I've never seen them row this badly, not even in practice," and admitted he knew the crew was cooked by 750 metres, i.e., even before the halfway stroke. Ben Rutledge of Cranbrook, B.C., used the word "panic" about running out of gas at 1,500 metres, "I gave it all I had and then just … nothing." So out of sync was he from pushing too hard he fell out of his seat. Said Edmonton's Andrew Hoskins of the rumbling, bumbling, stumbling row: "This is the most painful experience of my life so far. But then I've never given birth."

**DAY TEN, Monday, August 23, silver**

The pickings were slim again, a single silver, which, if you're still counting, is five medals in 10 days. Wrestler Tonya Verbeek, a native of Beamsville, Ontario, and at the end of a long and accomplished career, earned her Olympic podium despite losing to world champion Saori Yoshida of Japan in the gold-medal match of the 55-kilogram division. "It's a great moment, and I would not change this feeling with everything else in the world," she said.

Feelings of another kind were in people's minds at the gymnastics hall when Shewfelt lost a chance at a bronze medal through no performance of his own but what appeared to be blatantly illegal judging and/or scoring malfunctions of a human kind. Shewfelt held third as Romania's Marian Dragulescu made his final approach. Dragulescu stumbled on his landing, but after what any TV viewer would judge an overly generous judges' score took the bronze with 9.612 points, leaving Shewfelt in fourth. In launching a formal protest, one Canadian official said Dragulescu's final vault score was "impossible by any reading of the rules." The appeal eventually failed, but through it all Shewfelt oozed class as a poster boy for sportsmanship.

**DAY ELEVEN, Tuesday, August 24, gold, silver**

As a big-picture day dawned, we were actually looking good to prove we belonged as we had a headline crew of medal contenders. In baseball, we were in the semi-finals against Cuba, but in baseball, perhaps more than any other sport, "on any given day" applies. In diving, Alexandre Despatie, of Laval, dominant and dynamic, led going into the finals of the three-metre springboard. On the track, the most popular of our strongest gold medal favourites, Felicien toed the starting line with her biggest rival, American Gail Devers, missing after going down in a tumble over a hurdle in the semi-final the day before. Our stars were finally aligned it seemed, and when little known 37-year-old cyclist Lori-Ann Muenzer of Edmonton opened the day's proceedings with a standout gold as she out-muscled Tamilla Abassova of Russia 2-0 in the sprint final, it had us seeing stars. As with Shewfelt's gold medal, it again came out of the blue, Muenzer becoming the first Canadian to win an Olympic cycling medal. After, this amazing physical specimen of a 37-year-old exulted, "This week is the fittest I've ever been, the fastest I've ever been." Suddenly, we were looking at perhaps four golds over the next two days, three today, baseball tomorrow, and now we're talking. But not for long. About four hours in fact.

Eighteen days earlier, Felicien had won her event at the Weltklasse Golden League meeting, the final pre-Olympic meet and her sixth straight win. Felicien received so much pre-Games publicity it put her into a different world: "It seems like all I do now is talk about myself. It makes me feel that I am so vain." Carly Simon couldn't have said it much better, please note the word "feel." This day, racing in Lane 5, she hit the very first hurdle with her right leg and fell hard into the next lane, taking out Russian Irina Shevchenko. "I don't know, I have no clue what happened," a shaken Felicien told the CBC. "It's my worst nightmare come true."

Despatie was first after the preliminary round in the three-metre springboard, as expected, but as unexpectedly and inexplicably as Heymans before him, chunked a finals round dive in world-class style. How fine is the line. Going into the third of his five dives, Despatie was sitting second behind China's Peng Bo, who had a superb day. Despatie attempted a tucked reverse 3½ somersault, a dive he'd performed for six years and with which he had scored 91.5 in the preliminary round. But he missed it from the start and hit the water with a splish-splash, earning 64.05 and kissing goodbye the gold which had seemed destined to be his since birth. World champ that he is, though, his last two dives earned him silver. "I made a big mistake, but I'm very happy I was able to come back strong and have a good finish. I thought it was over after the third dive, that I wasn't in the race." And yet another Olympic first and another reminder of our feeble Olympic success rate: Despatie became the first Canadian male to win an Olympic diving medal — but gold had to have been the only goal.

The blow to conclude this fateful day came after our baseball team stared down mighty Cuba. Leading 3-2 in the bottom of the eighth inning, third baseman Peter Orr, of Richmond Hill, Ont., one of Canada's best players up to that point, threw away a routine double play ball to open the floodgates in an 8-5 loss. To add heartbreak to misery, the potential game-tying home run off the bat of Kevin Nicholson of Surrey, B.C., was caught by the Cuban leftfielder at the top of the fence for the final out.

It was a roller-coaster, Heartbreak Hotel day that ran our total to seven medals in 11 days.

**DAY TWELVE, Wednesday, August 25, medal-less**

We absorb a good old-fashioned thrashing on the diamond in the bronze medal game and the heartbreak comes full circle. A soon-to-be Seattle Mariner named Kenji Jojima had four RBIs to lead Japan to an 11-2 romp. "We are disappointed but we should be pleased because it is our first time in the semi-finals," said Canadian manager and ex-Blue Jay Ernie Whitt. "Canadians should be proud of this team."

It's not a day to be watching the medal table. Our slide was in only one direction and we were absent from the podium for the sixth time in 12 days. Uh-oh, there's that disturbing pattern again. Back home, and looking back on the previous day's pratfalls, the day's edition of The National Post hit the nail on the head with a stunning mock-up of what the headlines and sports pages could have been, given Day 11's helter-skelter act, noting it would have been the first time Canada won three gold medals in one day. Looking at the reverse of reality, I started wondering what's wrong with this picture and the only thing I could come up with was nothing, if not winning big-time is Canadian.

## DAY THIRTEEN, Thursday, August 26, medal-less

Off all podiums for a second straight day, seven in 13. But at least not a totally disastrous day. In canoe/kayaking, Canada qualified for 10 finals, duplicating its best showing in the event in the boycotted 1984 Games in Los Angeles. Displaying perspective, "I honestly don't think we've achieved a very high level of success," said Adam van Koeverden, the team's biggest medal threat. "It's not time to celebrate. It wasn't my goal to come here and make the final." In the men's triathlon, defending Olympic champion Simon Whitfield of Kingston, Ont., but long based in Victoria, finished 11th. "It was a strong-man's course, and I'm not the strongest man," admitted Whitfield, who sat back and let the leaders get too far ahead during the cycling portion of the event, a decision he referred to as a "tactical mistake." "I took a gamble and it failed. I can live with that."

## DAY FOURTEEN, Friday, August 27, silver, bronze

Legs and arms are us, we earn our eighth and ninth medals — passing American swimmer Michael Phelps who has eight — via silver from mountain biker Marie-Helene Premont and bronze from van Koeverden. Premont, who finished 59 seconds behind Gunn-Rita Dahle of Norway, who won in 1:56:51, was fifth at the previous year's world championship and placed second in two World Cup races this season. "I knew I was in good form, I had a good feeling all week. Everything was perfect here. I wasn't stressed at all, I didn't have any pressure," said Premont, from Chateau-Richer, Que. With a beam a mile wide this rookie Olympian said afterward, "I'm really happy. It's so incredible, there's no words to describe it." Van Koeverden gutted it out in the K-1 1,000-metre and managed to hold off Australian

Nathan Baggaley. "In the last 50 metres I gave it my all to win the medal from the Australian and I felt pain," said the native of Oakville, Ont. "Now I'll try my best in the K1 500 (the next day)."

**DAY FIFTEEN, Saturday, August 28, gold, silver, bronze**

Not a day to complain about. Kayakers van Koeverden and Caroline Brunet won gold and bronze; Ross Macdonald and Mike Wolfs teamed up for sailing silver. Van Koeverden became our first double medalist in these Games and in the process established another Canadian first, as in solo kayaker medalist. It was our first canoe-kayak gold since 1984 in L.A. and he did it in style, again beating Baggaley, a two-time world champion, in the K-1 500 metres final. "It hasn't sunk in yet," he said. "I just went to the bathroom and looked in the mirror and didn't recognize myself for a second. It was like, 'You just did something pretty incredible.'"

Brunet, a 35-year-old from Lac-Beauport, Que., and our most successful female kayaker with two Olympic silvers already in her trophy cabinet, settled for bronze in her fifth trip to the Games. "I was worried about the wind," Brunet said. "I woke up at 2:30 a.m. and I was thinking that the race will be postponed or delayed. I gave it my all at the end of the race to finish third. I'm happy with the bronze medal."

Macdonald, from Vancouver, and Wolfs, from Mississauga, who joined forces only seven months earlier, were third in the standings heading into the day's 11th and final race, but finished second to take silver. "It was a tough day as far as conditions go," said Macdonald. "Our plan was to try and get a clean start and work the middle of the track and it worked out." Macdonald also won bronze in the event in 1992 at Barcelona. "I have to admit the novelty of the bronze wore off a few years ago," he said. "And this one is just sinking in. It's great."

In the men's platform diving finals, Despatie's performance is not up to snuff as he finishes fourth. "I'm hoping people feel disgraced now," said Despatie's coach Michel Larouche, on our medal failures as the post-Games hand-wringing commenced before the finish line. "And from that, move forward — exactly the way Australia did after '76." Australia dramatically boosted funding for athletes between 1976 and 2000, and lo and behold its medal count. Larouche says Canada is falling behind in the world of sport and money is one of the reasons why. "I'm one of the lucky ones that has a sponsor and gets support from a major corporation," Despatie said. "If that's the difference, maybe people should wake up and support athletes."

**DAY SIXTEEN, Sunday, August 29, medal-less**

... for the eighth time in the 16 days of competition, a great stat if you're facing MLB pitching. Time (Canada) Magazine's pre-Games top picks: rowing eights, no medal; Felicien, no medal; Cockburn, silver; Maryse Turcotte, no medal; Despatie, silver; Mark Boswell, no medal; Jill Savege, no medal; Shewfelt, gold; Diane Cummins, no medal; Brian Johns, no medal; Dominique Bosshart, no medal; Nicholas Gill, no medal; Ryder Hesjedal, no medal; Christine Nordhagen, no medal; Daniel Igali, no medal; Sherraine MacKay, no medal ... let loose the Talking Heads.

"We are proud of all of the athletes who competed here in Athens. We congratulate those athletes who achieved success at these Games and we share in the disappointment of those who did not achieve the results they had hoped for," said COC President Michael Chambers. "We initially believed we would exceed our performance from Sydney, but this goal was not achieved. This reinforces the need to make further significant changes in the Canadian sport system for our athletes to be more successful."

Mark Lowry, the COC's Executive Director of Sport, hammered home the statistics behind Canada's failure to live to up medal expectations, noting only 27% of Canadian athletes ranked fifth or higher in the world going into the Olympics ended up turning in similar-level performance at the Games. "How did we do? Not as well as we thought we would. This is what we're facing with the rest of the world — they're leaving us behind. We need reinforcement if we are to strive for higher performances. We have athletes who are just as good as anyone else in the world. It is not acceptable to have athletes within striking distance but not achieve their goals." Lowry continued: "We have a coaching situation which is unacceptable. Until we take a position that coaching should be top of the list, it cuts down on athletes' performance. We need to recognize the bench depth in this country; there is usually one athlete who represents the sport, but no other who can step in and take over in their absence."

Let's give the silver lining its due. Canadian athletes achieved the highest success rate ever in terms of top 12 finishes. But as the Games ended, IOC President Jacques Rogge said, "It would seem that government funding would be needed to help Canadian sport," and that he would soon visit Canada to encourage increased government investment before 2010. Rogge said similar requests are typical prior to any nation hosting the Games, but his remarks were of considerable comfort to the COC. "At least someone's listening. If it takes President Rogge and the IOC to wake some folks up on Parliament Hill, I'll buy the ticket," said Chambers.

The day after the Olympics ended, and for the first time in 17 days, the sports news on the front pages of the nation's newspapers changed to the hockey World Cup, in which we immediately restored our tattered international pride, at least for a short while.

Three weeks later, a front page headline in the Victoria Times Colonist blared out: "We're too nice to win, says coach". Victoria's Jim Fowlie, who had just assumed the reins of the national swim, detailed a meeting with parents of top B.C. swimmers in which he outlined a program where the best would advance ahead of the pack. "What the parents said to me was that was 'favouritism.' You would never hear Russian, American or Aussie parents say that," said Fowlie. "The question any national team program in Canada has to ask is how do we nurture a winner in a society that likes to pull everybody down to the norm when we need to be elevating people to the highest level? How do we make a champion? That's not only a sports problem but a cultural problem in Canada. The question is, will we allow our athletes to step outside the norm? While we try to balance equality, the Aussies definitely go for winning and back their winners and make no bones about it." He went on to say, "Sure, it's absolutely as much a cultural, if not human nature, issue in Canada as it is in sports. But sometimes we're harsh on ourselves. In some ways this reflects well on our people. There are a lot of athletes from a lot of places who would trade their gold medals for our nation's peace and serenity." To the eternal quandary of how do nice guys finish first, if it makes you a greedy nice guy to pursue both, so be it.

As for the dreaded evil of favouritism, sport is naught but a combination of play and exercise. Sometimes we play for fun, sometimes we play for keeps. Sometimes we exercise to ensure our health, sometimes we exercise to the max in combination with our natural athletic ability. Is it really elitism to assist natural talent? Should we pretend it doesn't exist? Campagnolo, in an address to the Cornwall Kiwanis Club, 1977: "At the Munich Olympics, we ranked 21st in the world. It is hard to think of any international endeavour where Canada would rank so low in world standing."

While we are a nation that will apologize for decades-old "mistakes," no more apologizing for winning. No more just being happy to bring the pizza to the party, no more just being there is good enough, this is sports we are talking about for crying out loud.

The Speech from The Throne on October 18, 1977, in Ottawa, was spot-on as it echoed Campagnolo's beliefs about our sport delivery system: "The goal of this government is to ensure that the athletes, at whatever level of competition, are regarded as a full-functioning, productive member of society. The goal of this government is to see that sport, fitness and recreation are acknowledged by one and all as full-functioning parts of that culture which is Canada. No more the sweaty athlete syndrome. No more the denigration of the athletic scholarship. No more the culture which is divided between artists and athletes. Athletes are artists and some artists are athletes."

Note the denigration. It's still sadly but firmly in place and points to where this missive is heading. It didn't, doesn't, have to be that way. It wasn't once, truly, unbelievably, beautifully, once, and that process produced our female athlete of the 20th century, Nancy Greene-Raine. No more the shunning of this approach toward scholarships by a handful of university presidents who are myopic on the subject. Their dim view has a huge impact our country's athletics, and because of that consequently our recreation participation levels. No more university athletes playing sandlot ball. No more the mentality that brings this about. Shunned Campagnolo certainly was, by a very powerful quarter, university sport as an entity. Read the existing Canadian Sports Policy and hit the search button for the word university. It stops twice. For the word colleges, once. More's the pity.

Peter Webster of Vancouver, multiple sports hall of fame inductee and awarded the Daryl Thompson Award by Sport B.C. in 1995 for lifetime service to sport (society really), offered up this while taking his turn at the Talking Head dais. "Our sport system is so disconnected, when you start at the recreational level at the local park, from there to the Olympic podium, there's no connection. There's no connection at the junior level, there's no connection at the university level, no connection at the college level, no connection with the sport governing body and no connection with the Olympic body." Why? "Because we try to be everything to all people, one, and we've got turf towers like you can't believe, we've got egos you can't believe, and we forget that it's for the good of the country and the good of society that we should be looking after these kids." Why is that so hard for others to see, are we a country of me-firsts? "Yeah! Why don't you ever see the university guys work in cooperation with the sport governing bodies?" Webster says don't look to the government to connect things, either. "But that's our sports system fault, not the government's. Governments, it's like everything else they do, they apply 50 cents to every word, they give 50 cents to everybody so everybody thinks wow, the government is looking after us but they don't make you accountable for your 50 cents. That's the problem. When you take it out of government hands and do it as a free enterprise thing, then you are accountable, you are accountable to your donors, you're accountable to your sponsors, you're accountable to who's putting the money up."

Chapman as echo/harmony: "I think we have to take the whole sports system out of the hands of the bureaucrats. That's the one part of the Australian system that I think is important: to have the management of our sports system in the hands of private enterprise, or a separate body. It is now tougher because [the feds] decided they couldn't support the sport system anymore so they kind of dismantled the whole concept." Piecemeal? "It's scattered." Nothing unified? "Nothing." How insane is that, if you care to go on the record? "Oh, it's pretty insane, I'd say that," said this past president of the Canadian Coaching Association, past head coach of the women's alpine ski team, past Olympic racer. Pretty insane, all right.

When your eyesight is fine but "what's wrong with this picture?" keeps ringing in your ears, the rest of your senses demand an answer. One frustration too many it dawned on me and I woke up to playing a game of chicken with the CIS. At least it wasn't CSIS.

# Chapter Two
## How The West Was One: Take One

In the spring of 1963, a very small Catholic Liberal Arts college in the Queen City of the Kootenays, Nelson, B.C., was awarded university status by the Social Credit government of Premier W.A.C. Bennett. Thus began Notre Dame University's true legacy, as simultaneously it embarked upon the most innovative university sports scholarship program in Canada — to date.

The concept of a full-ride sports scholarship had always been anathema to certain Eastern Establishment types but all the Notre Dame program did was serve as the physical and mental fountainhead for the creation of the Canadian alpine ski team, which led to the crown on the career of Nancy Greene-Raine. It came at a time when Senior hockey still had major impact and was semi-pro in everything but name. The scholarship program served to put the Nelson Maple Leafs of the Western International Hockey League back on secure footing only two seasons after the team had ceased operations, even prompting dreams of establishing the squad as a farm team for Father David Bauer's then-fledgling Canadian National Team. The fact that NDU's approach remains anathema to those certain Eastern Establishment types is ludicrous when seriously considered. As Greene-Raine herself phrases it, "They don't have the right."

But of course "they" do, via voting rights and the right to uphold personal misconceptions. It's infuriating that for a century they have exercised their democratic right, even if it seriously undermined Canadian sport. Ridiculous! To stand behind an argument just for the sake of stubborn tradition doesn't exactly tax brain cells, and these are very intelligent people.

That Nelson, with only 10,000 inhabitants, would lead the country forward would have only slightly bemused the local citizenry, if they had ever stopped to consider it, because that's what this progressive city has done throughout its entire, remarkable history. Every community fosters and harbours the senses of self and pride, but for its size, there is no other which has contributed so much to Canada's — albeit primarily through B.C.'s — maturation process.

The Ontario pooh-bahs who determined sports policy in our universities operated on the basis of fear, anti-Americanism, loyalty to an elitist British mentality, and to put a little sniff of nasty in the air, a combination of snobbery toward and jealousy of successful athletes, coaches and administrators. Nelson, and by extension Notre Dame, simply got on with what it's always done: the day-to-day job of making things better. Upon Notre Dame's graduation from college to university, A.L. Cartier, principal from 1950-54, saw fit to comment, "[NDU] will live to be a thing that the city of Nelson has been proudest of in all its achievements."

Not that it's always been smooth sailing for this postcard-perfect locale on the shores of the West Arm of Kootenay Lake, in southeastern B.C.'s Selkirk Mountains, where all you need is a quick sniff to get clean air. Nelson has seen more than its share of ups and downs since it was incorporated in 1897. So what? Who or what hasn't? Although it has had more than its share of opportunities to do so, it has never rolled over and played possum.

"It's died how many times?" asks Peter Webster, a big-city type, Quebec City and Montreal to be precise. He journeyed west in 1965 at the tender age of 22 to become manager of the still-new national ski team based at small-town NDU and has since made Vancouver, an eight-hour drive, his home. "It died once with the university, it died once when the CPR [Canadian Pacific Railroad] left, it died once when KFP [Kootenay Forest Products] left, and died once when the [provincial] government [offices] left — and it always came back. When you think of all the people, all the original things that happened there in Nelson … I can't think of another one," said Webster when asked to map Nelson's contributions to Canada.

"This is continuous, it's gone on. For argument's sake, the Penticton V's [1954 Allan Cup and 1955 World Champions] were one thing; this place has a series of achievements, even to the extent of just four months ago, for the first time in British Columbia history, there was a memorandum of agreement between the RCMP and a municipal [police] force to cooperate, in Nelson. You know, we don't recognize the good things that we do in Canada … that probably comes easily when you think of Nelson because there's so much good that has come out of Nelson."

For those of European descent, the first good thing to come out of Nelson was silver in 1886. Along with gold, coal and other minerals discovered throughout the Kootenays, both East and West, Nelson first boomed as a center of mining activity. By 1894, it was served by two railroads, the Canadian Pacific running east-west, and the Great Northern north-south across the border. But it didn't take long for forestry to move to the fore as the Selkirks are just one of a handful of tree-covered mountain ranges between B.C.'s Okanagan Valley and the Rocky Mountains astride the Alberta border. Towering highest over Nelson was Kokanee Glacier, which was to play such a key role in Canadian skiing history seven decades later. By the time Nelson was incorporated on March 4, 1897, 3,000 people called it home, the city itself home to B.C.'s first hydro-electric generating plant, and eventually B.C. Tel and Greyhound Bus Lines, as well has the operating base for Burns Meats.

No maple syrup, sorry, but women were playing hockey there near the turn of the century.

Canadian hockey fans who don't know of the Patrick family's import to the game are likely to still have pimples or baby cheeks. Webster, who moved to Montreal aged 14, was but one of several in a pipeline of innovation and innovators between the two cities.

The Patricks arrived in the West Kootenay in 1907, father Joseph and family including son Lester, son Frank leaving McGill University to join them a year later. As the brothers were making Nelson the regional powerhouse on the ice, while also freelancing their talents to the holders of the biggest hockey purses both West and East, the family ran a logging operation.

The clan made a small fortune through its sale in 1911 and proceeded to utterly revolutionize the game we so love. The Patricks' "Nelson" money resulted in the first indoor, artificial ice arenas for the emerging professional game in Canada in Vancouver and Victoria, and the rest, as we're so fortunate they say, is the history of the National Hockey League.

Father Joe was the original businessman, sons Lester and Frank were the stars on the ice and the greatest innovators the game has ever known. At the time of their passing in Victoria in the early 1960s, more than 20 NHL rules were of the brothers' making.

Natural resources made the Kootenays rich, and Nelson shared the wealth. A recent book detailed how the city of then 7,000 raised more than $8 million in Victory Bonds during World War I. Then, remarkably, in the middle of the Great Depression, the city fathers undertook the province's biggest building project. Upon completion, the Nelson Civic Centre boasted an indoor arena and curling rinks, badminton hall/gymnasium, arts/movie theatre, playing fields and library — in one location — and suddenly Nelson was the cock of the sports walk across Western Canada.

When the new rink opened on the weekend of November 29-30, 1935, "The whole community was in a state of euphoria," the Nelson Daily News reported.

"In its day, it was the finest facility of its kind," former Nelsonite Leo Atwell said in his book documenting the history of the B.C. Amateur Hockey Association. "It brought many intra-provincial senior playdowns to the area, the first being the Western Canadian final between Kimberley and Prince Albert. Kimberley won the series and went on to be the first team from B.C. to win the Allan Cup later that year."

Wayne "Fritz" Farenholtz, a city councillor from 1966-74, recalls those heady days. "We thought that a new era in the life and history of this town had developed finally. We had everything we needed down there. We had the best facility in the country ... Everybody knew about Nelson, and there was tremendous pride in the community."

The Civic Centre also helped pave the way for the arrival in Nelson of one Ernie Gare, who signed on the dotted line to play defense for the Nelson Maple Leafs of the Western International Hockey League in 1950, a year of no small import to this city of such, and who, more than any other individual, brought athletic scholarship to town. Let the real story begin.

---

"Notre Dame University of Nelson was born in 1950 of the pioneering effort of the then Bishop of Nelson, Most Rev. Martin M. Johnson, in order to offer needed academic facilities to aspiring students, teachers and others living in the East and West Kootenay areas interested in improving their educational status."

So begins Notre Dame's recorded history as set out in its calendar as it proudly recalls its humble beginnings, from a meagre but eager-beaver 12 students in an abandoned bakery, through to the breakthrough event on March 27, 1963, when the B.C. government announced legislation making Notre Dame the first private and joint second/third university in the province. For a multitude of reasons, Notre Dame was not to go down in the history books as a shining success, as one would envision an institute of higher learning could or rather should be, in fact closing its doors only14 years later, but, for those who envisioned and fought for a better future for Canadian athletes, nothing rivals the home of Canadian university sports scholarships.

Notre Dame was guided from college to university status by Father Thomas Aquinas, a Franciscan from New York, who had no delusions that academic concerns were a university's sole raison d'etre, unlike some of his prima donna peers in Ontario. Two months after Notre Dame was awarded university status, he announced that a dormitory must be built and in answer to those who said higher-learning facilities should come first, he replied: "Only part of our teaching is done in the classrooms. The other part, the greater part, is done living with the students."

Hockey, our nearest, our dearest, was the first to benefit from NDU's sports scholarship benevolence, then skiing, as soon as it caught wind of what was possible on its side of the yet-to-be-invented half-pipe. Father Aquinas once said "In my experience with sport, I find that the man who pulls his weight on the field also excels in the classroom. If he loafs while he plays, he loafs while he studies." For an article which appeared in the gone but not forgotten Weekend Magazine on November 10, 1966, Father Aquinas sat down with Vancouver-based journalist Patrick Nagle, one of the few in Canada to really grasp the impact of the unfolding events.

Nagle describes him as a *"lean, chain-smoking down-east Yankee priest. When excited, Father Aquinas invokes the Spanish Inquisition ("Holy Toledo!"). His favourite themes are the university and the athletic program. "I just don't think it's fair to the kid to let him lie around and be a hockey bum," Father Aquinas says. "As long as he's capable of education above the secondary level, he should have it. My opinion has been that the professional leagues are not encouraging kids to go on for higher education. More than this, I think their methods of putting pressure on high-school kids – particularly the use of money – makes hockey appear more attractive than education.*

*"In the long-term view, of course, this is absolutely wrong. The hockey executives say a boy loses experience if he finishes his education. I don't believe this. If a boy gets a hockey scholarship and plays good hockey, say he graduates at 24. He's missed a couple of years with the pros, that's all. And his future is much brighter. Besides, I think with the education, experience and maturity, he could last a couple more years up there anyway.*

*"Now this would not make hockey more genteel. And I don't want to insult those men who are running hockey so successfully right now. I do think the time has come to sit down and do some long-range*

*planning, and I mean really long-range planning. Not like our present national team who are – I think – still a short-range proposition. Those kids are definitely sacrificing some of their education for hockey.*

*"If you connected good solid farm teams to the universities you would have the natural material to draw on for a national hockey team in depth, and you would also be supplying the expanded National Hockey League with the best type of player in the years to come. I would like to prove this combination of university and sport is successful. We should act as support and supply for the National Hockey League, the way the colleges supply football players in the United States."*

Nagle soon brings in Webster, by now the university AD as well as ski team manager, as Gare had taken a sabbatical. *"I think bringing the national team to Nelson is the best thing that ever happened to skiing in this country. And Father Aquinas is great. He's really keen on the athletic program. We talk every day about it. Now that we've got the ski team here, I think we should try to get the hockey team here too."* Very Canadian thinking, only to be topped by an American when Nagle returned to the good father.

*"I've got a secret urge,"* he confesses. *"You know, I'm an American, but I think it's kind of sad to see Canadians going down there year after year in hockey, even though it's the national sport. This is at least partly the fault of there being no long-range player development for a national team.*

*"The universities are the ideal place for this kind of development, but they're all working independently. Nobody's interested in the national picture. That's really what I'd like to throw a little light on. That's really what I want this program to achieve.*

*"It may be a long time off, I don't know. U.B.C. hockey teams haven't been back here since the year we tied Father Bauer's national team and beat their Thunderbirds. But I would like to see regular, strong inter-university competition. I hope it comes soon. It may be closer than we think. People seem to be noticing us. If we win some more, they should notice us more."*

To be sure, people were noticing Father Aquinas's sports and education philosophy. The first, if not so undoubtedly then certainly most intimately was Gare, a Nelson Maple Leaf when Father Aquinas arrived at NDU in 1958, Ernie, as he was known to everyone about town. He was named Athletic Director of Notre Dame College in 1962 after serving as Nelson's Recreation Commission Director the previous five years. It would be impossible to overstate his contributions to not only Notre Dame, but to sports, and particularly to Canadian hockey. And wouldn't it have been wonderful to be a fly on the wall when he and Father Aquinas got together for a fusion of the minds.

"Problems? Probably there will be a lot that we don't even know about," Gare said in the summer of 1964 after the Canadian Amateur Ski Association formally named Nelson and Notre Dame as the home of the first Canadian national alpine ski team. But he was a "there are no problems, only solutions" kind of guy. "Ernie was a hero!" says Currie Chapman, of a man who didn't demand respect but acquired it effortlessly through the natural side of his nature.

His own university education having been adjourned because of his playing career, which brought him to Nelson, Gare became convinced that athletes and education are two sides of the same coin, that the former needs to be exposed to as much of the latter as possible, that athletics and academics are naturally tied at the hip. At the same time Father Aquinas was engineering Notre Dame's transformation from college to university, his athletic director was in his good graces for displaying a blatant disregard for the hidebound mentalities which ruled the CIAU at the time and putting the pieces of what really shouldn't have been a puzzle together to bring those visions and beliefs into action.

In matters of the mind such as this, even more than five decades after the fact, the moment of germination of Notre Dame's scholarship program in his mind is fortunately not lost to us.

From an April 30, 1965 Notre Dame news release: "Negotiations for this program started through the efforts of Mr. Gare, who is a member of the hockey executive and a former player on the Nelson Maple Leafs. The idea started in 1961when the Kootenay International Junior Hockey League was formed at NDU. "I saw the potential of the players and the program at that time," said Mr. Gare, and the next year he recruited several hockey players at NDU, and came up with the 1963 KIJHL championships. "That year we lost three games out of 27."

Although within only two years the hockey scholarship program was thriving and made its name at Notre Dame with the Senior Leafs, it was anything but Gare's original intention, a position which was to initially flabbergast and then downright anger Leaf enthusiasts, his friends. In the spring of 1963, he submitted to the university hierarchy a six-page proposal on "The Consideration of Athletic Scholarships at Notre Dame University of Nelson". It makes for telling reading and absolutely emphasizes that for him, it was all about the combination of a university education and athletics, and the worldly benefits derived by the university and its student-athletes, first, foremost, maximus.

Fortune had smiled on the Notre Dame Knights, who debuted with that stellar 24-3 record under coach Gare. They also had the town's hockey spotlight. That season the Maple Leafs withdrew from the WIHL due to, what else, financial woes, marking the end of 60 years of Senior hockey in Nelson, according to the press reports of the time. When the Rossland Warriors also folded their tent, the WIHL ceased operations. That winter, league and Allan Cup champion Trail Smoke Eaters, behind coach Bobby Kromm, represented Canada at the World Championships for the second time in three seasons, after having lifted the crown in 1961.

But Senior hockey across Canada was nearing the beginning of the end of its long, losing battle with the professional game, this WIHL season a perfect case in point. It provided the Knights with a fortuitous vacuum to fill, which they did to a tee. That off-season, Gare wanted his fledgling university squad to pound the final nails in the Senior Maple Leafs' warmed up coffin — right then and there. Wrote Gare:

"The general public should be informed that the college is going ahead with a planned program which, in the future will provide a strong permanent team. The announcement of such a program would serve the prime purpose of deterring the general public from supporting ANY revival of Senior hockey interests. This movement or program would have to be initiated as soon as possible so that it would serve to kill any attempt to formulate plans for any Nelson Senior entry in the old Western International Hockey League." Strong words that didn't come to pass, however, as events were moving quickly all those years ago.

Honesty and trustworthiness as reflections of strength of character are very persuasive elements and Gare was loaded with them. Combine that with Father Aquinas's abiding belief in the power and value of university sport and it's only natural that on August 5, 1963, the following announcement was made of the first step toward the only full-ride university sports scholarship program in Canadian history:

*NDU Approves Athletic Service Scholarships*

The athletic director of Notre Dame University of Nelson, Ernie Gare, Friday announced that the NDU board of governors had approved the granting of eight athletic service scholarships for the 1963-64 academic year. Mr. Gare said the majority of the scholarships will be allocated to the 'Knights,' NDU's entry in the Kootenay International Junior Hockey League. He pointed out that 1962-63 was the first full season for the Knights and the initial year of the league's operation.

By granting these scholarships NDU is endorsing the university's hockey entry in the league and attempting to put its team and the league on a more solid footing. Students wishing service scholarships for athletics should contact Ernie Gare at NDU.

"Successful candidates must fulfill usual academic university entrance requirements and must maintain a 60 per cent average through the school year," said Mr. Gare, and he pointed out, "Last year eight students were required to withdraw from varsity hockey and basketball teams because of failure to maintain academic standards."

The service scholarships require also that the student assist in the university cafeteria.

The KIJHL includes: Gonzaga University Bulldogs, Trail Junior Smoke Eaters, Cranbrook Junior Canucks and Notre Dame Knights. Mr. Gare said, "This is a step in the right direction and as a result, we hope to be able to field a more competitive junior hockey team which will be a strong contender in the KIJHL".

Go Knights Go, but hold on, history and university hockey fans. Neither Senior hockey nor the Maple Leafs were done and just a few weeks later Nelson returned to a rejuvenated WIHL. Right then and there, it was just so many fired blanks for Gares's hopes and dreams of the Knights reigning supreme in Nelson. But malice? Are you kidding? That '64-'65 season, a few Knights on NDU hockey scholarships were transformed into Leafs as call-ups to a bruised Senior team. Gare was able to convince the executive and Booster Club of the revitalized Maple Leafs that the players on scholarship at Notre Dame could also play for the Senior Maple Leafs next season, and that the Leafs would benefit if the team itself coughed up some cash for scholarships.

Suddenly everyone in the local hockey circles was talking amicably again — at least for awhile. As the season unfolded, it became apparent that now was the time to take this bonhomie up to the university atop the mountain. On February 1, 1965, Gare, who once tried to put the Leafs out of their misery, presented the university with the second step to those elusive full-ride scholarships:

*NOTRE DAME UNIVERSITY ATHLETIC DEPARTMENT BRIEF REGARDING HOCKEY – STUDENT SCHOLARSHIPS.*

*PREAMBLE: Because of a lack of job opportunities within the City of Nelson, the Nelson Maple Leaf Senior Hockey Club have always found it very difficult to provide suitable employment in order to recruit hockey players for the hockey team. This season (1964-65) the Senior hockey executive embarked on a program of recruiting student-type hockey players for the local team by offering a University scholarship in lieu of playing hockey. To date, six players on the Maple Leafs are receiving financial assistance from this plan and are also attending Notre Dame University. Two players are on full scholarship (approximately $1,500.00) with the balance, four, on partial scholarships of $400.00 to $500.00 each. This financial assistance is being supplied from three sources: (A) Gate receipts of the Senior Hockey Club; (B) Nelson Senior Hockey Booster Club; (D) [sic] Private or Commercial donations.*

*FUTURE PROJECTIONS: The present executive plus the local hockey fan are very pleased (as indicated by attendance figures) with this inaugural part of the program. It is tentatively hoped that an increase in the program can be tackled this summer prior to the 1965-66 season. This increase would include additional student-hockey type personnel, which would naturally increase the scholarship program.*

*NOTRE DAME UNIVERSITY: The University derives benefits from this program: (A) Recruitment — There are six students who are enrolled on this program who would not have been here, if the program were not in effect. (B) Publicity — The national wire story that covered the new approach to recruiting of senior hockey players, publicized the University's cooperative attitude. (C) Intercollegiate Competition — The University's Varsity hockey team has utilized these six players in intercollegiate games and thereby made it possible to compete against larger institutions. The scheduling of these games (if you compare the enrolment figures of Notre Dame University and of some of the larger institutions) is only made possible because of this program. A University of this size could not compete in this calibre of league from drawing on an enrolment of 400-500 students.*

*RECOMMENDATIONS: The program has been initiated and built by interested outside individuals who have spent time and energy to promote the entire program. It is recommended that since the University derives benefit, in the areas mentioned, that the University assist on sponsoring the program by instituting (5) full scholarships for the 1965-66 season.*

*SCHOLARSHIP VALUE: — Each scholarship would cover full tuition and board and room as set up by the University. Value of $1,200.00.*

*ELIGIBILITY: — Each successful applicant must have the necessary academic qualifications as laid down by the University.*

*CONCLUSION: — The eventual goal would be to have the Senior team based at the University with the majority of the personnel being University students. The coaching situation could be solved by having a member of the P.E. staff or academic faculty hired in a dual capacity, as both instructor and coach. This would place the leadership of the team in the hands of someone familiar and in agreement with the academic responsibilities of each student-player.*

*It is essential that community participation be retained at the executive or booster club level. This is necessary for the promotion of local fan support which would be so important in order to maintain the present revenue from game attendance. Also community interest is required and needed in order that the "Team" remains as an image of a "local" team and not strictly in the sense of a University team.*

*The mechanics of recruiting athletes and joint-operation could be detailed at a later stage in development and are not included here because of the essence of space and time.*

*Financially, there is always the capability of the gate receipts paying off all or a portion of each scholarship that is awarded by the University. Commercial or private scholarship assistance donations do not expect any possible return of their money.*

*Basically, the new program needs additional scholarship assistance from the community and from the University.*
*Respectfully submitted,*
*Ernie M. Gare, Athletic Director.*

During this 1964-65 season, Knights Shelley Atwell and Mike Laughton of Nelson, Miles Desharnais of Cranbrook, B.C., Carl Chawacka of Melville Saskatchewan, Danny Calles of Kimberley, B.C., and Murray Owens of Kamloops, B.C., skated for both teams. The Maple Leafs represented Western Canada in the Allan Cup, losing to Sherbrooke, Que.; the Knights defeated the University of British Columbia Thunderbirds and University of Alberta (Calgary) Dinosaurs twice each in intercollegiate showdowns. Gare, by now a member of the Maple Leafs executive, convinced Notre Dame to push the envelope and at the end of April the third and final step was taken:

*1965 Master Copy*

*PROPOSED SCHOLARSHIP AGREEMENT Between*

*THE NELSON MAPLE LEAFS HOCKEY CLUB (SOCIETY #5042)*

*And NOTRE DAME UNIVERSITY OF NELSON, B.C.*

    *PREAMBLE*

    *The University Athletic Department presented a brief to the N.D.U. Board of Governors requesting five (5) athletic scholarships, value of $1200.00 each, to assist the hockey experimental program now in its first year of operation.*

    *Since that presentation to the Notre Dame University Board of Governors has agreed to issue five (value $1200.00 each) hockey scholarships with the provisions that:*

    *The Nelson Maple Leafs Hockey Society or its affiliated group provide an equal number of scholarships (value $1200.00). If the Hockey Society supplies less than five scholarships then the University will only provide an equal number of scholarships as supplied by the Nelson Maple Leafs Hockey Society and its affiliates.*

    *That the University will award these athletic scholarships, only, when this agreement is ratified.*

    *SCHOLARSHIP COMMITTEE*

    *It is essential that a "Scholarship Committee" be established with membership of this committee coming from within the Nelson Maple Leafs Hockey Society and representatives from Notre Dame University.*

    *PURPOSE & DUTIES OF THE COMMITTEE*

    *To establish and set in motion recruiting procedures and issue proper applications forms to applicants.*

    *To recruit successful candidated [sic] who are capable of meeting the requirements as outlined by this committee.*

    *To select successful candidates and make these recommendations to the Nelson Maple Leaf Hockey Society.*

    *To have the authority to suspend any scholarship, if the candidate(s) violate the regulations as laid down by this committee. [as approved by the Nelson Maple Leaf Hockey Society] [Agreed. NMLHC.]*

    *To make recommendations in writing, to the Nelson Maple Leaf Hockey Society on or about any aspect of the aforementioned*

*"Hockey Scholarship" operation that directly affects scholarship students.*

*These are the main goals and objectives of the "Committee" and an operational manual for this "Committee" is attached to this agreement.*

*NOTRE DAME UNIVERSITY SCHOLARSHIP PARTICPATION*

*The Notre Dame University Board of Governors have agreed to provide an equal number of athletic scholarships (value of $1200.00 each) to a maximum of five (5) or on an equal basis as provided by the Nelson Maple Leaf Hockey Society or its affiliated organizations.*

*The University agrees to this system of scholarship participation with the following conditions: That all players attending Notre Dame University of Nelson must be allowed to participate in eight (8) intercollegiate contests during the regular hockey season for the Varsity hockey team.*

*I. That the University through its membership on the "Scholarship Committee", constantly supervise the academic achievements of the scholarship students.*

*That the University receive an audited year-end statement of season. That if any profit exists at the end of a season, after five hundred dollars ($500.00) has been set aside for fall training camp expenses, that this profit be split on a basis of 50%/50% between the Nelson Maple Leaf Hockey Club and the Notre Dame University for the sole purpose of applying to future scholarship commitments.*

*That the league playing schedule be reduced to a maximum of forty-games (40) or a minimum of thirty-six (36) games. This would afford the scholarship player a much better opportunity to remain at a higher academic level.*

*That the Nelson Maple Leaf Hockey Society employ a "Coach" that realizes the value and principle of education combined with athletics. That this individual will support actively this type of program. Also that regular monthly meetings be held between the coaching staff and the Scholarship Committee to assist in carrying out the aims and purposes of this agreement in the operation of this program.*

*CONCLUSION*

*It is not nor should it be the intent of the University to control any or all of the Nelson Maple Leaf Hockey Society operation, but only to concern itself with the areas of student-scholarship as related to the hockey team. The Nelson Maple Leafs should always retain the image of a "local" team so as to maintain the interest of local hockey fans and booster club members even though a number of players are enrolled at the University.*

*Also from a practical hockey viewpoint, the actual operation of a senior calibre team should be kept in the hands of the most experienced people, those who usually appear in the Senior Hockey executive circles. The University's greatest area of concern would be in the academic achievements and progress of each student-player. The functions of this Committee does allow this participation and protection for the University and its students.*

Abracadabra meets presto in the form of a full-ride university sports scholarship through a little city and a small university. The glory years of the Nelson Maple Leafs scholarship program through Notre Dame were at hand.

One of the first "big names" to emerge from the program, which was to gradually grow in scope over the next decade almost to the point of Gare's hoped-for 50% plus one, was Mike Laughton, the local multi-sport star who reached the NHL. Along his path, we return to the value of the Civic Centre: "When I made the NHL everybody said, 'you are so lucky.' I would say to them that I didn't really see too many of them at 4:30 in the morning on the way to the rink. It was there for everybody, but I just loved it so much." Laughton was figure skating at that particular time of the day, continuing the sport until 16, and then focusing on hockey. "[Figure skating] was important because that's what I base my success on, that I was a pretty decent skater."

For Laughton, taking university courses while playing for the Leafs was to be a part of Nelson's hockey's heyday, when the Leafs were the proverbial hottest ticket in town. "You couldn't get in. For playoffs people would sleep on the streets to buy the tickets the next morning. When the games would come you had people sitting on the beams and the fire chief threatening to close the place down."

Upon the NHL's expansion from the Original Six in 1967, Laughton was drafted by Charley Finley's Oakland Seals. He laced up the infamous white skates for 189 NHL games over the next four seasons, scoring 39-48-81, collecting 101 PIM. A three-year run in the WHA produced a line of 43-49-90 and 90 PIM in 203 games played, before eventually returning to Nelson and finishing his playing career with the Leafs in the late '70s.

Gare's efforts to get an NDU faculty member into Maple Leaf management bore fruit in his own person, fortunately for this amazing program he valiantly nourished. He was either on the team's executive, or was manager or coach of the Leafs, for most of the next decade. But university people flowed through the system.

In 1966, 10-year-minor leaguer Frank Arnett, at age 33, signed both his coaching contract with the Maple Leafs and admission statement as a mature student with the university. "It's really hard for me," the tough-as-nails Arnett told Nagle. "I've been away too long. And I wasn't that interested in school after I left home to play hockey. Now I've got a lot of catching up to do.

"Some of my marks aren't so good. But you can put down my maths marks. I got 85 in that."

When Gare stepped down as Leafs coach on Nov. 21, 1975, he handed the reins to the recently returned Laughton. Team captain Hugh Hooker said, "It's hard to realize anybody doing a better job than Ernie. It's possible, but it all boils down to discipline. The guys will miss him. They liked and respected him. A few of them came to our club just because of Ernie. I don't see where the coaching change should make that much difference unless Mike decides to play. He's a heckuva hockey player."

Hooker, who began playing for Ernie a dozen years earlier with the NDU Knights and Leafs, was by now a teammate of Ted Hargreaves for the second time. This Canadian Olympic bronze medalist and teammate of Nancy Greene in Grenoble found himself a minor leaguer in the Toronto Maple Leafs system before arriving in Nelson as player/coach in 1971, following a nasty ankle injury. Recuperation complete, Hargreaves reached the pro game with the WHA's Winnipeg Jets in the 1973-74 season. That one year of pro was enough for Hargreaves, who morphed into an NDU/Maple Leafs scholarship student, wearing those classic green and white uniforms before he graduated with his teaching degree and spent the rest of his life in Nelson. Hargreaves, held in the community's highest esteem until cancer claimed his life in 2005, was one of a small group of school teachers to come out of Notre Dame, easily the most by per capita education-centric location in the country.

He and his peers came to Nelson as young men and players in the bigger hockey world, all part of that vast majority for whom the NHL just wasn't going to be. Picture it. Suddenly a university on a mountainside in a city on a lake appears on your horizon, and just as suddenly, hallelujah just doesn't seem to quite cut it, as they recall it today.

Diminutive by hockey standards but productive winger Tom Foxcroft, by July 2005 nearing the 30-year mark as a high school teacher, comments on events in 1970: "I was offered a full ticket, Michigan Tech, Cornell, University of Denver, fly there, fly back. Hockey Canada was going to give me $400, total, and I remember my dad saying $400, how many $400s? I said Dad, I think he's saying one $400. And you know what, I would have stayed in Canada, I mean I'm a Canadian, I've always been a Canadian, and that was as much as they were going to give anybody.

"Today I teach at Mount Sentinel Secondary school and all these volleyball kids, they're all going to the States, all going out of Canada to play. It just makes me sick. To think for one second that you can't recoup, by having good athletes in your house and then sell tickets, I mean it's absurd. This scholarship program here, I remember because I went and played pro and then I had to sit out a year to get a scholarship again, and when this came about, I thought I had died and gone to heaven. I remember Frank Selke Jr. was negotiating my contract with [NHL] Oakland (Seals) and he said 'Foxy, this is as good as it gets, you're going to play for this town, you can walk right in and play, full scholarship', and they sponsored me to come here and I never left. To keep my rights, [Oakland] paid me to come here. Because I was going to leave [the organization], I hated Providence [Rhode Island] and I wasn't going to make it in Oakland. They wanted to keep my rights but I said, well I'm outta here! And they said well, wait a minute, what we'll do is help sponsor you, so they were paying me money every month to keep my rights while I was going to school here and the scholarship was paying for my education – hello?!" He laughs and laughs.

Smooth-skating center Leroy Mowery originally landed in the WIHL with the Trail Smoke Eaters, which provided him with a job in the Cominco smelter. Now a retired high school teacher, he is quoted in the Nelson Daily News, July, 2005: "At that stage of my life all I was interested in was making money. My intent was to make money and buy a fancy car. I worked on the hill at Cominco for a few months and I thought that maybe I should get an education. To this day I'm grateful that I did."

Goaltender Bill McDonnell, fellow retired high school teacher, and Ontario product: "I looked all around, and there wasn't anything available to me. Financially, I couldn't afford to go to school on my own, and my parents couldn't afford to send me to school. It was only with incredible good fortune that I got a phone call from Nelson two weeks before school started asking me to join their program. My wife and I look at it as a defining moment in my life. Looking back at Ernie's personality, I think his goal and premise behind combining the academics and athletics in a scholarship program was to present opportunities for student-athletes. I wasn't the strongest student in school but I had an incredible desire to learn, and to play, and between the two of them, I was able to make a marriage.

"It wasn't easy when I first came out because I'd been out of school for four years. I had been working, and that first term, to keep my head above water and on the ice as well was a real challenge. It was really quite interesting because following my first year here, both [Maple Leafs teammate] Gary McQuaid and I were invited to the national [team] camp in Ottawa and when it came down to staying or not, I decided not to stay. I wanted to come back to Nelson. Well, I was going to the Philly camp shortly thereafter, my first pro camp, and then I made the decision to not stay with the eastern-based national team. Although I never spoke to or met Father Bauer, I understood he was quite upset that my preference was to come back to play for the Nelson team and Notre Dame rather than play for the national team. I must admit that's the only regret that I had, because I really believe in the Olympic movement, and the national program, I really did, and I still do. When we talk about pure, I would like to be able to see us compete at the amateur level in the Olympics, but that train's left the station, I still believe in wooden hockey sticks! But this program out here met so many of my needs, both academically and athletically, that I didn't want to put that in jeopardy. I had the opportunity to sign with Philly and probably play for their team in the American Hockey League, but at that particular time, education was such a strong goal of mine that I passed on it.

"[Notre Dame] was also a defining part in my life. As an individual, I grew immensely. I was quite, quite introverted through my teen years and my expression basically came through sports; now I had another avenue to express myself and that was through academics and thinking. And that confidence, that's a key word, the confidence, the opportunity that was presented to me to grow my confidence in myself, as a student, as a person and as an athlete. I'd never trade it. People have asked, especially my wife: 'Do you ever regret not staying with Philly?', and I don't, ever, ever regret that because there was a lifestyle choice that I made. It was more than just what I was getting with the university and the Nelson area, more than I envisioned in a professional environment, or a large-city environment. So yeah, when you look at it, it was a perfect fix for me, it fit perfectly for me."

McQuaid, long known around Nelson as McGoo, history grad, minor hockey coach, man sometimes happily playing gadfly in its good sense about town, is an original gift of the gabber who never met a fellow conversation addict he didn't like, even if it doesn't always sound like it. He told the Nelson Daily News: "A lot of guys hadn't gone to [post-secondary] school before. [NDU] really paid attention to the books instead of just the hockey. It took a while for that to happen. Everyone got along so well, but if someone wasn't paying attention, Father Aquinas told us scholarships were a two-way thing. It's not just athletics. We've got both things going. We're proud of the program and we're proud of the way you play sports, but if you're not going to keep your marks up, you're not going to play." Study hard, boys.

When Mowery first arrived in Nelson he commuted to work at Cominco in Trail. He and fellow 1966 newcomer, Brian Russill, luckily survived driving back and forth every day with Kromm, now coach of the Maple Leafs but one of hockey's worst drivers. Trail is one of Canada's pre-eminent hockey communities, the home of Minor Hockey Week. The Smoke Eaters 1961 World Championship team was to be Canada's last for the next 33 years. The Cominco lead and zinc smelter provided employment for many a Smoke Eater over the decades. The team wasn't named after the smokestack but a player who picked up a lit pipe thrown by an irate fan on the ice and skated off puffing it, as the story goes. Imagine that crowd. It was a classic rivalry, cities 50 miles apart, one blue collar, one educational white. Senior hockey in both cities expired, as did NDU, only Cominco remains.

From original letterhead:
*TRAIL SMOKE EATERS*
*WORLD CHAMPIONSHIP 1939, 1961*
*ALLAN CUP 1938, 1962*
*3775 Dagwood Drive*
*Trail, B.C.*
*Aug 27 / 70*
*Board of Directors,*
*Notre Dame University,*
*Nelson, B.C.*
*Dear Sirs:*

*On behalf of the Trail Smoke Eaters Executive, I as one of the members am interested in knowing whether or not talented hockey players playing with the Trail Smoke Eaters who are desirous of furthering their education would be entitled to a scholarship. We at the present time have several players who have shown interest in attending N.D.U.*

*We realize it would be a benefit to the Smoke Eaters, but it would be an incentive for the players to obtain an education while pursuing a hockey career and also increase hockey calibre in the W.I.H.L.*

*We of course would recommend athletes who would meet the high standards of entrance requirements of N.D.U.*

*We realize N.D.U. has scholarship commitments with other teams in the W.I.H.L. and we certainly would not want to infringe upon their rights but we are hopeful that N.D.U. would give consideration in granting similar scholarships to deserving students playing hockey for the Trail Smoke Eaters.*

*Sincerely yours,*

*Allan Tognotti*

*CANADA'S OLDEST CONTINUING SENIOR HOCKEY CLUB*

It never came to pass, but you can't help but admire the effort, and from this perspective, the recognition, the pat on the back, well done, from a rival.

That clause, stipulating that Leafs on the scholarship plan were also required to play for the Knights, but only for a handful of games a year? There was no valid intercollegiate league at the time, and eventually even that requirement, and the Knights, simply faded away, much to the chagrin of some, if not others.

Nelson businessman Peter Godfrey was part of the no longer dormant 1963 Maple Leafs Booster Club under new club president Jack James that provided the Leafs with those first two scholarships. He eventually joined the team executive and later the WIHL executive, and offered this on what transpired off the Civic Centre ice those 40 years ago: "In my opinion, I don't think there could have been Senior hockey in Nelson without the scholarship program because we simply could not have afforded it, the revenues wouldn't have supported bringing these guys in without the help of the university through the Roman Catholic Diocese and so on. Obviously, Ernie was the one that got the scholarship program going and it saved Senior. I guess Ernie originally intended for it to be a university scholarship program for university hockey but as it came full circle, it saved the life of Nelson Maple Leafs Senior hockey."

While a few dozen hockey players were finding personal lifelines to nirvana in Nelson, the university's willingness to offer and support these opportunities were immediately noticed elsewhere in the Canadian sports community, right from the get-go. It couldn't have been any other way, given the restrictive, archaic approach of the CIAU. Notre Dame, by virtue of its private status, thank you Diocese, was not affiliated, this in a country where sports scholarships actually had evil connotations to some people.

An alpine skiing scholarship at first glance seemed tantamount to bordering on the absurd. The knives did come out. How can you compete at the international level and still go to university asked the unimaginative. You study while on the lifts?

The Notre Dame brain trust knew it could be done, and in partnership with the Canadian Amateur Ski Association, head office in Montreal, proved it. Welcome back to that Nelson-Montreal pipeline again and welcome to the formation of the Canadian national alpine ski team.

Unbeknownst to the few particular individuals involved, serendipity truly ruled those formative days. Considering the somewhat ramshackle if well-meaning approach of the Canadian Amateur Ski Association to the development of the competitive element of the sport to that point, and a distinct disconnect, there's that word again, between western and eastern cliques within the national ski community, the fact Notre Dame emerged onto the national landscape, even if 99% of the country was unaware of it, helped save the proverbial day and laid the groundwork for the Crazy Canucks of the 1970s, who raised not only awareness but heart-thumping respect for Canada in every alpine skiing country across the globe. Canada is so vast that eastern and western cliques are a fact of life. But whoever said two cliques can't click? Four decades ago, B.C. and Quebec were Canada's skiing bases, together they found another way to spell C A N A D A.

We return to Trail, situated on the Columbia River and at the base of a short but extremely steep highway up to Rossland, which, in turn, sits at the base of Red Mountain, Rossland and Red being the twin homes of Nancy Greene.

Cue Don Sturgess, Vancouver-bred, ski racer, mover and shaker, Cominco engineer, Canadian Amateur Skiing Association

(CASA) executive member. Today he says of Red Mountain, "until I came to Rossland I had no idea what a real downhill could be." Of events circa 1963, "I'd been coaching kids both in the east and the west, both in Rossland and in the Laurentians and the Eastern Townships. The parents of the kids, and the kids, were concerned that if they went into a national team program, would they be able to keep up any kind of education at all or would they be sacrificing their potentials for careers? A lot of them had very good academic grades and they already had ideas of what careers they were going to go on to. They had models in their own families, and previous skiers, and at that time the chances of having a professional skiing career were very, very limited."

Sturgess paid a visit to the Notre Dame campus, where he talked to similarly-minded individuals. The picture suddenly just became a lot clearer, didn't it?

First, we must step into what was not a pretty background. As if all Canadians had somehow lived on the prairies our first 80 years, Canada's then medal haul at alpine World Championships or Olympic Games was in the hands of two women, Lucille Wheeler of Saint-Jovite, Quebec, and Ottawa's Anne Heggtveit. As a toddler, Wheeler was a Wayne Gretzky, a Tiger Woods, on skis, AKA healthy body, healthy mind, the Canadian junior champion at age 12. Her parents bearing the costs, Wheeler spent several years racing and training in Europe before the 1956 Winter Olympics in Cortina d'Ampezzo, Italy, where it all paid off as she became the first alpine skier from North America to win an Olympic medal, bronze. Two years later, at the World Championships in Bad Gastein, Austria, she won the downhill and giant slalom titles, narrowly missing out on the combined title, earning her, among other plaudits, the 1958 Lou Marsh Trophy as Canada's outstanding athlete.

Wheeler's breakthrough inspired Heggtveit, her 17-year-old teammate in Cortina d'Ampezzo. Four years later, in Squaw Valley, California, Heggtveit won Canada's first Olympic gold in alpine skiing, as well as the FIS [Federation Internationale du Ski] and overall world championship slalom titles. And, of course, she also won the Lou Marsh Trophy. Both women are enshrined in their deserved Halls of Fame and are recipients of the Order of Canada.

But aside from these two shining stars, who'd volleyed back the question of whether Canadians could ski with the best — the dominating Europeans and the emerging Americans — the slate was clean. A new approach was due, especially now that young Canadian ski racers had just been shown precisely how big their dreams could be. You think Nancy Greene noticed?

Cue yet another prominent Montreal-to-Nelson transplant, Dave Jacobs, 1957 Canadian downhill champion and national team member until 1962. "In those days, we had a national team in name only. We only got together in December and then we would go to Europe to train with a coach and a manager you might have just met on the way over. Those teams had to get into condition by themselves and there was a big void between the juniors and the top. The team was serving the pinnacle — not the base." Not for long.

Webster: "We had a problem in Canada. It was easy for the kids to get to Europe from Eastern Canada. And it was very difficult for the kids from Trail-Rossland and Kimberley to get to Eastern Canada, so yours truly started the Canadian National Ski Team fund. The idea was to level the playing field, so the eastern guys and the western guys had the same opportunity to go over there and meet that coach we had, that nobody in Canada had ever met! Think about it. The joke was whoever could show up in the Geneva Train Station on December 2, under the clock, the guy with the red hat is our coach. Well, it wasn't really like that, that's part of the mythology, but it was more or less like that."

Nancy Greene-Raine: "I was on the national team starting in 1960 but back in those days the team was just a list of names and they would put a team together a month or so ahead of time and go to Europe, prior to the world championships, or Olympics [at that time held in rotating two-year intervals]. 1961 was the first time they sent a national team to Europe, in an off-year, and I was on that team, and the next year they picked a world championship team and I went to Europe again. But it was only a very small group, there were usually about eight guys and five or six girls and that was it. So apart from that, there was no program for anybody in Canada. People would do that for a year or two and then retire. There was always a big gap. There was no progression. So after the world championships in 1962, there were big discussions, everybody said this is wrong, and they said we need to have a training camp out west in the early season, have trials and then pick a team to go to Europe. You just can't invite everybody and pick the top eight who have the money.

"So in 1963 we were going to do that and then, at the last minute, the Quebec division said no, we're going to send our kids to

Europe because it's just as expensive to go out West as it is to go to Europe, and why should we spend all that money coming out west. And there wasn't a mechanism in place to fund people to come out to the camp, so all of a sudden there was a split. So the team went to Europe, and had European coaches like they always had. There was lots of anger and there was lots of emotion. We said we were forming the Western Canadian Ski Team — it was the Western Canadian National team!" If there's a better sense of disconnect than having two teams representing a single country, someone please spell it out for me. "Oh, yeah!" Greene says as she does so. "When we broke, when we formed the Western Canadian ski team, we raced as and we called ourselves that. In our minds, we weren't on the national team and in our minds when we went to the Canadian championships we went down there to beat those other guys. We had a really strong mentality at those championships and we did beat them." Feisty, feisty, but that's Nancy. A relatively recent brief written by Ken Read, now the head honcho of Ski Canada, describes her as "one of Canada's greatest treasures," just to remind you. My, my, long have forces west and east played kickball with the Canadian fabric. Enough, already, of politics, but yes, The Little Tiger was right, something had to be done.

For half the answer, we return to Jacobs, who took time in the summer of 2004 in Nelson, on the occasion of the 40th anniversary reunion of the founding of the national team and formation of the country's first bona fide university sports scholarship, to explain his head of the class role. He graduated from high school in Montreal at 16 but then "flunked out" of McGill University, went to work for his father's manufacturing company and ski raced in the winter.

"In 1955 I remember going down to Stowe, Vermont, for the North American championships and all the Europeans were there. It was a really big race, all the kids from Western Canada were there. We're up on the training hill and I see these American kids, four or five with the same colour jacket. I skied over and said what's the big deal here and they said, we go to Dartmouth, we ski for the university, we're their team, and they were there with their coaches. We're down there hanging out in the wind and here are these college teams? I said wow, that's amazing. I started looking into it and found that St. Lawrence University had one of the top teams in the east, and Otto Schniebs was a very well-known coach.

"I said to my Dad, I want to go back to college, I want to go to St. Lawrence. He said, 'Well, you went to McGill and flunked out!'

He was an engineer and said, 'I'd like you to be [one]. If you want to be, I'll send you back.' St. Lawrence was a liberal arts school, but they had a three-two program with MIT, where you take three years at St. Lawrence and if your grades were good enough you'd finish up two years at MIT and get a four-year degree so you'd take all the lab work at MIT and all the theoretical stuff at St. Lawrence, the math and everything.

"So I said OK, I really wasn't interested in it, I just wanted to get on the team, I wanted to ski, so I said OK, I'll do it," said Jacobs, sounding like the teen sports fanatic of every generation. "My Dad said fine, so we applied for an athletic scholarship at the time but he was making too much for me to get it, so he paid for the tuition." Jacobs never saw cause to continue his two-fold education in Canada: "It wasn't even a consideration, because going there and racing in the Eastern U.S., I realized that was where the competition was, those three big universities, Dartmouth, Middlesbury and St. Lawrence. That's when I found out they had athletic scholarships. I talked to the racers and asked about costs. 'Well, we're on a free ride,' they said, and I said, 'really, you get paid for everything, you get a coach and you go to the same races I'm at? And you have uniforms!' I thought wow, what could be better than that, geez, so yeah, it was an eye-opener." The CIAU had put such a kibosh on the notion of sports scholarships having any validity — or chance — in Canada, that Jacobs asserts he had never even thought about them previously. Thus, for these purposes, began his real education.

"I went there and made the team and saw what the program was like. We had incredible dry-land training and this is where I learned it all, weight training and endurance running, and intervals and running up sand hills. I got in better shape than I had ever been in my life! So that was '55 and '56 and then in '57 while at St. Lawrence I won the national championships in downhill in Canada. Dartmouth had Chickie Igaya who won the Olympic Giant Slalom in Squaw Valley in '60, Tom Corcoran, Ralph Miller, these were all the best skiers in the country and that was my university circuit. There was a Norwegian who went there too, Guttorm Berge, he was one of the best in the world.

"So then I got a sense of what was possible. Actually my father died at the time, and I did end up going to MIT, kind of. I was accepted but I dropped out because my heart wasn't in it. I went back to St. Lawrence and got my science degree and graduated in '61 and then ran ski schools in the east, in '62 and '63. I was still racing then. I raced pro," he said, sounding exactly like the world calibre athlete, coach and businessman he became.

In his milieu, Jacobs, of the English Canadian Quebecer tribe, made some invaluable contacts with the elite of the French ski world. This would have momentous impact on Canadian skiing, primarily because of what Jacobs had absorbed in and outside his university classrooms, what he brought to the table in his own right. "The lesson that I learned was that these kids are driven, to be at that level you are driven and each one has, whatever drives them, a fire in the belly. Their whole focus is on competition. When I was at St. Lawrence, I wanted to be the fittest guy in the country, and that was my drive because I would think, when I was lifting weights or running, I was thinking there is probably somebody somewhere doing an extra 10 pounds. So I'd push myself. That was my drive, somebody was doing that extra wind sprint or something. Everybody had their own drive and I think it's pretty much similar at that level. That's the focus."

So here's Jacobs, former national champion in a dysfunctional system, professional racer, university graduate, imbued with a "sense of what was possible," in the spring of 1964. "I'm from Montreal, and one of my mentors was a guy named Raymond Lanctot who imported French products, Dynamet skis and Rossignol skis, and through him I got to know some of the French national team racers. When they were racing in the U.S. they would come through Montreal. Raymond would host them and I met guys like Guy Perrilat, who was one of the best in France at the time and a guy named Charles Bozon; these are guys who were Olympic-calibre skiers. So [wife] Fay and I decided to go to Europe to Chamonis and skied with Guy Perrilat and Charles Bozon. Talking to them about their national team program, they explained their system, with the Espoirs, who were young kids that would aspire to the team, and these were nationally-supported programs where they got equipment and coaching, fulltime coaching. Honore Bonnet was the French national team coach, a full-time coach, and as the racers developed, when they got to the national team level, he would guide them in summer camps and training camps and travel with them so he really knew them.

"To me, it was such a stark contrast. I went to the world championships for Canada in 1958. At that time, I was the national downhill champion and so I was named to the team. John Platt was on the team with me, and I had never really known John, he was from the west, but we all met in Montreal on the plane and then we land in Frankfurt and we are introduced to our coach, Mukke Claussing from Germany. Here was a guy that had never seen me before in my life, had no idea how I skied. We'd go up to Garmisch and up to the Zugspitze to train. He spoke English, but it was a completely disjointed process. In the '60 Olympics, Franz Tritscher was the coach and there was a little more contact in the winter time so it had evolved somewhat. But the French team, they trained in the summer under the coaches, so it was a continuous process, an interactive process. I came back and I don't know why, but I just started thinking about it."

The result of those brain cells firing was a lengthy letter he addressed to CASA President Bill Tindale, in which he proposed a radical departure from the norm, which self-paraphrased 40 years later goes something like this: "I can foresee a process in Canada whereby you take athletes, hire a fulltime coach, center them at a town that has a university so the coach has an opportunity to train the athletes, monitor their process, and they can get an education."

In the Canada of the time, that mentality was almost as rare as the number of Canadian men who had won international ski medals. For all sports, the ruling heretics back east said it couldn't be done, while kindly offering intramurals to soften the blow for our more hyperactive youth. "I really felt it was important that athletes get an education at the same time because I was a college graduate, and a national-calibre athlete, and there weren't many in my era," Jacobs poignantly notes. "I suggested UBC. I didn't know anything about Nelson or Notre Dame but UBC and perhaps Garibaldi? There was nothing in Montreal or Toronto. I sent the letter to Bill Tindale. He forwarded it to Don Sturgess who was chairman of the international competitions committee.

"Don writes me back. He says 'Thanks for your letter; as a matter of fact we're researching a concept like that and have identified a university in Nelson, British Columbia, called Notre Dame, [your letter] is exactly what we are thinking about and would you like to apply for the job as head coach of the new program?' It was a serendipity thing. I wasn't looking for a job, I hadn't thought of coaching, and we had just finished with this [ski area] process. I was at this stage of my life and I said to Fay I'm going to take the job and we're going to move to Nelson, B.C." Serendipity as in a new job he really wasn't looking for, serendipity his being on the same wavelength as a suddenly — Wheeler, Heggtveit — invigorated

CASA, which was looking to cement these recent achievements via Jacob's preferred radical departure from the norm, by building the pyramid from the bottom up through incorporating education as the bottom line.

A year earlier at the 1963 AGM, Sturgess, Arnold Midgley of Ottawa, and Grant Boyd of Ottawa were named a three-man committee tasked with finding a solution to the ongoing tug-of-war over pursuing ski racing at the expense of scholastics. If one Ernie Gare is universally regarded in this parallel world as the hero of this script, then there are dozens upon dozens up dozens of co-heroes. One can't leave that note unsung and they were there right from that mystical Day One. Sturgess, an elegant elder citizen these days who carries his lanky frame with ease and is partial to the most civil of conversations, 43 years later retraced those long-ago first steps.

"I think the thinking for it started around '63, the year that we kept the [Greene's so-called National Western Canadian] team back from going to Europe and competed against the Americans. We had to assure ourselves that we had an adequate level of competition here in North America in order to justify a program, so as soon as we had such a good year competing against the Americans, in other words establishing that we really did have a very competitive environment", it was off to the races.

The trio delivered a master plan worthy of the bottom line. "It was to expand our base because the base we were drawing from was tending to be only skiers who were satisfied with giving up their educational activity. So if that was the limit we could see we weren't going to have the depth in the future. And there was a big age factor to it, especially with the girls. If they were going to have to go to a national program at age 14, how could they be expected to stop finishing their high school? Girls typically were reaching the peak earlier, their competitive level at 16, a lot of them, so how could you take away their opportunity to finish high school?" To which a non sequiter is the only rationale reply. Platt of Trail, who did much of the CASA's legwork out west while Sturgess was busy back east, said of those parents who curtailed their teen's ski ambitions to enforce an education first: "Maybe intelligently too, because we didn't have a structured program." At the time.

"As the skiers came up so fast, we needed people to identify them and keep an eye on their progress much earlier. So of course that facilitated communicating with their parents about their future. It was interesting," noted Sturgess, "there were so many aspects to it that we were unconsciously considering. I was just reading a paper, some international sports psychology thing, looking at the German team and all the factors that they think are most important to get a skier to an international level, and it includes things like parental support, motivational aspects for the skier and those kind of things. We were kind of unconsciously looking at precisely these areas to identify the ones with potential. At the same time, we didn't have it formalized in any kind of written selection process or anything like that. But we knew we had to identify a bigger group in order to have the top of the pyramid the best place we could draw from." The three committee members, acutely aware of Father David Bauer's university-based National Hockey Team then based out of UBC, and the rapidly-expanding U.S. collegiate ski-racing environment in the northwestern United States, over the next year produced this absolute gem of a report, authored by Sturgess:

*CANADIAN AMATEUR SKI ASSOCIATION*
*INTERNATIONAL COMPETITIONS COMMITTEE*
*ALPINE*
*Bulletin # 6*
*I.C.C. Chairman*
*659 Champagneur*
*Outremount, Quebec*
*August 20th, 1964*
*CANADIAN AMATEUR SKI ASSOCIATION*
*PROPOSED ALPINE NATIONAL TEAM PROGRAM*
*NELSON, B.C.*

*INTRODUCTION*

*The training programs organized by the Canadian Amateur Association during the past five years have resulted in great improvement in the level of Canadian competitive skiing, both at the National and International levels. However, because of the length of the time involved in attending such intensive programs on a full time basis, some National Team members have not been able to take part, while others have sacrificed educations and careers in order to partake in these programs. It was proposed at the last annual general meeting of the C.A.S.A. that a permanent type of training program be developed that would allow team members to continue their education while training for National and International competition. A committee consisting of Don Sturgess, Arnold Midgely, and Grant*

*Boyd, was formed for the purposed of studying this problem. The following report is the conclusion of this committee as to the best manner for future training of Canada's national Alpine Team.*

*AIMS OF PROGRAM*

*The chief aim of this program is to provide the best skiers possible for Canada's International Teams, without imposing serious restrictions on the educational opportunities of team members. The secondary aim is the development of more top-calibre Canadian racers, thereby adding depth to the National Team and team nominees.*

*SUMMARY AND CONCLUSIONS*

*The program proposed involves the training of National Team members from September through April each year, in Nelson, B.C. where participants could continue their education either at High School, Notre Dame University, or at the B.C. Vocational School, at the same time training and competing in major meets. Pre-season training could take place at Notre Dame University in Nelson, with initial slalom training at Kokanee glacier, near Nelson. Early season slalom training would be most feasible at Red Mountain near Rossland, with daily slalom and giant slalom training possible from January through March at the Silver King hill, only 10 minutes from Nelson. During the competitive season it would be possible to attend intercollegiate meets in Canada and the U.S. giving team members ample opportunity on F.I.S. calibre hills against top-ranked U.S. racers. Tentative schedules for the next two years are shown in the appendix. The total cost for this program would vary depending upon the numbers taking part, the totals estimated at $31,440 for 24 ($1,310 each) or $18,720 for 12 ($1,560 each). It is further proposed that a plan for financing this program be developed, with suggestion that industry be approached to underwrite one half the balance remaining after the Fitness Council grant is allowed for, the other half to be paid by the areas and individuals concerned. It is proposed that a Canada-wide committee be established to make industry contacts this summer, the incentive to industry participation being the development of individuals suitable for future employment in industrial positions. It is submitted that this program will aid the development of Canadian skiing, therefore immediate acceptance of the principle and general outline is recommended so that work on many of the details can be further refined.*

There's much, much more to it, of course and it's important to note that the entire report was approved unanimously. So when Jacobs forwarded his education/athletics thoughts two months later, it couldn't have resonated more loudly than in, oh, a few hundred receptive ears.

Sturgess: "That was one of the main reasons that we were really happy to be able to recruit him in the first place. He had an understanding of the U.S. collegiate system and he knew about racing down there. He knew about the Eastern half of it, as well as where it was going to happen, here in the West. Because, we wanted a person who understood education, international competitive skiing and then could buy the philosophy because nobody was going to come and take that job if they didn't buy the philosophy. We already had had coaches around. Well, first of all, none of our coaches were anything but European up to that point. None of them had any education at all. Of course ours was even more of a challenge because we were going to go to an international level. You had to bring them up to that level of competition and still be able to be in Nelson for 80 per cent, 60 per cent, whatever time it was going to take." Which Notre Dame bought into and assisted? "Exactly."

Buy it? Jacobs was selling it without trying. For him, the component of an academic education in an athlete's development was a no-brainer. As he notes, "I was a product of the system," even though he ruefully admitted that system was only available to him south of the 49th. Jacobs was hired not only by the CASA but also by Notre Dame to instruct mathematics. "So I guess that's how it started. My theory, or hope, was the athletes would work hard at training and skiing, and also their studies." Done, from Day One. "They went to school in the morning, a lot of them were in my math class, and we dry-land trained several hours in the afternoon. When we traveled to races in the U.S., Schweitzer Basin and so on, we took a tutor. His name was Dip Saraswati, I'll never forget, after training and after dinner in the evening the kids would sit down and have their study programs with him. As a matter of fact, in the winter of '65 we spent three weeks in Europe and Dip came with us then. That was the genesis of it and it came together perfectly here."

There was also the national team factor, rather, mostly non-factor, to consider. "Actually, Nancy gave me some of the old reports I wrote for the Canadian Ski Association in 1964, I just read them again, and can't believe I wrote that stuff. But one of my theories was that because my experiences with Canada had been such a disjointed thing, I didn't really feel a part of the Canadian team. I just met the guys from the West for the first time and it was like, we're on the Canadian team but we weren't a team. It was all individuals and we didn't have a coach. It was all that. My theory was I wanted them [national team] all here and I wanted them all to wear the same uniform, because of my experience from St. Lawrence. I talked to manufacturers and we designed jackets. Everybody had the same training, sweat clothing, same ski jackets; I tried to make them feel that they were representing Canada.

"Part of my drive was to talk to the press, so for the first time I really started talking to reporters and we got incredible press. I talked to Volkswagen Canada and said we need buses; I want them to have their own buses, so Volkswagen donated those two with Canadian National Ski Team logos. I wanted them to feel like a national team. They trained so hard, they suffered together. You bring back that bond. You suffer together, you bond together, train together and represent the country together. Just by reading the articles about themselves, they got a sense of, hey! We gave them a purpose almost bigger than themselves, to represent Canada. At the same time I tried to instil in them [that it should never come] at the expense of humility, and I'd say to them you never believe your own press. You have the purpose to improve yourself and be the best that you can be but as soon as you start believing in what you read about yourself ... The approach wasn't like many American universities where football players are given a token grade and they just wanted to play. No. [NDU] expected them to do well, they weren't throwing any bones at the athletes, they were treated just like regular students. Except they had that allowance," for working as much or more on their academics outside regular classroom hours as in. "They gave them an allowance for doing that — and that's what we needed."

Selling it, buying it, living it. "I think it's great, make no mistake; my experience with the national team program here was the best experience in my life, and the benefits for the kids were huge. I just value the participation of sports in life's lessons, anything that will contribute to that is beneficial. The fact that some universities won't give athletics scholarships doesn't make sense to me. These kids have driven themselves to be athletes. Sure, they might go to universities for athletics but they are going to become good students, they have it inside of them. So what if the motivation is athletics to begin with, so what? How can anybody judge? You can't play god, how are you going to play god?"

Echoes Webster: "Well, in my opinion, there's no question that pure athletic scholarships work. Now there's no question that society's changed, systems have changed, competitions have changed, education's changed, equality's changed, but there's no reason why you can't take that groundwork we did in the '60s and modernize it, right?" Good question, but you don't have to ask that of the converted, it's the nay-sayers that need their little worlds rocked.

Before arriving in Nelson, Webster was active in Quebec sports and business circles (after realizing early on he wasn't a top-notch racer) and working for the Royal Trust Company of Canada. "It was an outstanding company and this shows how progressive they were. If I was going to go and get my MBA, my manager could have said go and come back, but because I was going to go and run a ski team, I had to talk to the president to get permission to go. And he gave it to me without even blinking an eyelash, because he was a former athlete himself. He let me go for $1 a year. I kept my position in the Royal Trust Company of Canada, he paid me a dollar a year to hold me, to keep my position, continue my pension, continue all that kind of stuff. And as a result of me being a pioneer, two or three guys in our office played hockey for Canada, they were Trust Company guys," apologizing for not remembering their names 40 years later.

"One other guy went off and did something else in sport, because he told me afterwards when I came back, did you realize you opened the gate? I didn't at the time. That was the type of the cooperation that Canada had from the corporate world, then we moved into the sponsorship world and we lost some of that togetherness. I mean, I will never say a bad word about Mr. Harrington and the Royal Trust Company, because they gave me an opportunity I would never, never, never have gotten in my life."

As to why Webster was also so easily able to "buy" into the new CASA development formula, "I don't know where this came from. I think it came a little bit from my dad because my dad sponsored Linda Crutchley, who was a great Canadian ski racer. He always liked education, and so he helped her do her skiing and her education and so that worked. It came down to me somehow, and I also saw that a lot of the guys who came off the national team became ski instructors and sports reps and ski reps and stuff like that and it was really my dad who turned around and said 'you see that guy there, he could be a lot better than he is, but he needs to be educated'. Oh, [Dad] was an Olympic athlete and I was very proud of Canada and our

Olympic movement and all that. I thought, well here's a chance. I was 19 or 20 and I started promoting the hell out of it and then somehow, I forget who came to me and said, 'do you want to [manage] the national team' and I said oh, alright," with an actor's skill of feigning a lack of humility.

"We were learning as we went. The idea of having an athletic table was way out, an athletic training table where we had the meals. Mrs. Anderson, who was [team member] Vern Anderson's aunt, worked in the kitchen and she did special meals that Jake and I designed. Where we got that from, I have no idea. We gave everybody stress tabs, which is a Vitamin B supplement, because we heard you guys are under so much pressure, training and travel, and blah, blah, blah, you should have more Vitamin B in your system. So I got these things called stress tabs, big bloody things like horse pills. They used to pee bright yellow, and so I knew if everybody was taking them," he says over his own guffaws. "I want to see you write your name in the snow!" which of course is an applicable test only for certain team members.

"When you think of the pioneering stuff that we did, I mean very few people ever did dry-land training. We were so far ahead of it, we took tutors to Europe. It didn't really work but the concept was there. It was too much of a varied amount of kids in different classes and different progress. We were really working hard every single day, to get the kids to come back, slow down, and get their heads together. But you know, we tried it, in good faith we tried it. We really tried to be ahead of this game. No other team ever, think about it, no other team ever left Canada with a team doctor until 1966. Doctor Al Carner came with us, and he volunteered. So we tried these things, right, and look at our buses, we had team buses, who else had team buses? We had uniforms, we had suitcases that matched, thanks to Mr. Woodward. Mr. Woodward was very good to us, he gave us razors, and gave us slacks, and gave us nice Canadian plaid suitcases."

So many little, little things, such a big, big vision.

"We operated, the sport system operated over the university system, as opposed to the university system operating outside the sports system, so we worked hand-in-glove with our university and we were the best in the country. We brought in the best in the country, the juniors, we brought them into the high schools, we got them to art school, we got them to the university, so we controlled the kids, the university didn't control the kids ... I guess I could say they controlled

50 per cent of their time and we controlled the other 50 per cent of their time, but we had the ultimate voice so we turned around and helped the university enforce the scholarship. It was a partnership; we had the club: if you don't perform in the classroom, if you don't perform on the hill, you're outta there. Most of the kids wanted to be on the national team, there was nobody that packed it in at all. We didn't have to send anybody home. There's no question that the odd time some kids stayed home from weekend races but nobody lost their scholarship, nobody."

Bottom line, then, Mr. Webster, is why Notre Dame University, but, god forbid, not the rest of the CIAU? "I don't have an answer for that, because I believe the education system screwed up and I believe the sports system screwed up. You look at our program, our program was copied by water polo in Kingston, Queen's University, basketball I think was St. Mary's University, badminton was UBC, swimming was in there somewhere too and this was in cooperation with the O'Keefe brewery. They brought in the best coaching in the world and O'Keefe paid for it, the corporate world, and they created these programs at universities and they did that after us because we were heading for the '76 Olympics. They took the basis of our program, which was the education portion of it, and the university model and plunked them in there. But don't ask me, you'd have to analyze it and see why it didn't work but the concept was starting to develop and it was starting to get funding involved and all that stuff. I don't have an answer today. I know the ingredients are out there in the system and it can still be done, it can probably be done far more efficiently than it is being done today — but there are too many executives in sport."

Yes, but if you have the right executives. "We never had everybody in the same uniform before," Jacobs told the Edmonton Journal's John Korobanik in 2004. "Everyone had a sense of purpose. This was Canada's national ski team. It gave everyone tremendous incentive. We went to the first races in 1965 in Aspen. Billy Kidd and Jimmy Heugo had just won their Olympic medals. And Peter Duncan, Nancy Greene, Bob Swan ... they pretty much cleaned those guys. Sports Illustrated wrote this big article, 'Canadians Raid Aspen'. And it took off from there."

Currie Chapman remembers the team's mission as well, well, at least Father Aquinas's pet goal. "We had to go down and win that NCAA title against Denver and Colorado and all those teams, in skiing. We won the title twice, I think. That was part of the deal, is that he would allow us to go [to NDU] on full scholarship as long as we would bring him back an American title, because he was from New York, he loved the NCAA kind of thing, that whole aspect."

While Chapman was eventually to parlay such grand experiences in Nelson into his position with the women's national team, The Little Tiger, AKA Nancy Greene, flew the highest because she went the fastest. In 1967, she won six individual races and the first-ever women's overall World Cup title. One year later, she defended that title and at the Winter Olympics in Grenoble, France, won Olympic gold and silver medals. The spoilsports countered that it was her, not the program. Pssshhhhaw, she says, pointing out that Jacobs' introduction of intense dry-land training in the fall, the CASA's summer camps at Kokanee Glacier and the chance to ski against the men — all part of the NDU program — made the difference.

As she told Korobanik, "For me it was the perfect situation. I trained a lot with the guys so I always had somebody around who was skiing better than I was, who was training harder, that I would have a hard time catching up to." She might have had a hard time catching up, but she certainly passed well. She retired after her incredible Olympic year, and two years later the national team was relocated from Nelson to Montreal under husband to-be and new national team coach Al Raine, but in her footsteps followed the likes of Betsy Clifford, Kathy Kreiner, Laurie Graham, Karen Percy, Kerrin Lee, Gerry Sorenson.

"The whole idea of being on the national ski team came out of that era and is really, in many senses the genesis of what the concept of what a national team is today," Jungle Jim Hunter, an original Crazy Canuck, told Korobanik, the Sports Editor of the Nelson Daily News during the ski team's stay in Nelson. "I'm not talking about just a ski team. I'm talking about the concept of a national team in any content. The national team back in the '80s and the whole concept ... was pretty powerful. To me it was enormous."

Korobanik heard this from no less a source than national ski head honcho Ken Read: "There's no question that the establishment of the team gave a focus to stepping up the whole Canadian ski program. That brought a structured program that really is a continual link to the team that is getting ready for the 2005 world championships and the 2006 Olympic Games. The reason is that the Nelson program was way ahead of its time. They had what was in effect a national training centre and a lot of the things Alpine Canada is now trying to recreate. Educational initiatives, a summer training facility on glaciers, albeit now quite a bit more sophisticated. But the concept is very much the same as they were doing it 40 years ago,"

Forty years ago, 21 young Canadian ski racers that first year were given the opportunity to set their own horizons. "They had a full plate and they did an incredible job. I really respect what they did," said Jacobs.

A few more than 40 years ago, there was also a struggle between east and west over the home and direction of the national ski program. We couldn't have our best skier only representing half the country, could we, really, even if Nancy Greene and her team-mates got a vicarious thrill out of it?

"There was definitely a tug of war in that sense," said Sturgess, as visions of a superman holding up a collapsed bridge come to mind. Down East, "The feeling was the mountains we had here weren't really that well developed, either, developed in the sense of having a lot of choices. After all, we only had Red Mountain at the time, Vancouver had nothing, it didn't have the vertical drop there so that you could do a serious race and you couldn't count on the weather ever cooperating. There were too many negative factors. You had Banff, in either 1948 or '50 they held some kind of world championships in Banff. They definitely had that international class of hill to race on but there was a feeling that it wasn't the kind of a place where there was enough going that we could center on and have a lot of races there and keep sending people out.

"Sure, they were right about the competition, if they went to Europe they could compete. But what we were seeing was what was going on in Colorado and even in Washington State and maybe to a lesser extent like Utah, they were very serious. In Idaho, the Harriman Cup had always been an outstanding international race, they always attracted a top field. Avril Harriman, who started Sun Valley, had the race named after him and he made sure they got the best in the world coming there and that went right back into the '40s and '50s. We used to go down there from Rossland for a long time. They had a base there and were well known, and the skiers from Vancouver went there. So there was international racing going on here in Western North America. They had the hills to justify it and they had the ski organizations to hold it and they had the local competition base and things like that so it was growing and one of things we felt — it wasn't

B.C. or Canada, it was the whole of the Western North America was going to have a much more powerful ski base."

Platt chimes in on the subject: "It couldn't just be looked at as a Western Canada group, it had to be national. It had to have the support, really, of Quebec and Ontario. Pierre Alain did a lot of the groundwork back east to make sure of support for both the eastern and western, and that it was going to be a national entity. It took a fair amount of convincing for the clubs to give up all their autonomy because the clubs were very strong and in a way didn't want to lose that tradition."

They surrendered it up for a piece of a more tasty pan-Canadian pie. Says Sturgess, "I think there was always a tug of war back and forth about where you should have an event and who were the best racers. I think that putting together the Notre Dame thing was a positive thing, I mean the east and the west together under one agreement with one concept. We always thought [Nelson] was the only place we'd be able to do this kind of program in Canada successfully. We weren't going to be able to get a world-class hill for downhill in the East at that time. Mount St. Anne was the only one that had the kind of vertical drop but it wasn't developed then and of course we would have a lot of problems with a bilingual education. That came later so it wasn't even an option in the first place. But I think there was an agreement that we needed to broaden our base and here was an area we could do it, so we went ahead and did it in what was the most logical place at that time."

Especially when you have Ernie and Notre Dame University awaiting you with open arms. "He was very positive about the idea. I think probably partly because there was a parallel with what Father Bauer had done, and I think that was very much in Ernie's mind. I think having a national-level team was appealing to them and I think that the university also was looking for things that would bring their credibility to a higher level. If they were doing something on a national scale [it would be] bringing more attention to the university as a place to go. I think they might have thought that it might be a good way to attract enrolment through the skiing because it would have pointed out to [outside] people the recreational opportunities in the area because they might not have known, Nelson was never thought of as a skiing town just because of the proximity to Rossland."

Sturgess remained actively involved in the management of the program until he returned to post-graduate studies of his own in 1967.

"That would have been the fourth year and they were still attracting a good enrolment of students to it. They were building up toward the '68 Olympics and they had a fairly good core team in terms of overall talent." As Grenoble proved, but in 1970, almost under the cover of night, the team, but not the scholarship program, relocated to Montreal. Guess that most charming of Canadian cities felt it was time to take something back after all the gifts it had bestowed upon the Queen City. Just joking, there.

"I don't know if there was maybe some kind of let-down that was coming after that in terms of being able to keep attracting people or what, but I know that certainly sports, skiing, in the world was getting to be a more professional thing and it was already being recognized through the World Cup, that kind of model, that level of competition. The skiers were better subsidized by the equipment companies in one form or another, it was quite a bit of professionalism with the top 10 amateurs in the world. There was money around and the countries that had the big names, Austria France, Switzerland and so on had the money certainly to fund their programs adequately, better than we did. So I don't know if that led the ski association to a more professional kind of approach to it," says Sturgess, who admits the end of the team's education component hurt then and now.

There was of course some spirited gnashing of teeth in Nelson in losing such a valued possession, but one has to keep in mind just how small Nelson really is. When the team established its base there in 1964, the population inside city limits was 10,000. When it moved to Montreal, the population was around 10,000. It still is today — although twice as many drive across the bridge daily to their homes along the West Arm rather than live in Nelson proper.

Among those upset to see it go was Platt, who took over Jacobs' head coach duties at his request following the World Championships in Portillo, Chile, in 1966, where the Canadian team again turned heads, proving they were on the right track. While Sturgess was preparing his initial report back in Montreal, Platt prepared for the terrain for the 1964 summer camp on Kokanee Glacier, the camp that really started it all for the country's first national alpine ski team.

The former Red Mountain racer was perfectly attuned to the skiing/education wavelength the CASA was now broadcasting. "The philosophy of everyone involved was to tie it in with the educational aspect because you can spend a lot of time in athletics and maybe only one person like Nancy will succeed. You wanted them to have an opportunity to go on and do other things in life. Father Aquinas wanted to give them the opportunity to go to university, use their intellect and brain, because you can't train all the time, and if you can have other kinds of focuses it helps the athletics. But it does take some integration and it takes some money, so they have that sorted."

Platt also suggests that Greene always downplayed her academic activities. For her part, she dispels the rumour she was all jock. Having already attended secretarial school, she at first worked in the registrar's office and admits to only enrolling fulltime in the fall of 1966. Then came her first overall World Cup title, the next year her second straight and two Olympic medals, and with them the education of a lifetime. Today she is chancellor of Thompson Rivers University, chartered in 2005.

Platt was with the team through those Grenoble Olympics. Sure, the World Cup was mushrooming from its infancy, and sure Nelson wasn't the easiest place in the world to get to, but "It does take someone who believes in it to keep it there, so if anyone has got any apprehension like Al did about the academic part … Al didn't really buy into that. I'd say Al had more of that [more training, more racing] philosophy than really carrying on and trying to build something in a university environment. And I'm not saying that he's right or wrong because at that time they definitely did need more summer skiing on a more demanding basis for downhill and giant slalom."

In attempting to explain what he "bought" into, Platt tells a tears-of-joy-jerker. "I think that was a lot to do with Don Sturgess and Pierre Alain. How are you going to put it together that makes some sense for the athlete and for the club per se? It was determined that the facility and an opportunity like in Nelson would bring this together. Dave Jacobs was a very good spokesman for it because he's a good public speaker, he could inspire people to think about it and with articles from these papers and other aspects people started to realize that this was a unified national team. So people would actually come in and say 'OK, I'd like to give an award to the national team.' I remember Dave, the first donation was $5, it was from somewhere on Vancouver Island," he says, half chuckling with a hint of the incredulous. "Yeah, some lady had read in some newspaper article on what the objectives were, you know, having the ski team there and having the athletics and receiving international recognition and the education and the whole bit and she was quite taken by it and she sent

$5. So I remember, Dave sort of took this letter, 'Thank you very much, can you imagine that?' And I always remember that, he was very, very taken by it, this real kind of … innocence."

As for his specific time at the university, Platt recalls: "Ernie could contribute because of his athletic background so he was good for feedback, and critique, for any of that. He also set up a lot of the exercises and the weight training. Ernie was always looking down the road at what you needed. You could only do so much weight training before you start to lose your flexibility. Ernie found out that down in Western Washington University there was a professor that was an expert in this. He could measure all your various movements so we went down to Western Washington and took a week-long course from him. Then we brought him up to actually test the kids, because academically he was far better equipped — and interested. We measured the flexibility of all the team and then could see that some of them were actually very flexible. And you had these types of opportunities in a university environment. Ernie was a big supporter of it because Ernie could realize the potential of having that type of an organization there and he could also see the same within the hockey environment. Ernie was basically an athlete, eh? He excelled in hockey, but he liked athletes, so he didn't differentiate. He was very supportive of world-class athletes coming there — and having the opportunity to work with them too."

Gare would have been the first to recognize being home to the national ski team was NDU's coup and his good fortune. It sadly is no flight of fancy to recognize a prevailing sense of academic egoism on the part of those Canadian university presidents who for so long maintained the separation of church and state that tarnished athletic scholarships as undesirable. They would deny this of course, and offer some other deflective rationale; understandably, they have their personal egos to prop up and maintain. Their reasons date, boy do they date, but of course, the earth was once not only thought flat but the center of the universe as well.

What is more a pity is that they were in a position to implement the impediment, to the detriment of generations of Canadian youth. It boggles the mind that developed minds such as their's would stoop out of pettiness to prevent the talented youth of Canada from reaching their full potential, but the thought does emerge. If Notre Dame University had subscribed to such an approach, none of this would have come about, imagine that parallel world. Ironic, isn't it, that a belief system as dogmatic as Catholicism can be, would in fact be responsible for such a forward-thinking and innovative approach to self-development as Notre Dame University offered up on a platter to the first Canadian National Ski Team.

---

"The first qualification is not mastery of subject matter, that you know a lot of history, or English. It's character, and the second one of course is ability. When you have character, that factor enters into every aspect of your life, whether it's art, music, teaching, playing hockey or whatever it is. It transfers from one to the other. And then the learning part, without the character, without the initiative, without the drive and the will to do something, then it really doesn't matter what the subject matter is because you take your character with you wherever you go. If it's for the good and if you instil the right habits, learning, completing a task, or putting all your energy into what you are doing, it applies equally to the sports area, the artistic area, to the academic area. It's that that makes it possible for an athlete to be good at academics and a person in academia being a good athlete. That transfers to what I felt about the program at Notre Dame and it's because at that time I was fortunate enough to appreciate that factor about people and what they were capable of doing."

Such is our introduction to Mary (Pat) MacMillan, education professor and Dean of Women at Notre Dame when Father Aquinas and Gare were looking to the future and throwing off needless shackles as fast as they could identify them. Today "Mrs. Mac" is a fairly robust 94, still plays a destructive or exemplary game of bridge depending if you're sitting adjacent or opposite her, and lives alone in a semi-assisted seniors' complex in Abbotsford, B.C, all three daughters within a couple hours' driving distance. Her education bona fines are exemplary; you don't emerge without such from a teaching career that began as a teenager in a rural Albertan one-room school, to her decade at Notre Dame, to in her 50s being selected as state curriculum designer in Alaska — following a full 50-state search, of which she says she is most proud — to having your services requested as a consultant on the education of troubled youth when in your tenth decade. When you're her age, you don't worry too much about pride coming before a fall.

"And then there was this other factor that I was very conscious of. You don't tell people what they know already, or what they can do already, or the habits that they have already. You don't interfere with the habits they can acquire on their own by virtue of the fact they have a strong character or vent of some kind. You don't tell them or preach to them. My belief at the time was that if they had the habits and the character to do the athletic part then they also had the character to do the academic part. One of the remarkable things about my involvement in that [NDU] program is that I cannot recall one incident where the students in the sports program failed to satisfy the requirements of the academic program. And I worked with them because I prepared course work for them when they were out in the field and I knew after a day of skiing that you would be tired, that you would be exhausted, that you could hardly keep awake and that it took strength of character in order to do the assignments I'd prepared, and like I said, I can't recall an incidence in which one student failed to do what was expected of them academically."

Isn't that interesting, because isn't that precisely what the nay-sayers in the CIAU were certain is exactly what would happen: that, and allowing free-range student-athletes on campus would prove poisonous to their establishments' hallowed halls. If such a small group of people could do such harm, a look in the mirror might have reflected a house of cards. But, then, what did those "educators" really know about the education potential of Canadian athletes? It was certainly different than what they thought.

"When I think of education it's not what we tell people, it's not what we lecture to them about; it's what they do with what they're told, it's what they do when they discover for themselves, it's what they do when they have the character that says I'm going to be the best at what I can be. When parents instil this in children then they're giving them the greatest of gifts, because it's like money in your purse, you can carry it around with you wherever you go and it's easily transferable because it comes from within a person.

"There is no such thing as an athlete who has succeeded because he was coached well. A great athlete has a quality within himself that utilizes the coaching. If that doesn't exist, then nothing happens. It's the same thing with education, same thing with artists, it's the same thing with the businessman. It's how they use what is presented to them that makes them great. And it can't be directive; you present people with a plan or ideas. No matter how good a coach is, there's not going to be an athlete unless they put in what they have taught him ... and it's the same thing with education. It's the same thing with any field of endeavour, whether it's business or sports or education. We know from our experience with great sportsmen that when they turn to another field they were as successful in that field as they were in their sports field — if they transfer the same habits and attitudes. Because what is it? It's being the best you can be every time you step on the ice, it's being the best you can be every time you do an assignment. You ignore the fact you might be able to get away with less than you are able to do."

Quick questions, quicker answers, after the breakfast dishes at the pancake house were cleared away. Seldom, I'm sure, has an interviewer curious about the academic side of university sport had a better brain to pick or an easier time of it.

Can athletes be better students because they are athletes?

"Yes: For the same reason they were successful in one field, it wasn't what they were told and had demonstrated, it's what they put into it themselves. That's a quality they can carry into any area because the great people, the people who succeed, are not the people who were lifted and carried over. They are the people who did it themselves. It doesn't matter what field you're in. It's a very personable attribute. Being the best you can be, wherever you are and whatever you do, is the key to achievement.

"So that's why I think great athletes can be great scholars or great scholars can be great athletes. Also, considering if you are five-foot-six, you mightn't be a hockey player. But any athletic endeavour they went into it would be possible for them because of character, habits and attitudes. That's why an academic sports scholarship is ideal because either the outcome will be the development of athletes or the outcome will be academically successful people. One way or the other, they will fit in better than the person who has a one-track aspiration."

How do you teach "dumb jocks"?

"My experience has been, and I'm very happy to be able to say this, as an administrator at the university level I admitted students who were reported to be less than able academically, but because of their character they not only succeeded but were very successful. You can have an athlete with the right attitudes and habits coming into higher education with what would apparently be inadequate preparation being turned into a good scholar. Because, you see, the reality of it is we don't know, we can't look into a person's mind, we can't know what's there. A person might seem inadequate because they didn't have an opportunity, because they didn't put enough energy into it or didn't have enough interest in it. But once they developed an attitude of optimism or interest it changed their whole appearance.

"They could change from an indifferent student into an A student in a remarkably short time because learning in any endeavour is what comes from within a person: When I change, the world changes; when an athlete changes his world changes; when a student changes his world changes. People are in control of their own destiny and the sad fact is that there are too many people who don't realize that, who don't understand that, who don't have the confidence to believe that. The real crux of the matter is that it's what comes from within a person that determines whether they succeed or not. If they feel they can't succeed, that's what will happen. If they feel that they can, that's what will happen to them, they will succeed. I'm very much in favour of an academic athletic program, combined, because I know that it can happen and I know that students don't necessarily need to suffer academically because they are interested in sports."

Why did Canadian academia say "no" to sports scholarships?

"When you are thinking of limitations, you get limitations. So it's a lack of understanding, this basic thing of aptitudes, habits and character. And I admit within the academia there is a perception that if you are a dedicated sports person, then that's enough, you can't do both. But I've seen enough successes, in my work, not only at Notre Dame but in other work in Alaska, California and Michigan, that people have infinite potential. When they have the attitudes and habits to succeed in one area all they have to do is transfer them to another area. And I feel very strongly that there is a tendency to underestimate the potential of people generally, and maybe there should be more of, 'I trust you to think for yourself. I trust you to try something. I will not deny you the opportunity [to] succeed if we allow you to do it.'"

Was it some sort of jealousy that led the university presidents within the CIAU to say "no" to sports scholarships?

"It was because they genuinely believed that you couldn't pursue two paths. That might be alright if you're walking through a forest but that doesn't apply to what your mind can do, to the power of your brain, to using your resources, because let's face it, the general consensus is that there aren't many of us who use our mental resources to the best of our ability. So I think there was a general feeling that people can't be good at hockey and philosophy both, or can't be good at hockey and chemistry or whatever it is. But maybe that's because it hasn't been done, enough. Maybe it's because we've closed our minds to the fact that you carry your self with you wherever you go and if you are a certain kind of person in one field you are carrying that into the next field. If you succeed here you will succeed there because you carry your self wherever you go."

How about those successful student-athletes?

"Just bring yourself along, here's the opportunity. Because in the long run the person who has ability in sports and is interested in academics is a well-rounded person and has many interests in life and lives a good healthy life, and has a lot to offer. We see it in a lot of our athletes. Because one of the things that happens in your life when you're a good athlete is there are diversions like late hours, liquor, drugs, you can't indulge in those if you are a great athlete. You have a lifestyle, you have a goal, you have an objective, you take care of your health, you take care of your body, you're a team worker. When you get an instruction or a suggestion you have what it takes to turn that into action, to turn that into learning. There wasn't a great athlete because of the great coaching, there's an athlete that did or carried out something the coach said. It comes from within. So if an athlete wants to enter an academic program he brings that 'I have this gift, I have this capability, I have this drive. I have this enthusiasm,' right along with him. That's when you see marvellous things, magical things, happen."

Ahem.

You loved playing baseball, didn't you?

"There's another thing to be said for athletics, too: It's an interest that carries you all through your life and if there's one thing that's paramount in living is that in every stage of your life it's not so much what you are going through at the present time but your preparation for the future, the interests you have, the outlook you have, the enthusiasm that you have and these become part of your increasing age. People whom you might say "become old gracefully" are the people who carry these interests, these enthusiasms, these observations. So who are we to deny people the opportunity to go into academics if they are sports people? It's their choice. If people want to try something, we should be enough advanced in what we understand about the brain and what the brain reveals about people who have enthusiasm, what the brain reveals about people who are frustrated, what the brain reveals about people who don't get opportunities, we have all the information now in a way we didn't have before, so we should be saying to people if you want to try it, you're the one who knows what you are able to do, or what your capabilities will be if you get the opportunity. It makes the world a different place."

Thoughts on the teaching profession?

"I guess you say the problem in education, or the goal in education, or the objective of education, is that we in education say to a person, this is who you are, this is what your potential is. Maybe we should focus more on that than test results, the standardized tests. And let me say something about standardized tests: If we put a child into a standardized test and he's not very sure of what he can do, he's immediately incapable of doing the test properly, because he feels he's a failure, or he feels that it is too much for him, or he's afraid of what it will show about him. We put him in a position where it's impossible for him to show what he is able to do. Maybe this is what happens with a lot of people. When we deny them a chance to try something, when we say this is what you are good at but it's not possible for you to be good in another area, maybe we are denying them the opportunity to show what they can do when they take themselves into a different situation. If people are athletes and they want to get into the academic side, they shouldn't be denied. They should go with our blessing."

From a professor's perspective, what was it like working with student-athletes for the first time?

"None of us regarded it as a hardship, or resented it, I'm positive about that, and we would have if the students hadn't done the work. That's what made it a success, the students did the work, and they did it satisfactorily, because I wasn't one and neither was Dip to say, well you know, you did it any old way and that's acceptable. Mind you, we made some adjustments but we didn't feel that the students took advantage of it. We felt that they gave it an honest try — there was no just handing any old thing in and expecting to get credit for it. There was nothing, nothing, like that at all, because neither of us would have accepted that. We knew that Ernie and Dave probably put on a little pressure. Maybe not, because the students had the greatest respect for Ernie. I know that every student that ever worked with Ernie would have the warmest feelings and the greatest respect for the time they spent with him.

"There isn't enough ... I guess you could say he had a vision that he persuaded the rest of us that it had worth and he put every effort into making it come to pass and it was marvellous, it was a marvellous experience. I tried as much as possible, for instance if a student came to me and said can I do an independent study on that part? I would allow that. It didn't happen very often but it happened a few times. I got superlative work, I got astounding work, work that I couldn't do myself from people who decided 'I want to do an individual project'. It was because they were doing something outside of the class. And I still think that is a good system. A combination. I sometimes wondered if that would be possible in very large classes, and I still think it would be. If other students had resented it I would really remember that, but there was never a suggestion that they were being favoured or anything — to the last individual, every individual on that ski team, that's really an accomplishment. We didn't have the embarrassment or the confusions, saying you know you're going on [ski] trips but you're not doing your [school] work. It was a given that when they were in the university they were students coming in Saturday and Sunday and working all day. No, it was wonderful."

Forty-some odd years had passed, let us not forget, between Mrs. Mac's having lived through this and now recalling it. But if anyone could present a better case for Notre Dame's approach and Notre Dame's people, they can try to top this.

Why Notre Dame?

"There were a number of factors. Ernie Gare and Dave Jacobs were key. Their enthusiasm, their own work, the work that Ernie did in the university in his courses and in his coaching and in his guiding of the young people was a real force. You couldn't diminish that. There was the willingness of the instructors to join the plan, not just the willingness, the enthusiasm. Even though I was teaching a great many courses, I was very enthusiastic in the beginning and gave it my full support. What Ernie asked of us was if we would be willing to prepare courses or assignments for students when they were out on the road, and let me repeat again that I never had an incident where students failed to respond. There were very many excellent students there. Curry Chapman was an absolutely fantastic teacher of junior high students, as well as a great athlete, a great administrator, all of those things. And he was one of the ones that responded to that program.

"So, it was a combination of factors. The facilities were in a place where skiing was possible, and it wouldn't have been possible without Ernie Gare. I mean he demonstrated in his work and his interests in the academic side of the university as well as the sports side that it was possible and his enthusiasm and our respect for what he contributed had something to do with our willingness to go along with the program. And none of us ever regretted it, there was never one word of regret for entering the program from the academic side. As a matter of fact, we had a great deal of pride in what these young people accomplished. And you see, again, the character, the drive, that they evidenced in their skiing transferred to the academic side. It was their character.

"Subject matter was secondary to the character and that is a theory or an ism that holds true. I mean character comes first, attitude and habits and what you are as a person is the first consideration. And that's what Ernie did, he saw what people could be and by what they were rather than what we asked them to do. It was a successful program, a very successful program. And the students ended up succeeding, because when you go into an athletic field you can't all be gold medal winners but you don't let that fact deprive you of the interests that you have and you don't let that fact say well, if I don't succeed then what'll I do? There is no other avenue because I haven't explored any other avenue? Ideally, a well-rounded person is what we want in our citizens."

Were you aware it was the only program of its kind in Canada?

"We were aware of it but we didn't think of it as doing something extraordinary or unusual. Ernie had a way of, I can't recall any resistance to the plan, ever. Maybe it was because of the kind of students we had. Because it wasn't just we agreed to it because of Ernie, but we were enthusiastic about it, and we were ... and nobody said well, it isn't possible, that I recall. To this day I'm very convinced athletes can have an academic program and succeed at it. And in fact I think it's a good thing to develop both sides of your character and your interests, in anything that you do."

What was your role as Dean of Women when the scholarship program first came about, seeing as how you were the one and only in Canadian history overseeing a full-ride variety?

"I remember that distinctly because Ernie and I worked together quite a bit. I don't know if Ernie first made a point of it or whether I did, but we discussed the students, the skiers, quite a number of them were in my classes. We talked a lot. On occasion we would discuss students who were having problems and what we could do about them. It evolved because we worked closely, just in informal ways, because Ernie, and I think we were the same, we were pretty dedicated to the students that we had, we wanted them to succeed, and I think that's why both of us got to the university — because Father Aquinas knew we would work hard. That's saying a lot, yes, the reason I got there was because of the way I worked [while teaching] high school. But I know that Ernie and I did a lot of talking about the students he was working with and the students I was working with and it just became sort of a habit.

"I would talk to him about a student who wasn't doing well and am certain now that when I look back at it that Ernie would have that student in and say what can you do to bring your marks up? He was like that. Every individual was of paramount importance to Ernie, and I can't ... as a man, as a friend, and as a colleague, there isn't enough I can say about him to really express my admiration of his character, his honesty and his integrity and of having the privilege of working with someone like that. And you see it's always a privilege to have a friend like that, to know that you have something in common because in a way you're a reflection of what he is ... it's difficult to express it in words."

Thank you Mrs. Mac for so innocently contradicting yourself — you just did so perfectly. Gare, a father of six, was all honourable actions and emotions. If not effortlessly, then at least self-effacingly he maintained that rare higher ground most of us can only dream of, personably, eminently, always admirably, until he was struck down by Lou Gehrig's disease in 1980, fit as a fiddle when his incurable disease struck. The very special ones, the fortunate, are able to recognize it at the end if it comes their way too soon: there is such a thing as living legend status. His eldest son, Ernie Jr., tossed this line over his shoulder while walking up mom Cathy's front door steps for dinner, some 25 years after his death: "Dad was way ahead of his time." Twentieth Century Renaissance Man comes to mind.

On his passing, the BCAHA inaugurated a coach-of-the-year award in his honour, recognizing him as the "ideal coach." For good reasons, here's but one example. In 1978-79, with Bill McDonnell assisting, Ernie coached the Nelson Midget Reps to a top four finish in the provincial finals held in the Civic Centre. Five Nelson Minor Hockey graduates, including his son Morey, played for the Nelson Junior Maple Leafs that season. Ernie and McDonnell crafted a team of nearly all first-year Midgets, led by future NHLer Greg Adams, into a squad emphasizing hockey sense and talent built on fundamentals. In the first round of the playoffs, Nelson survived an overtly physical mauling from a bigger, year-older Trail team in a best-of-three series that required four games because of an overtime finish in Game 3, before it skated off bruised and battered — but with it-hurts-to-laugh chuckles. In 2002, son Danny of NHL and Team Canada fame joined his father in the B.C. Hockey Hall of Fame and in 2005 had his No. 18 jersey retired to the rafters by the Buffalo Sabres. Imagine those emotions for a son who credits his father unconditionally for his success, whose brothers are NHL scouts, and whose brother-in-law Tom Renney was elected to the B.C. Hockey Hall of Fame in 2004, and today coaches the New York Rangers. His eldest and youngest daughters, Glenda and Jennifer, married "hockey guys", Mary-Anne a strapping Irish mason. Google the Ernie Gare Scholarship Society and you learn that it is "Canada's first and longest-running athletic scholarship program". Gare, and his extended family, underpinned all that goes by the name of a life well lived.

Nelson has had its Montreal connections, its Civic Centre, its Notre Dame University, its hockey hey-days, its national ski team, its people. Today its website proudly proclaims its standing as "The Greatest Little Arts Town in Canada". If you've ever seen the Steve Martin-Darryl Hannah movie Roxanne, then you'll know the producers couldn't have found a location more appropriately surreal. At least it sure seemed like that at times there, especially for all those like Mrs. Mac who became friends with Ernie Gare. He, Ted Hargreaves, Nancy Greene and all athletic scholars from Socrates on down are a part of Nelson, B.C., which, glory be, was all spruced up and looking idyllic on January 13, 2007, when CBC's Hockey Day In Canada skated into location. Let it snow, let it snow, let it snow (which it did), we all know. What we heard anew was through this interview:

Ron McLean (from Nelson): "Your mom Cathy, by the way, has been a hero this week, she's embarrassed when I call her the Matriarch of Hockey in town, she is, and she's been a superstar, but let's talk about your Dad Ernie, and first of all, a little about the Notre Dame college, now it's called Selkirk, but tell us a bit about the school."

Danny Gare (by video-link from Columbus, Ohio): "Well, it's interesting. Dad, you know, played for the Leafs for many years, and that's all I ever really wanted to do, Ron, was to play for this team here that had the jersey with the Maple Leaf on and there was a lot of players that I watched you know throughout the years when Dad was playing, Shorty Malacko, Frank Carlson, Marsh Severyn, a number of players, Frank Arnett, you saw Howie Hornby talking about it, so, a lot of players that I looked up to. And even when he started the scholarship program and went to the university as the Athletic

74

Director, you know there were players there that really played and shone for the Leafs and throughout the collegiate play in Canada. So to have that scholarship and be around those individuals like Murray Owens, and Carl Chwacka, and Hugh Hooker, Buck Crawford, Brian Russill and so on and so forth, I could go on and on, they were great figureheads for me and I used to stick-boy, I used to go to practice, I used to be around them all the time, but one of the things Dad always said to me was, lookit, you know, you've got to be determined, you've got to make sure that, you know, you work hard every time you get a chance to go on the ice.

"He was obviously my mentor and really made the difference for me to get to where I wanted to go, you know the pins on the wall story. You want me to tell that? OK. Well, it was funny, we won a Bantam championship in Nelson and we hadn't won I think a championship — ever — for a provincial championship, and I remember beating out North Shore Winter Club and coming home on a fire-truck ride, the town was ecstatic. There was Pat Price on the team, Dale McMullin, Wayne Naka, Marc Severyn, a lot of great players that played and went on to junior.

"But I think the one thing about it was we were so caught up in it and we were in high school, and well you know we didn't work out for about a three-week period or four-week period and we were riding high type of thing and one of the things that was funny about that was that I went up to the university after maybe my third week of not working out or training at all and Dad says to me in the weight room, he says, "So son, what do you want to do?" And it was one of those questions of a lifetime. I said, "What was that, Dad?" and he repeated the question. "What do you want to do?" So I said I want to play in the National Hockey League! You know, like every kid did. So he goes come on upstairs into my office and in his office, overlooking where you had the dinner last night in the gymnasium, he had a map of Canada behind his desk, and he said: "Son, there is a kid in every town in Canada that wants to do the same thing you want to do." I said, yeah. And he said "No, I'm serious." He was very serious and very adamant about it.

"And he said: "But what you have to do, you're small, there's assets you have to have. One, he says, is you have shoot 300-400 pucks a day. Two, you have to come up and fill out your upper body, lift some weights, and three, you have to learn how to box — because at that time it was a tough game.

"So, I said "OK, Dad," but he said "listen, I tell ya, there's a kid in every town that wants to do the same thing you want to do so what we're going to do, every time you work out I'm going to put a pin on Trail, I'm going to put a pin on North Shore Winter Club, I'm going to put a pin on Castlegar and so forth, every time you come."

"So, to make a long story short, and I tell this story to kids all the time whenever I get up to talk and talk about goal-setting, when I was drafted by the Buffalo Sabres in 1974-75 in the second round, that map of Canada was full of green, yellow, black, blue, gold pins, so, it was a great way to have incentive but also a great way to reach your goals."

McLean: "Magical story. Now the foundation, Cathy and your sister received a check yesterday, Jennifer, I don't know if we have a shot of that presentation right now, but tell us a little bit about the foundation and what it continues to do, Danny."

Gare: "Well, you've been out and you've supported it and we appreciate that. We've had some great names that have come out throughout the years, Harry Neale has come out, Gordie Howe came out one year, and we've had a lot of interest from Johnny Bucyk, people from that area that have always come out and stars from around the area like Horcoff and Ferraros, and the Kootenay boys that always seem to help out, Greg Adams, and so forth, Pat Price, all these people came out to always support it. But it's also the people that have gone through the scholarship program that have come back. The National Ski Team came back with Nancy Greene a couple of years ago and we had a big reunion for that, Emily Beauchamp did a great job of putting that together, Peter Webster, he was another part of that, but I think the key about all of that is the fact that he started the first athletic scholarship program ever in Canada and it still goes on. We try to raise money every summer through golf tournaments, street hockey, soccer tournaments, whatever we can do to raise money and continue his legacy in his name and give out bursaries to youngsters, either, any sport within the regional district and it's been outstanding, the people support, the volunteers, which is your model this year, has always been there, and the merchants and the business people around Nelson, so we can't say enough about it and it's great. I'm sure my Father is still looking down very proud."

# Chapter Three
## How The West Was One: Take Two

The B.C. Legislature's focus on university education in March of 1963 was dramatic in scope. One Act made Notre Dame the first private university in the province. A second Act upgraded Victoria College to university status, and created Simon Fraser University (SFU) in Burnaby as well as junior colleges in Kelowna and Castlegar. It's improbable the Social Credit government realized the entirety of the forces those Bills unleashed on Canadian university sports, although, to its credit, almost a couple decades later one of its successors was to take the ball and run with it.

Simon Fraser came alive before its location atop Burnaby Mountain was even finalized. Much more significantly, SFU loudly and proudly announced it was going to offer athletic scholarships before a single student ever set foot in its registrar's office. Father Aquinas, meet Dr. Gordon Shrum. Ernie Gare, meet Lorne Davies.

To what could only have been gasps of disbelief, indignation and even horror back in the power corridors of the East, Dr. Shrum most effectively let the Canadian Interuniversity Athletic Union (CIAU) know it was irrelevant, moribund and an archaic leftover of what was then, and still is today, a front for a discriminatory philosophy more in tune with Puritan and Victorian mores than with the projectile-like developments of 20th-Century society.

*Vancouver Sun, March 13, 1964*
*Headline: Simon Fraser to Offer Athletic Scholarships*
*Subhead: Grants Will Help Stem Flow of Talent to U.S.*
*By Denny Boyd*

*There is new hope that the annual flow of British Columbia's finest athletes to United States colleges may be stopped.*

*Dr. Gordon M. Shrum, chancellor of the new Simon Fraser University, proposes a vigorous athletic program that will offer athletic scholarships, the finest professional coaching and tutorial aid to Canadian students who combine athletic and academic proficiency.*

*Like many educators, Dr. Shrum is alarmed at the number of Canadian athletes who are accepting scholarships in U.S. schools simply because there are no such opportunities in their own country. In many cases, these students give up their Canadian citizenship to accept rewarding jobs in the U.S. after graduation.*

*Because of this situation says Dr. Shrum, Canada is sacrificing a vital resource – people.*

*Dr. Shrum said Thursday that he wants to apply to athletics the same high standard that he applies to academics – a dollar and five cents return from every dollar spent.*

*He said, "We will have three faculties, arts, science and education. Education will be a large and important faculty because we will be training teachers for our B.C. schools. It is imperative that we have the best training program and facilities in physical education. Indicative of the importance we place in this program is the fact that the first building on our campus will be our gymnasium and swimming pool which is essential for both the use of all our students and our physical education department."*

*Dr. Shrum said it is a serious mistake to underestimate the importance of physical fitness in our daily life.*

*"I don't say that athletics is the panacea for all our problems but I feel that, in young people, athletics are as much a driving force as sex.*

*"We live in an affluent society. We have more leisure, a five-day work week. And I think that the fact we have the Beatle craze and an average of 125 drunks arrested every weekend is symptomatic of boredom – boredom that should be channelled into healthy pursuits.*

*"I think even people of moderate means will agree it is better to be taking part in a thing like, the high school basketball tournament than to be sitting in a beer parlour or a cheap movie."*

*Dr. Shrum said that every Canadian athlete who goes to an American school takes with him something that Canada could have used. "These people, all of them can make an important contribution. Most of them become physical education teachers but there are limited job opportunities for them in Canada. Many more become doctors and engineers, people we need.*

*"To keep them around, we must encourage them."*

*To do this, Dr. Shrum proposes a three-point program which he will press for at SFU.*

*"Our coaching must be of the best professional level available. I would be in favour of bringing in coaches from the United States until our programs supplies us with our own coaches. People ask, 'Why isn't Harry Jerome (Vancouver's world-record sprinter now attending University of Oregon) running for UBC?' But what has UBC to offer in the way of coaching for an athlete of Jerome's excellence?*

*"And really, how can any one expect Frank Gnup to wield a competitive football team at UBC without the help of a big, experienced coaching staff? Personally, I would like to have a person like Russ Jackson (Ottawa Rough Riders quarterback) as our football coach. He is a brilliant young man, a mathematics teacher and an excellent football player."*

*"The University has to show interest in the athletes by providing tutorial encouragement. I would not for one moment condone the development of athletics at the expense of academics nor would I ever push a student through his exams simply because he plays football. But I do feel that university can give extra tutoring to a person who is carrying both academics and athletics."*

*Dr. Shrum says athletic scholarships should be made available in all sports, providing the athlete measures up to the school's academic standards. He also pointed to the athletic facilities at SFU: gym, swimming pool and a network of 21 playing fields.*

*The former dean of graduate studies at UBC said, "When I came to UBC in 1925, it was four years before we had a gym, which the students themselves built. We had no tennis courts until the students built them in the second year. And what playing fields we did have had been raked and seeded by the students."*

*Dr. Shrum reiterated that the most pressing problem is to stop the flow of athletes to the U.S.*

*"I can think of a number of brilliant men who were fine athletes in Canadian universities. Wallace Sterling was a football player at University of Alberta and even coached Calgary Stampeders for one year. Now he is president of Stanford University.*

*"Wilf Hull was a fine lineman at UBC in the days when the football team had to practice at 7 in the morning. Now he is president of Dominion Tar and Chemical.*

*"And our Prime Minister, Lester Pearson, paid his tuition at University of Toronto by playing semi-pro baseball in the summer. He even coached the university football team one year. Think how much history might have changed had Mike Pearson accepted a scholarship to an American school.*

*"That's why I say, we must keep our athletes in our country and we must give them every opportunity to receive an education."*

Sis boom bah! Hip, hip, hooray! Rah, rah, rah! Three cheers, for he's a jolly good fellow! Well done, Dr. Shrum! He tapped Davies, another UBC product, to be his henchman in this heretical approach to serving the total needs of some of Canada's most talented youth, prime Canadian beef, not cake if you will. Davies steered the fledgling program through its inevitable growing pains with a more level-headed approach than his chancellor's grandiose, ground-breaking vision, and spent 30 years as SFU's athletic director compiling a list of achievements arguably unparalleled in Canadian university sports. In doing so, he aptly demonstrated exactly who the heretics were. Today, Davies still has an office at SFU, from which he coordinates the Terry Fox Run. One of Canada's most celebrated heroes was a Clansmen Junior Varsity basketball player before cancer struck. It was there, in the fall of 2004, that Davies spoke of the course charted at Simon Fraser that not only exemplified the famous explorer's courage but that also starkly exposed the blinkers of choice worn by his and Dr. Shrum's peers back East.

"We always complain about our kids not doing as well as we'd like, but the amount that we do give them is a pittance," were Davies' first words. The social do-gooders in the country who decry funding sports as a means to an exemplary end are not all missionary workers among the downtrodden and brow-beaten, the truly deserving; in fact, some of them are even ex-Olympians and holders of the Order of Canada, which seems almost impossible to believe but is located in the sad but true file. Suffice to say, Dr. Shrum and Davies thought and felt otherwise. Their approach was belief in potential, a belief which harnesses the good as opposed to the CIAU's misguided attempts at warding off, ooohh, the devil.

"The history in the country for scholarships has been thought of by many administrators as an evil, as if there was something inherently evil about the word 'scholarships'. And I'm sure you're well aware that the word scholarship pertains to scholastic achievement and so, therefore, they find it to be somewhat of a misnomer to have the words athletic and scholarships, those two words together," said a wry at best Davies, whose university was to exorcise those fears of the demon in honourable fashion.

"But the thing is, they should be aware, and I've always believed this with all my heart, a scholarship doesn't make you a good athlete, doesn't automatically make you a world champion or conference champion, but it provides you with an opportunity to spend time honing your skills and developing your skills. A scholarship is not a cure-all and it's not an answer to every problem, but it provides an avenue through which a young person can come to a university, instead of having to work part-time and giving up a sport, or to having to possibly miss an opportunity in a sport. They can develop their skills through the competition; you've got to have good competition for them, you've got to have good coaching for them, and you've got to have good facilities. Put those together and you give a person a scholarship so that they can devote their time to really concentrate, you're going to turn out what I think is a good quality person. And that's what it's all about, it's about people."

The Ontario university presidents and athletic directors who for so long staunchly refused to consider the validity of top-flight athletic endeavour within the Canadian university environment weren't paying attention to those very people, thereby demeaning not only those capable of great achievements both physically and mentally, but the very intrinsic value of sport in this ever-changing world in which we live in.

Visionaries are usually dreamers — give peace a chance — and Davies' chancellor was no exception. "When we opened here in 1965, actually prior to our opening, Dr. Shrum was wise enough to realize that talking about athletics would give him and the university a certain degree of recognition, instant recognition. So he made some statements — he did have a great love for sports, I don't want to denigrate that — but the concept of him knowing what it cost, he didn't have any real concept," noted Davies with a chuckle. Davies did have a fieldworker's grasp of the situation because of his, gasp, American university experience, any taint of which the CIAU nay-sayers long attempted to keep from the pure North proud and free.

Davies had attended Western Washington University just across the border in Bellingham, first as a student and then as a coach, before moving onto the University of Oregon in Portland to complete his Master's degree, and coach. Prior to taking up his post at SFU, he had taught and coached at UBC. "I was privy to the knowledge of who was getting scholarships and what amounts they were getting," said Davies. Dr. Shrum obviously wasn't.

"So he made statements, things like that we would play in the Rose Bowl eventually and things of that nature," said Davies with a twinkle of amusement in his eyes. "When I was hired in May of '65 my first question, because I'd heard all these pronouncements about scholarships, was OK, what types of scholarships are you going to have and what amounts of money do you have? When I asked, they had no answers. They had no answers as to who was going to be allowed into the university from outside of the province, what procedures there would be. After I was given the amount, I asked do you have any forms of any type, any applications forms, they had nothing. To go back one step, when I finally got an answer to how much scholarship money I was going to receive I was told $10,000," and never mind the twinkle in the eye, now it's a full-blown chortle. "I thought that was maybe for one sport but it was for all three sports, that would be basketball, swimming and football, and of course you realize they were all men's sports, in those days women were not given scholarships, nor were they given opportunities.

"Subsequently I started to look at what I could do with $10,000 and realized that I couldn't have a full football team on tuition type scholarships, or a basketball team or a whole swimming team. So what I did, and I apologize, I can't remember so I can't give you the exact amounts, but I gave approximately 10 scholarships, tuition scholarships, to basketball, and I gave it seems to me about six or so to swimming, and the remainder went to football." The first three Clansmen teams were now securely in place at 101 Scholarship Place Drive, as it were. To keep it in perspective, "The amount of money, the $10,000, as I told Dr. Shrum, was less than the tape budget at the University of Washington that year."

Davies, his hand forced but in partnership with Dr. Shrum's rock-solid determination and beliefs, did the only thing possible, which was to look outside the SFU treasury for financial support. And, as will be amply re-demonstrated later, it was and still is there if one but looks for it. Some money came from a family which owned a large department store, more from the owner/operator of a heavy-duty equipment company which specified the contribution must go to a football player. It wasn't much, but a start, mere mortar around the bricks, but that first trickle, as Davies described it, enabled SFU to offer Karen Magnussen, yes, that Karen Magnussen, Canada's last women's world figure skating champion, a scholarship. "That was a tuition type scholarship and an attempt for us to try to show that we wanted to encourage people of a very high international level to come to the university," explained Davies calmly, for which the applause should be never-ending.

"The situation was that there were no ground rules. They wanted to give me personally $10,000 in my account, my budget. I wouldn't accept that because I could be accused of giving amounts of money for people to buy a car," said Davies, well aware of the unsavoury practices at some, repeat some, American universities and that having his hands on that money would inevitably lead to suspicion and thus erroneously straight into unfounded innuendo that SFU was following in those nefarious footsteps. One can almost imagine certain CIAU hands wringing with glee had he accepted that original proposal.

What he did instead, and oh, the too-often underappreciated value of common sense, was to request that the university establish a three-person committee "made up of two faculty people and one from the staff. Basically, I didn't want an athletic person in there, including myself," said Davies, "because then they could say we were pressuring people or whatever," neither bothering nor having to define "they" to his particular audience of one. He would then submit a list of candidates for athletic awards to the committee, the key criteria being a need to meet the university's academic standards, no ifs, ands or buts. "Within the country itself, we were either looked at as renegades because we had these evil scholarships, or we were looked at as some type of heroes. The other thing was as soon as you said the word scholarship, for every person it conjured up something different. One person thought room and board and books and so on, but another would think it would be a tuition scholarship, another might think it was $100, to help the fees, or whatever."

Coming out of the starting gate with a pro-athletic scholarship stance even as the home sod was being turned "up the hill," Canada's newest university guaranteed itself critics for this decidedly pro-American approach. Davies simply went about doing his job of providing a hospitable environment in which Canadian student athletes could excel. In what must have seemed to some as a second thumbing of the nose, this devil incarnate chose to compete south of the border, for what were sound reasons beyond proximity. "I had seen the level Western Washington played at in the Pacific Northwest, I saw the level UBC played in Canada West, and my impression was that some of the schools in Canada West would have got eaten up and spit out by schools in Washington and Oregon. Again, our philosophy was simply this: If you are going to do something, then do it well, and that holds true in chemistry, or physics, or music, or English, or whatever. Why should it less in the area of athletics?"

The program began slowly, first year against junior college or junior varsity teams, second year it challenged small four-year schools, its third year it faced a full schedule of four-year schools and has since.

Playing teams from south of the border also had its mystique, as Davies labelled it, especially when it came to getting the school's name remembered by certain Grade 11 and 12 students outside the provincial postal code. "We were doing well against American schools. Along with that was the fact that every year I would schedule at least one game in California, so if you were in Toronto, or in Hamilton, or whatever, it was pretty exciting to think you were going to California for one of your away games."

The perils of recruiting, of course, have always been a CIS bugaboo, a stance singularly aimed at a fear of the worst. Davies was actively and openly revolting, period, full stop, knowing the qualities required. "Subsequently our biggest problem at one time was not trying to find kids, it was trying to select. We would do things like timing them and we'd do some strength things with them and so on, but the underlying factor — no matter what — wasn't their speed or size, it was their grade point average. If they couldn't make the standard here, they weren't coming with us, there was no way we were getting them in or attempting to get them into school.

"I can recall going to a CIAU meeting in Halifax where the major issue was a vote about whether or not Canadian universities would have scholarships. I had been invited as a guest, so I said a few words to assure them scholarships were not inherently evil. It was the administration of scholarships that gives scholarships a bad reputation or black eye. I don't know how pleased they were to hear those words but they voted for them, but the following day they voted again and turned them down. If I recall this correctly, a fellow who was the athletic director at Trent, they didn't have a pure intercollegiate program, he had voted for it the previous day when I was there and then after I had left they re-voted, he voted against it, so the scholarships were in for one day and out the next day."

The fact that SFU was standing on its own two feet outside the Canadian system made Davies's recruiting forays in the feeder system easier, nay, honourable. He subscribed to Toronto newspapers to peruse their sports sections. Throughout the history of the CIAU there has been an East-West divide. Obviously not so with Davies, who described his efforts as being akin to preaching to and converting the great unwashed. Picture him in Toronto, map of the city in hand, his target talented high school athletes.

"It was fascinating because, when you'd go up to the desk of a secretary in the school, you'd hand her your card and she'd look at the card and say you're from Simon Fraser" he recalled, mimicking amazement, aghast amazement. "I'd say, yes, I'm from Simon Fraser. It was like missionary work, because what I'd do from there, she'd give the card to the vice-principal, then he and the principal would come up and I'd talk to them and then they would ask me if I would speak to a group of their teachers and tell them all about Simon Fraser, so I would spend half of my time," to the accompaniment of more chuckling, "explaining about what Simon Fraser was doing academically as well as athletically. In some areas the high school coaches couldn't have been more supportive because they were having so many of their students go to the United States and they, being proud Canadians, wanted their fellows and girls to stay in this country. It was also interesting to note for me when I went into Toronto, the coaches, a great many of them were graduates of the U of T, or schools in that region, and they had no allegiance to their school. In other words, it wasn't a matter of, oh well, we've got a pretty good kid, but I'm recommending he goes to the University of Toronto. They were bending over backwards to give us details, information and so on."

Asked if it was a love of the scholarship or a lack of empathy for their University of Toronto, Davies never hesitated, laying it on the missing. "The U of T is a very powerful, very fine academic institution and subsequently they had athletes going there that didn't continue with their sports. They would get almost overwhelmed by the number of people, the size of the institution, and so on. They wouldn't play again and their coaches were disappointed in that because if you coach a young kid through four of years at high school, you'd like to see how they'd play at an upper level."

Not to be juvenile, but. The juvenile part being the idiotic hammerlock just a few individuals within the CIAU had on recreational sport being the be-all and end-all requirement for our academically and athletically talented youth. "I was there in 1964, with the [B.C.] Lions; we were playing in the Grey Cup and worked out at Varsity Stadium. Varsity Stadium had, the one day we were there, an intramural football game going on, and in my opinion, they had better talent on those two intramural teams than several of the schools in Western Canada had. I realized what was happening is that it was very difficult to break into [the varsity] for some of these young kids so they would either play intramurals or they would stop playing. And their coaches, although we were a long way, were very strongly in favour of them playing in Canada. And, my thoughts were very straightforward — if every good kid went to the States, how would we ever build up good programs in this country?"

Which, of course, raises the $64 gazillion question of why the CIAU never objectively entertained such thoughts.

"Our scholarships were very minimal, so we'd wave the flag a lot, the idea of trying to have good athletic programs in Canada and for you to stay here and help us build it. I went into many parents' homes and talked to the families as well as the coaches. It was amazing how many people were in favour of that even though it meant their son would have to come all the way out to the West Coast. And, we had a certain mystique about us."

The core belief behind that mystique was, of course, repugnant to the CIAU, but that was OK out here on the Pacific Coast, as the dictatorial and hypocritical practices of the CIAU centered around The Great Lakes were themselves repugnant.

"I had somebody come in from the CIAU while the university wasn't even finished; the offices were downtown at Dunsmuir and Seymour, and this fellow came in and the first question after he introduced himself was: 'Hello, I want to know, we, the CIAU, want to know when you're coming into the CIAU,' said Davies, putting on the bluff act of his self-righteous visitor/inquisitor that day. "I said, wait, we're just starting and I'm not certain we're coming into the CIAU. So he was a little abrasive and my thoughts were if the rest of the CIAU is the way this fellow is, I don't know if we will ever go in. He didn't make a good first impression."

It gets worse.

"I mean, if you said to me, explain the definition of how a person would get a scholarship, I'd find it very difficult. On top of that is, a friend of mine, Jim Young [Dirty Thirty of the B.C. Lions to CFL fans], went to an eastern university, he turned down an opportunity, if I'm not mistaken, to go to Syracuse, because he got a better arrangement at an eastern university. I was at two meetings, one in the West and one nationally about scholarships, and the old guard would very emphatically deny they had any scholarships. However, there were things being given under the table, behind the back, by influential alumni that I found really disgusting and distasteful. Because if I'm dealing with you as a coach and I say we can't give you a scholarship but if you phone this number this person will take care of your travel, will take care of room and board and your books, it means that I am condoning something that's dishonest."

By banning athletic scholarships, the CIAU, predictably, invited abuse. There's a long — and current — history of it within the organization. "I find that's a great sadness," said Davies. "When you coach a young person you're not only teaching them how to play the sport, hopefully you're teaching them how to overcome things that are difficult physically and emotionally in their lives. At the same time you should try to teach them to do that in an ethical manner. And I find it to be, you wouldn't in a ..." as he searches for the right comparison, "if you were teaching a class, an academic class, you wouldn't say to the students I'm going to leave the room and right here on my desk is a book that has all the answers in it. You wouldn't do it. I don't think it's acceptable, [it's] absolutely unacceptable," to suggest sports alone, or of necessity, breeds cheats.

"Now, of course," he continued, "there are all kinds of ways of looking at scholarships. If scholarships are given with no thought of the person receiving the scholarship attaining success academically, then that scholarship should not be given. They should be given to," and he emphasized this, "students. I've always been a strong believer in this as well, that not only should students in athletics be given scholarships, but students who are outstanding musicians, who have great voices, students who have leaderships skills. Those are all qualities that should be encouraged, as should the development of them."

And now that we're really getting on the CIAU's case, it gets not only worse, but amoral. "These things just pass by me as far as dates," said Davies, perhaps just being polite, perhaps purposely obtuse, "but I can remember meeting with the president of the CIAU; I can't recall the other fellow, but there were two of them who were very high up in their organization. They were smooth-talking us into becoming members of the CIAU. I'd heard a lot of stories of things that were happening, so we had lunch and during the lunch they talked about a variety of things, so I finally asked: What would happen if you found out that one of your member institutions was doing something wrong. You don't have scholarships? 'Oh, we don't have scholarships,'" said Davies, mimicking their straight-faced answer.

So he said to them, "What would you do if you found out that one of these institutions was giving money of some type?" Long pause. "Then they look at each other, and I said, would you do something to them, as far as taking a title away, or not allowing them to compete, or ...? And they said we wouldn't do anything. Right then and there, that's the end of the CIAU, I mean if that's the type — they wouldn't do anything. If they found out ..." they'd just turn the proverbial blind eye? "That's right," and as a tad of personal indignation spews out of his listener's mouth, Davies was quick to jump in and disclaim, "I'm sure it must be different now, because we're talking 30 years ago. I think they're still a little bit behind in their all-out acceptance of athletic scholarships. That's just a personal opinion, and you can see it by a couple of things; the fact Canadian institutions are still losing a lot of qualified students to the U.S., the second factor is a number of them not having the ingredients necessary for success — good coaching, good competition, good facilities.

"You go down and look at the University of Washington, at Alabama or Nebraska, look at the facilities. I'm not suggesting we try to copy those people, I don't believe in that. I think that what we have here is an opportunity to have something far better because of the rigid academic standards in Canada. The fact is we have quality kids, but we have to find ways to make sure these ingredients are in place. If they are, a lot of these kids wouldn't go south. If the Canadian universities would give some consideration to improving those types of things ..." not needing to add that we wouldn't have 2,500 Canadians on American scholarships. Repeat, 2,500 Canadians on American scholarships. Repeat again.

When one grows up in the sports world, it doesn't take long to hear the phrase "dumb jock." Take that adjective, put it in front of virtually any endeavour and you will find people who fit the description, but that usually doesn't tarnish the entire field. Powerful forces, however, across Canada seemed determined to keep the jocks not in but out of their place. Davies, on the bunch of them: "The interesting part of it was that not all academic people were 100 per cent in favour."

Upon reading the following from a 1977 Parliamentary Report: "A certain righteousness has arisen in Canadian universities which negate all the favourable aspects of the scholarships as a vehicle to encourage both academic and athletic pursuits," Davies wholeheartedly concurs. "That's absolutely true, absolutely true," and he should know, given the response he received as the devil personified for not only utilizing but promoting scholarships. The really interesting thing is that while the majority of Canadian academia was happy to turn their blind eye to the concept of individuals being able to achieve simultaneously in the academic and athletic spheres, being confronted with it right in front of them made believers out of the professorial community at SFU.

"It didn't happen overnight but we never had any kind of movement to get rid of scholarships from anybody in the academic areas. That was never, ever, to my knowledge, brought up and the reason for it was that we had such fine people. In their classes they could see them as good students. We had a fellow by the name of Ted Workington, he played football and basketball, first year, and then he stayed with the football team. He was a straight-A student, and eventually he went with the [B.C.] Lions, but to my knowledge he was our first Rhodes Scholar candidate from the university.

"And he was a jock, yeah, and I was very proud of that because of what it illustrated," namely the potential of student athletes and the achievement of maintaining two fulltime schedules, counting all the bus hours. "If you were with us on a road trip you might be gone Friday afternoon and you wouldn't be back until Saturday night or Sunday so that time was taken away from your normal activities, of which some of those would be study. But the kids like Ted Workington, he'd play a game, a heckuva game. We'd be coming back from Oregon or wherever and the light would be on in the bus and he'd be studying."

To this day, the mathematical equation for that is, competing in Canada West = travel time = Rhodes Scholar candidate or better, and it's time to bury the dumb jock syndrome once and for all in a dusty vault, along with the CIAU's use of academic abuses well detailed in some American programs as their rationale for forever just saying no. "It's like, saying something is inherently evil, wrong or evil, because somebody is doing something that is akin to it. It's like saying I will never drive an automobile because my pet dog was run over by an automobile one time and I just hate them. Hello? Ha, ha, ha," Davies chuckles, trying to understand how reasonable people can adopt such a narrow-minded philosophy.

"I felt that for educated people they were really very short-sighted, identifying wrong things. It doesn't mean because school X has PhD people who are cheats, that every university in the country has PhD cheats. It's almost unbelievable that they could be so small-minded. Again, I'm guarding my words by saying, yes, there's the other extreme, the person who says oh, let's have scholarships, I don't care what my coaches give the athletes as long as it doesn't cost me anything."

Upon reading another quote handed him: "One of the lines in there was to the effect that it's not reasonable for a [athletics] program to expect to be funded by the university. Why not?" Acknowledging the response, fears of elitism: "It's just silly. Our newspapers are made up of about 10 per cent sports, it's a huge part of society," and researchable in the humanities section of the SFU library. "It would be nice if the federal government would come out and give athletes a really good-quality opportunity if they wanted to go to university." Amen.

Davies was hearing few if any amens from among his peers when he first started out, which he now laughs about, recalling a recruiting trip that took him to Hamilton's McMaster University. Upon being introduced to the AD, "This fellow almost spit! I'd never seen anybody, in my life, it was almost like making the sign of the cross to keep this evil person out of his building. The problem, too, was the fact there was so much rumour and so much misconception. When you say scholarships, people conjure up, like WOW, these scholarships, well, they had no idea."

The CIAU had so blackened the name of the NCAA full-ride scholarship by this point that one director of that not-so-august body once sniffed that "We don't need that in our culture." Oh, to have vision to the end of one's nose. Certainly we don't need the mythical Basket-weaving 101, as courses at those academically-tainted U.S. programs came to be known, even though such abuses always were a miniscule part of the bigger overall NCAA picture.

Davies was well aware of it. "I had a fair knowledge of the Pac Eight in those days, but I wanted to also see what other schools were doing, so I did a fairly extensive tour of major northwest schools, I went to Oregon, Oregon State, Washington State, I went to Idaho State, etc., and tried to glean from them the salient points of having a good program and looking at the problem areas. And that's basically what I think Canadian university athletics should do, is take a look and see the abuses that have taken place south of the border — not every big school has abuses." Stanford, anyone? "Exactly! Harvard, or any of these other places. But the point being, why don't we learn from other people's mistakes?" Probably because some here might have to admit to some of their own.

SFU was immediately tarnished by the anti-scholarship brush by some quarters, but in a classic case of the tail wagging the dog, it was also tarnished with the brush of full-ride — tuition, books, room and board — scholarship. "And to be very candid with you, we made no effort to try to puncture that façade. We were kind of hiding behind it, made no effort to say, well, we really don't have very much. We just went on as if to say we had the NCAA scholarships, simply as a recruiting tool. But we were always honest, when we recruited. If your parents had some misgivings about you coming out here, I would assure them that I would look after you. In other words, you wouldn't be sleeping in the basement beside the furnace in some old dump." As well, each week each scholarship athlete reported in. "I don't want to say counselling, but it was close to counselling, you would have to come in each week and you would have to report how you were doing in each of your classes. We didn't want any surprises at the end of the semester. But I'm sure people didn't realize we were doing those things."

SFU broke ground in many ways.

"At one time, we were the only university in the country that had fulltime coaches. When we opened, the thing that I was available to convince the university is that coaching and teaching are synonymous. In other words, if you're a coach, you're a teacher, and if you're a teacher, you're a coach. Subsequently, I was also able to convince them that instead of us having one coach handling the intramural program and one handling the sports programs, and somebody else doing this and that, their involvement be sport-specific. Now that's happened at some places in the country and I think that's done a lot to bring up the quality of the coaching. That's the misconception that Canadian universities had, but they are changing. For a long time they thought somebody had to be in physical education, or you brought in an outsider. Well, the outsider couldn't care less about the academic ability, they are only interested in winning, having a team and winning. I don't want, under any circumstances, to give the impression that Canadian colleges are not improving, they are improving and have improved, immensely, but I still think there are some things they could do along those lines that would make them better," with regards to striving for success, not relegating sport to the simple realm of play.

SFU pursued athletic excellence and achievement the same way the academic community strives to achieve insight, only SFU simultaneously developed the whole person. "Winning and losing? Don't let me give you the wrong impression, I'm a strong believer in winning, because as the old adage goes, I wouldn't want to have a doctor operate on me if he didn't care if he won or lost, or a lawyer who didn't care if he won or lost the case. But there's sportsmanship you should be teaching, there are values, and realizing it's not just something that happens. It's really a privilege to be a part of a university program that has the ingredients I mentioned because you're there with other gifted people, and the old adage of iron sharpening iron does hold. You get among those kinds of people and you see their levels of dedication and devotion and it helps you raise your levels," continued Davies.

He concedes that the history of the CIAU's approach to truly significant athletic achievement was up to that point, essentially a snobbish form of anti-elitism: if even one member university wasn't prepared to strive for the brass ring, then none should, which in effect condemned Canadian university sport to uniform mediocrity. Such an approach obviously never crossed Davies's mind. While the CIAU could foresee problems and was only too content to not even contemplate putting one foot in front of another in case those steps might lead to a single one, Davies was fearless in that regard.

It might be easy to imagine rifts and divisions within any squad in which some players do and others don't receive scholarships, but there are always ways of dealing with difficult issues.

"Well, I think that, hopefully, they realized that a scholarship doesn't make you a great person, or a great athlete. Also, I instituted a program of challenges, and I think what did is it kept the door open if you were a walk-on. Dave Cutler, one of Canada's greatest kickers, was a walk-on. He turned up with his bag on his back and so, subsequently, it gave somebody like Dave Cutler the opportunity. If he walked in as an unknown he could work his way up through the challenge system and I think that had a lot of bearing on things. Instead of people grumbling, oh, I'm not getting a scholarship and they're not treating me very well, I think that dissolved most of that." In other words, if you work hard, don't grumble, because you probably won't have to? "Exactly."

The students were the easy ones to work with, the fun part of the job. It was the frontline periphery that was and still is the headache.

"You know, it's a very, very difficult ball of twine to unravel but really it comes back to what I've said twice to you, that the administration is the key, the administration of the university. First, you better have your president on side, because you don't want to have a person who has high standards and is very ethical as your athletic director if the president of the university does something that is totally off base.

"I went to a meeting and gave my apple pie and mom address and told them, hey, you can help these kids. They went around the room and it got to the far side and one president said I don't care what my coaches do, they can give their players suits, they can give them, you know, cars, they can give them anything as long as it doesn't cost me anything at our university and at that moment I realized that they were in the dark ages of the NCAA, the dark ages that the NCAA had been trying to fight for years. Why would you even think that? Because you know the next thing is the bidding wars start.

"So what have you got now? You've got this kid whose head is spinning. It's immoral, really, that's what it is, it's absolutely immoral to do that. But they do this out of their own misconception; they're students first, that's what it's all about. I've had parents in my office, and I'm not exaggerating, parents with tears in their eyes, mom crying, can you get my son into your school, he wants to play. No, I said, he doesn't have the grades. If you had an institution that was unethical — and this kid, he ended up going to a Pac-10 school and was a starter — they'd say well, we'll find some way to tutor him or something. And that's wrong. It teaches the kid something, it teaches him the institution is unethical."

Specifically addressing academia downplaying sports, "It's because they don't set something as a standard to look at. They look at all the rotten things that have happened," such as football star Dexter Manley graduating from university without being able to read. "There's a perfect example. But they don't see the examples, or, they don't glorify the fact that Wilf Wedman is a Rhodes Scholar, that Ted Workington was a candidate for a Rhodes Scholarship, and did all the things they had to do in their particular sport. They've got blinkers on, that's what they have."

So, to return to Dr. Gordon Shrum, who just like his peer Father Aquinas at Notre Dame, could not stand to be encumbered by those blinkers, and whose dreams and hopes and visions, to this day are on display. "He got instant recognition, he was a very bright, very intelligent man. I think certainly the success of the teams, certainly, justified him making those statements," about playing in the Rose Bowl, which was impossible in football but which proved possible in soccer.

"He had no idea and I say this not disrespectfully. His intentions were great, he had a wonderful feeling, he'd come to football games; if I close my eyes I can still see him up in the stands, rainy nights, old coat on and rumpled hat, sitting and watching the kids. He loved them! He realized, really realized there was an ingredient within the athlete that was very admirable. I've asked him, and I've asked a man who was the chairman of B.C. Tel, and I asked them individually, I said you hire a lot of people, what determines who you hire? And privately and individually, they said to me, 'I look for somebody who does something besides go to school, besides go to university.' They had respect for athletes because they knew how hard they work, they had respect for people in music and people in theatre, whatever these things were, in other words, for a person to have to go through all the discipline required to play on a team, they realize that person had some special drive and ability and so they wanted those kind of people as employees.

"So I think Dr. Shrum, in his inimitable style, he recognized that was of terrific value to the student and to the university and the recognition that we got. Like you said, I was like a skunk at the family picnic, you know, I was this evil scholarship person."

When the Shrum Bowl between the SFU Clan and UBC Thunderbirds football teams first began in 1967, Davies recoiled at some of the media coverage. "When we played UBC it was like the scholarship boys against the good guys." Like pros vs. amateurs? "That's right! The British amateurs!"

In 1976, the SFU Clan won the NAIA soccer championship — playing in the Rose Bowl. Dr. Gordon Shrum died at the age of 89 in 1985. Lorne Davies should hold court more often.

After he stepped down from his position in 1995, Davies was succeeded by Mike Dinning. Even after the Clan at that point moved six sports into CIS (CIAU) competition, with an eye to raising the university's profile within Canada, the remaining Clan teams operating south of the border took their winning ways to near perfection, capturing the university's fifth Sports Directors' Cup for the best overall athletic program in the NAIA with an unheard of four straight titles, culminating in 2000. At which point, SFU went back to its past when it named the aforementioned Wilf Wedmann as its third AD and it would be hard to find someone with a finer pedigree for the position.

Wedmann, as Davies noted, was SFU's first Rhodes Scholar, as well as the university's first of dozens of Olympians, competing in the high jump in the 1968 and 1972 Summer Olympic Games. Under Wedmann, the university's sports facilities have grown considerably and but for politics and money, SFU would have played a leading role in the Vancouver 2010 Winter Olympic Games. The former head honcho at Sports Canada is both a student of history and a forward thinker, which makes for some pretty compelling views.

By way of introduction, from his fingertips:

*Vancouver Sun Guest Editorial*
*Tuesday, September 21, 2004*
*By Wilf Wedmann*
*(Olympian, Coach, National Sports Organization CEO & current SFU Director of Recreation and Athletics)*

*Sometimes it's the obvious we fail to notice. As the Olympic debate calls for more funding, more paid coaches, and the need to look at the American sport model, we fail to notice the United States' school-based sport approach which won the most gold and total medals at the Athens Games.*

*Interestingly, the United States approach was explored by the 1969 Task Force on Sport for Canadians, which designed the blueprint of the modern Canadian sport system.*

*"It is strikingly obvious," wrote the Task Force (which included B.C.'s Nancy Greene-Raine), "that the ideal institution for the fostering and recognition of athletic talent is the school. Some schools in some places do all this but many do not. We believe there is a "hang-up" among many educators and teachers on sport which makes them downgrade it or view it as largely irrelevant in the learning process ...*

*"Canadians too often look at the major involvement of American education in sport and compliment themselves on our better taste."*

*Because education was a provincial jurisdiction, the federal Task Force limited its recommendations to areas of federal jurisdiction, and the opportunity to build a strong stable education foundation for Canadian sport was lost.*

*Another obvious often overlooked is that the nurturing and development of world class athletes is a 10-20 year investment. A stable system is required. Our federal and provincial governments' interest in sport is not stable. Nor are our volunteer-led sport organizations stable. Our provincial education systems, which are concerned with the development of our Canadian youth from elementary school through university, are by design much more stable, long-term institutions.*

*We sport leaders also need to realize that federal and provincial government funding is in short supply. Health care, education, municipalities, etc. all require more funding. We cannot simply demand more funding, but must also assume responsibilities for building partnerships to make much more efficient use of tax payers' dollars and provide our citizens with multiple returns on their investment.*

*The link between education and sport (from core physical education, recreation through to competitive sport and Olympic excellence) should be fully forged to bring multiple returns for Canadian education, health, and sport.*

*Simon Fraser University is an excellent example of the education-sport linkage and partnership approach I'm advocating. As a former CEO of several major national sport organizations, I'm astounded by the resources at my disposal at SFU compared to the national sport organizations I led: facilities, fulltime professional coaches, fulltime sport physiotherapists, access to research faculty with expertise in sport psychology, nutrition, kinesiology, etc., and fulltime staff in event management, media relations, marketing and fund raising. These are incredible educational assets that can work in partnership with the Canadian sport system.*

*SFU has in fact sought to do so. Our CLAN wrestling program has been involved in winning four Olympic medals in the last 6 Games. This was achieved by developing a long-term partnership with BC Wrestling and Wrestling Canada, which not only helped Canadian wrestling but also SFU athletics and recreation.*

*The same is true for SFU's partnership with Softball Canada, which made SFU the training base for Canada's Olympic Women's Softball team.*

*Our recent $3 million partnership agreement with the Vancouver Whitecaps likewise benefits education and sport. The new fields being built by the Whitecaps will double the current field usage opportunities of our SFU recreation members (students, faculty, and staff) and provide a year-round training centre for the national soccer teams, the Whitecaps and the Whitecaps' youth programs.*

*This is also why we extended our hand to the 2010 Vancouver Bid Committee to ensure a multi-decade legacy not only for the students of SFU, but also the physical activity, health, and human performance research community, local community recreation users, and the Canadian sport system.*

*There are more than fifty Canadian universities who could assist the Canadian sport system while also benefiting their education institutions. Elementary and secondary schools can do the same. A strong institutional link between education and sport makes sense in terms of providing a stable base and maximizing resources for both education and sport.*

*The opportunity to positively link education and sport was missed in the 1970s. The opportunity to do so recently with the 2010 Olympic Oval investment was missed just a month ago when the Vancouver Organizing Committee moved it to Richmond.*

*Hopefully, Canadians and federal-provincial governments will soon find the wisdom and the will to link our Canadian sport system with our provincial education systems for the long-term health and excellence of Canadians!*

Atop the hill, and a few minutes after Davies had signed off with a handshake following his recollections of the past, Wedmann sat down in front of a fresh blank tape. If anyone still doubts that the moniker "dumb jock" deserves to be consigned to every scrap heap except the comedy channel, read on.

Self-deprecating Wilf: "It was a bad year for Rhodes Scholarships! Har, har. Timing is everything to get to the right level, pick the weak year, right? I kept staying at this university until I could see it was a bad year," his sixth. Wedmann immediately turned to his aforementioned 1969 "Report On The Task Force On Sport For Canadians," which he described as "perhaps the best blueprint for Canadian sport versus anything we've done since. All the other reports are fatter, bigger, thicker, and perhaps get more detailed and complex. The beauty of the '69 report was that it was thin, and half of it was devoted to what we should do with Canadian hockey because that was, of course, what we love."

It was released after Canada "sort of had a replay of what we just went through in Athens, in a sense, it was a very bad summer," said Wedmann of our 1-3-1 medal performance at the 1968 Summer Olympic Games in Mexico City. The resultant outcry from concerned quarters prompted Pierre Trudeau to make an election campaign promise to deal with our international capabilities. Thus, The Task Force, which "said something to the effect that the most natural place where this solution should begin is at the education system. Virtually every Canadian kid is part of the Canadian education system, or the provincial education systems, the PE at the beginning, the intramurals at the elementary school, the intra-school stuff, it all leads up then to the next step, and then the universities are the next step.

"So, [the federal government], they saw that as really being the primary focus of attention. Tragically, they recognized that their jurisdiction was limited to the federal domain, and education is provincial. Even though they made the point that the American system [had its shortcomings] they made the point also that Canadian universities seem to hold their nose and look askew at the scholarship system. That was recognized in 1969 when the report came out. They wanted nothing better than to do that. It's been forgotten. They sort of addressed the same issue that's being addressed here and it was said then. Which is amazing — at the point where we started into modern sport we actually knew the right way to go and we failed to go that way because of the jurisdictional issues. It wasn't the Task Force's responsibility, it basically did what it could," but unfortunately, most unfortunately, could not prevail upon the monolith to move. Which does bring up, exactly who does the CIS report to?

And, look askew at scholarships? "It's that snootiness — without looking at the reality of what can be done. I guess the sadness is that we look at the American system and without being academically sound we make it that the scholarship itself is the cause of the problem. And it's the administration of the financial assistance/scholarship that's the cause. It always is. It's like the Olympics, we can say the Olympics are bad, you know? There have been abuses of the Olympics, but the Olympics are a tool. And if you use them well, they can be used for good. If you use them stupidly? Adolf Hitler in '36 used them for a whole different purpose than what it was meant. Tokyo in '64 used it to come out into the world. Mexico in '68 tried to do the same thing when it really wasn't ready and they killed a number of students with protests because of the Olympics, In that case, the articulation of the Games were not necessarily good, does that mean the Games are bad?

"It's the same thing with this issue. We give money for students who have incredible academic excellence. That's great. I have no problem saying you know what, if we've got great singers, or we've great artists on this campus, great dancers, we should give them financial assistance. So it's not that we're doing it only for athletes, it is about the diverse person and, if anything, universities should be about diverse articulations of human endeavour. Some of us articulate that in certain different forms. Not all of us are great writers or great mathematicians, but all of us who are in here have to be at a pretty sophisticated academic performance level and can benefit from what the university has to offer while also adding to the quality of life at a university and to representing university in the public domain, which is an important part of communications. That's where I think our sports programs add tremendously to the imagery of Simon Fraser University. And given that we are trying to administer them at the highest level, I think we do a heckuva job. Daniel Igali is a wonderful prototype of a human being, he is now doing his masters in criminology looking at terrorism, etcetera, he's an Olympic champion, a world champion," future Nigerian Sports Minister? "All those things. I mean, that's the power. You can also get it wrong, you can also screw it up, so you have to guard against that."

On that subject, and more particular the CIS's grand fear of jockitis lowering hallowed academic standards, Wedmann pulls no punches. "The only person responsible for that is the university administrator, the president. That's not the model that financial assistance is about. I think that Canadians, in some ways, have played that superior nose, failed to appreciate the power of what United States universities have done, failed to appreciate what a Stanford has accomplished. It's a pretty incredible standard at Stanford, that with its incredible academic standards it ends up winning athletically as well," emphasizing the point that awarding sports scholarships does anything but guarantee a taint to those hallowed halls. There's proof that it works. We've looked the other way."

And by the way, Tiger Woods attended Stanford, where Michelle Wie is to enrol at the appropriate time.

Getting to the point, as it relates to being a rookie university AD: "I came here four years ago and I realized what a gold mine I have here, compared to being at gymnastics or track and field. I've got an infrastructure, I have got actual facilities, I have an entire infrastructure of facility management, finance, legal, risk insurance, all of those things are here, and then when I come to my department, I've got a marketing guy, I've got a media guy, I've got an event guy, I've got a physiotherapy department, I've got paid professional coaches here.

"Then I looked around and thought, well, why isn't this part of the sports system?"

At which point the clapping and the cheering resulting from him preaching to at least one of the faithful drowns him out. He recalls running into a former associate at a downtown Vancouver hotel and finding out that the Canadian Coaching Association was holding a meeting he knew nothing about. "I've got 14 paid, pensionable coaches, which is a real difference, these guys here are actually developing pensions, and I'm sitting there realizing that I never get invited to come to a meeting because I am an outsider. All those meetings with coaching associations, the Canadian Olympic Committee, the Marion Lay Legacies Now group, these high-performance centers, I never get invited to them."

Bizarre.

"It is. But it is exactly the lesson, from my own experience. Mind you, I wish I could tell you that I was really bright when I was in Ottawa at the national level and was thinking I've got to get the universities involved, right?" says Wedmann, somewhat apologetically, as he actually ran the national show.

"I can't tell you that I'm not fighting with my university colleagues across the country on the very issue of financial assistance/scholarships. And I can't tell you that they are committed to high-performance/excellence. Even though the words they spout at times, the rules and regulations are to the contrary."

They aren't committed to high performance?

"Exactly. Then on the other hand, I started adding up what I thought was an average budget given we've got 51 universities, plus or minus a few that are coming in every year, but if everybody spent about $2 million on their sports programs ... that's $100 million, which before the latest Sport Canada budget was as much as Sport Canada was investing in sport."

Bizarre is the fact our universities are and aren't a part of a delivery system that recognizes the necessity of elite development, bizarre is the fact that elite is a swear word.

On how to affect the philosophical sea change necessary to restore sanity, Wedmann says willingness. "I talked to a Sport Canada rep who used to work with me at Gymnastics Canada and I said to him, I understand why you might not be working with us in a concerted effort to integrate us into the sport model if you will, but I don't understand why you don't think that you have to make us change.

"Because we're sitting here with $100 million in annual

expenditures and with the inventory of facilities we have, there's nobody that matches us. I wish there was, but there isn't.

"Imagine if the prime minister got on the phone and said to [then UBC President] Martha Piper, Martha, we're doing a lot of research investment in you, can't you get your athletic department to start changing its course and put a little extra research money into research for high-performance sport in your university? I'm sure we can have these conversations. But instead we are still outside. To just presume there's enough money for all the interests in Canada, that's stupid. But boy, we could add some synergy here, and that's where I was pissed with the Olympic Oval, pardon me. That was a perfect investment — up here. I understand why the sports systems and the centres might not necessarily love the universities because we don't deserve to be loved as people want, although there are pockets of high performance at a lot of universities across the country. I certainly believe the Western Canadian universities have a much deeper commitment to sport than the Easterners, aside from Quebec."

An ebullient Wedmann describes SFU's original decision to not compete in Canada as a "brilliant decision" because the CIAU "was too restrictive and silly in their behaviour." It remains so. He applauds the NAIA's policy of capping athletic scholarship amounts at the costs of going to university and pooh-poohs the CIS's current regulation which he calls "arbitrarily capped at the cost of tuition and fees. In Canada, we finally got that about five years ago. Well, ever since that was passed the Ontario and Atlantic provinces have been fighting like mad to whittle away at it, such that, right now in the next two years the cap is 70 per cent of tuition and fees."

The CIS has evolved from being restrictive and silly to somehow managing to be capable of doing a great job of running backwards chasing its tail.

He lauds the integrity of the NAIA programs, for which ultimate responsibility rests with university administrators. "The tragedy in Canada is that we are not recognizing the power of what a good strong athletics or recreation program can add to a university, and that's a tragedy." Why not? "I think part of it is because we have done exactly what you said, we've looked south and we saw the bad things, not the good things, and that's so unacademic, that we dare to do that, I think that's really unhealthy because an academic perspective is supposed to be a full perspective and a thorough analytical study and that hasn't happened by us Canadians, we just look down south and we like to see the bad things," in a false bid for self-gratification.

"That's right, and then we're better than you. So we don't compete. What bothers me about the CIS is the fact that we athletic directors don't operate like the academics do. Academics aren't as regulatory as athletic directors. We love rules. And so what we do is regulate, and then what we do is regulate all sorts of things away from it. Now we want to limit how much you can give away, because you're going to recruit kids and I don't want you recruiting away from me. You have all sorts of motivations behind this. Whereas the academic people, they have a few core principles you have to live by and they actually encourage diversity of approaches, etc, theoretically at least. The CIS should behave consistently with that. But given that we're good old jocks, we tend to work the rules and rules are often about stopping you rather than embracing them and encouraging things.

"We've become rule-bound. We athletic directors in the CIS are too much based on regulatory practices, as opposed to our living by our philosophy, our mission and what we are really about. And so in some ways, we've undermined our own credibility and we've done that within the university academic community and at the same time we've undermined our credibility within the sports system so they don't want to pay attention to us.

"At the same time we haven't done a good job of lobbying governments in terms of the sports side of this thing to say, you know what, we're a heckuva asset to you. So again you can come back and say the first problem is us, it isn't necessarily others. But part of this is recognizing that if you run a good program, and there is validity to it, you can have bright student-athletes, if you expect high-performances, you'll get it. The question is of the expectations and we in ourselves have not really come to grips with strong expectations, Again, I could argue with the academics but I would be beating on ourselves before I beat on them. I mean, if we're smart, we've got to understand that a university, its core business is academics and you can't disrespect that, you must respect the core business, hence I need to shape my work within that framework."

So, dearly departed foes, we can insist on academic standards of the highest integrity? "You know what's the one thing that all of this has taught me? It's that a good athlete responds to standards because it's the challenge you need to have and they're hungry for it. When we don't give them high standards, when we don't have high expectations of them, we're not helping them. In some way, I think today's parents are in the same camp. They think they're doing the kids well by helping them all of the time. You've got to let your kid get challenged and try things and fend for themselves because otherwise they never learn how to do that. I think student-athletics can be incredible and I think it is worthy of financial assistance or scholarships, but I think we need to demand more of us and I think the Canadian universities need to have more demands on them to challenge their students, not just in athletics but in all the walks of life because I'd love nothing better than we should have exceptional dance programs, exceptional music programs.

"I think the public should demand more of us, not in the sense of making it easier for my kid but in the sense of saying we want to have cutting-edge stuff at university. This is the other thing with CIS that drives me crazy. Because if I understand the academic community, they don't say they're trying to be the best in Canada, research is not just great research if it's validated only for Canada, it needs to be peer-reviewed on a global basis and a kind of principle, law or truth must apply on a global basis. I would liken them to global players. So then why as athletic programs are we satisfied with not challenging ourselves at the world level? Which then gets us back into high-performance sport, etc., and that real investment is needed if you're serious about what you're doing. If you're [University of Toronto Dean of Physical Education] Bruce Kidd, and you're interested in having the most varsity sports, but you can't finance them at the level needed to be the best, you're a recreationist, and that's wonderful, but it's called a high-performance program. And I don't understand why a university would want anything less than high performance?

"So again, when I go to my [fellow] athletic directors, it's why aren't we like the rest of our colleagues? We should be striving for the best in the world. Does that say we can make that easily? No. That's really hard, that's what it's about. And will we make it fast? No, we've got a lot of work to do but the minute we cut ourselves down by making regulations that limit what you can do, we are not going to strive high. That's the other sadness of this behaviour that perhaps is never thought about, it's we need to strive, we need to be into nurturing and that doesn't mean cheating. Why don't we think about it from that vantage point? It says something about us, right? I never thought I needed to cheat to get there," he says of his Olympics. "No, to be the best in the world I need to be stronger, build the best technique, build the best mental toughness, etcetera, etcetera. I don't think where can I get some cheated forensics, that is not the solution."

No, but there is one, and it's the teeter to the totter of the element within the CIS which refuses to recognize it even has a problem. It's called SFU's approach since Day One.

Hail the role call of Clan teams which have won national championships, and to save you from dozing off while the list drones on and on, it's 45 — 38 in the NAIA, six in the CIS, and one North American Collegiate. Recall all those Director's Cups? Heady territory. Casting an eye over SFU's Olympic contributions, the numbers come in at 86 athletes, 11 coaches, one manager, three gold, four silver and two bronze medals. Wedmann was the first SFU student-athlete to wear the Maple Leaf under the Olympic rings, first in 1968 in Mexico City and four years later at Munich. Debbie Brill, who with Dick Fosbury simultaneously but separately pioneered a new technique which literally flipped high jumping onto its back, competed in 1972 in Munich, 1976 in Montreal and 1984 in Los Angeles. At those Games, Sue Holloway and Hugh Fisher won gold medals in canoe, the university's third came in 2002 when wrestler Daniel Igali became a household name following his tears-of-joy kiss of the mat draped in a Canadian flag. Clansman Jeff Shue wrestled his way to silver in 1992; four years later Bob Molle won silver and Chris Rinke won bronze on the mats in Los Angeles. Wrestler Dave MacKay competed in Los Angeles and Seoul, and coached in Sydney and Athens. Swimmer Bruce Robertson won silver and gold in Munich (among the 16 international gold medals for Canada in his career). Gary MacDonald struck silver in Montreal, losing by 0.22 seconds in Canada's first but not last gold-medal shutout Games. Mike Renney coached the women's softball team in three successive Games beginning when the sport made its Olympic debut in 1996 (a team which featured one Hayley Wickenheiser in cleats). The SFU softball program began in 1991, but no Clan member made the team for Athens. In Sydney in 2000 there were three, in Athens there were five, with the entire Olympic team based at SFU in the run-up to the Games. The Clan's Jay Triano coached the team in Sydney, a team which featured one Steve Nash. In Los Angeles, Randy Ragan and Mike Sweeney played soccer, two years later and only slightly further south, they were members of Canada's one and only men's World Cup team. John Buchanan is revered in Clan history, not only for his considerable coaching achievements, but also for starting the university's now world-famous (if you're in that world) bagpipe band. Buchanan coached the first Clan soccer team in 1975 and was on the sidelines in the famous Rose Bowl championship game one year later. A bigger thrill and equally bigger relief might have been the semi-final game when the Clan entered the Guinness World Records for the longest soccer game in modern history by playing in a marathon 243-minute victory over Quincey College of Illinois. Buchanan was an assistant coach at the Montreal Games the next year. Navel-gazing, the Clan has produced more Canadian Football League football players than any other Canadian university, over 130 at last count, including the legendary walk-on Dave Cutler, and professional football's all-time leading scorer, Lui Passaglia, whose son is now on an athletic scholarship at SFU.

If you ever get tested on what Canadian universities can contribute to Canadian sport, re-read the preceding paragraph. There are now 52 and counting CIS member institutions. Do the math. However, the equation only works if you take the Clan's approach. Across the CIS, there just aren't enough pockets of the same, because the CIS, as a whole, has turned a blind eye and an upheld nose.

In June 2003, SFU announced a $10 million upgrade in its athletic facilities to coincide with its 40th birthday. In April 2004 the Vancouver Whitecaps, Canada's flagship soccer organization, announced an initial investment of $3 million at, in and through SFU to construct a new training home for all Whitecap teams, and really, so much more. Some comments from that day:

"This is a historic day for SFU because a privately owned professional sports franchise and one of Canada's leading universities have developed a partnership that will create a legacy of excellence," said SFU President Michael Stevenson. "With the generosity of the Whitecaps investment and our dynamic new relationship with the organization and the Canadian Soccer Association, Simon Fraser University students, student-athletes and the surrounding community will benefit from these lit turf fields that will more than double our current available field use."

"The purpose of this training centre is to provide the Whitecaps FC and Canadian Soccer Association with a permanent, year-round training facility," said Whitecaps owner Greg Kerfoot. "As an organization our objective has consistently been to develop a strong club structure and this facility provides the foundation to serve that goal. We believe that the centre will also provide a positive training atmosphere for Canadian soccer and establish Vancouver as the home of our national teams."

"This generous investment from our friends at the Whitecaps will help us to realize our dream of making Simon Fraser University the centre of sports and sports science in this country," said SFU Director of Recreation and Athletics Wilf Wedmann. "As part of the SFU Olympic Oval Legacy vision the university is planning to develop a sports science institute and sports medicine centre for the benefit of Canadian athletes."

"The CSA supports the evolution of this project and looks forward to being able to have its national teams use the facility," said CSA President Andy Sharpe. "We are delighted with the ongoing commitment shown by Whitecaps FC and owner Greg Kerfoot to the future of soccer in Vancouver, British Columbia and Canada. This is a major step forward in our quest to improve the quality of facilities across the country and the subsequent impact on the preparations of our national team programs."

The move brings to five the national team programs "Up the Hill," joining women's soccer, softball and wrestling, and men's wrestling, 2005 being a roller-coaster year for SFU atop its perch atop the mount. In April, B.C. Premier Gordon Campbell announced provincial investment of $20 million to assist SFU continue its tradition of athletic excellence with the construction of a new athletic centre and stadium. The premier was downright effusive (love those speechwriters) in making the announcement. "SFU has a proud history of training some of Canada's best young athletes, a history the province wants to help build on as we prepare for 2010," said Campbell.

"Supporting athletic infrastructure projects such as this one, which will support a culture of fitness on campus and in the community of Burnaby, is a critical part of our commitment to promote sport and healthy living throughout B.C." 10-4, Mr Premier. Where were you, though, later in the year when SFU somehow lost the right to build the speed-skating oval for those just aforementioned 2010 Vancouver Winter Olympic Games?

Can you say disconnect? While Wedmann cursed that call by VANOC, he took it in his stride. "Well, I would have argued that the University of Calgary Olympic Oval was a brilliant prototype. If there's anything we can take and say that was innovative leadership by whoever — federal, provincial governments, etc. — it was that they didn't leave the oval sitting out on its own like it's going to be in Richmond. And this isn't a rant against that because I don't really care, but what bothers me is that Calgary is such a vivid example.

"By putting that oval inside that university, not on a peripheral basis but inside, under the same department that has kinesiology, athletics and recreation, you had an integrated model. They had some challenges at the beginning, because, 'if you build it they will come' does not necessarily apply. But they then started programming and we've just got some innovative coaching and technological developments coming out of Calgary, the Oval. The sadness there for me is the centre couldn't get and make a commitment to the university, as a result that high-performance centre sits outside the university, as a pimple, and must negotiate everything. As opposed to where I work here and it's an inside conversation. It's very different than an outsider talking with facilities to negotiate something.

"So you've got this marvellous prototype in Calgary, and here in Vancouver we didn't follow it. I think that's moronic. You know? I hope they can live up the dream that [The City of Richmond] spun. Our university was not at liberty to underwrite the Olympic Games, I mean, our responsibility, first and foremost, is to the students, and we're a provincial educational institution, so we can't sit there with VANOC, you give us sixty million dollars and everything above that we can pay. Richmond has a tax base and if their taxpayers want to do that, that's their choice. If we knew it was that kind of definition by VANOC, we should have walked, if we knew that was what they really wanted, we would have withdrawn right up front because our president and our board, and I wouldn't allow it personally, because it's not appropriate.

"But it is the wrong decision by VANOC, the federal and provincial governments, in my opinion, because they've forsaken the legacy. For us, we weren't interested in the Olympics, being an Olympic site, it was the legacy of having five more laboratories, of research and physical activity and human performance, it was to have a national high-performance centre here. It was all that, and we've got a heckuva base."

SFU wasn't "interested" in the Olympics, per se, but the Games certainly would have been the whipped cream on the strawberry-rhubarb pie. "You've got it, yeah, that's nice, been there done it, not to disparage it, but what's interesting is what happened before and what's going to happen after and that's what that building is interesting to me for. But, you know, we will have to find another way to get a field-house built so we can continue our vision because that 2010 vision we had is still operational inside the university, that's still a goal we want to pursue and focus around.

"We want to have good recreation, we want to have good stuff for our Clan athletic teams, we want to have a sports medicine center as opposed to just a physio clinic, we want to have a European-style multi-sport club here, centred here. We're going to have 10,000 people living on the mountain, we've got 2,500 Clan alumni. The Daniel Igali model, or wrestling model that Mike Jones developed here, is brilliant because we have a club side and we have a varsity side. Daniel couldn't get into this university in the beginning, went to Douglas, got his grades up, trained with Burnaby Mountain Wrestling Club. Once he entered the university, he was part of the varsity program, graduates, now he's part of the Burnaby Mountain Wrestling Club. Again, at all times he trained in that little cubby hole down there and was trained by the same group of coaches that train all of our student athletes as well as community athletes," says Wedmann of near seamless connection.

# Chapter Four
## Vive Le Difference

There is one banner that's never hung at SFU. Hockey.

From 1966, again courtesy Patrick Nagle in Weekend Magazine: "I've talked to people here and around the country," says Simon Fraser athletic director Lorne Davies about his athletic-scholarship program. "Coaches and universities are pulling for us. We're trying to provide the best program in Canada. When the time is right — when we can get the proper coach, equipment and facilities — we'll have a hockey team, too. It's our national sport. We can't ignore it. We could get a good league going out here with all the universities."

If there is a perfect example of the disconnect of university sport within Canada how fitting that it should be hockey. We may not win 'em all, all of the time, nor should we, but how long has it been since we last feared lacing 'em up against anyone? But just ask yourself: which is your favourite university team, or player? Thought so. Aside from immediate family, and girl- and boyfriends, near absolute indifference rules the day. Any top high school talent, male or female, bound and determined to combine and utilize both their brain and their athletic ability, simultaneously and to the max, look south. Shame on the CIS, recall demanded. What's even worse is that CIS hockey today is extremely high-calibre, but its own approach has effectively neutered its appeal. There ought to be a law. We have enough wilderness in Canada that we don't need to designate our university hockey league another one.

"I think the CIS is really hoy-yoy, oy-yoy with these 30-year-olds hanging around. Get a life," said University of Winnipeg Athletic Director Bill Wedlake. "The CIS is not interested in the high school hockey player, they end up going south to play in top programs."

Before proceeding further down this path, kudos must be given to the CHL, the governing body of major junior hockey in Canada, which has a scholarship program for its graduating 20-year-olds. That's who mostly stocks our university leagues these days, and in the good old days would be playing Senior hockey at this point in their careers. As for get a life, that should be rephrased continue your hockey life, playing Senior AAA as it's known these days. Perennial powerhouse Alberta Golden Bears is often comprised entirely of ex-

CHLers, Senior AAA players in a re-retro jersey, and would win the Allan Cup hands down, should it choose to.

"I don't think NHL scouts are even scouting CIS hockey — period," said Jordan Little in November of 2004, then 23 and a third-year defenseman from the University of Manitoba Bisons, even though he is just barely technically wrong on that fact. Echoed teammate and former Kamloops Blazer Paul Deniset, "It's tough. It seems like it's a league that no one knows about. Even in the city of Winnipeg, you'll tell someone that you play for the Bisons, and they'll know nothing about it. I just don't think they realize the level of hockey." Only a few chosen or lucky do. "It's depressing, sometimes. When you played junior in the Western League you're used to playing in front of big crowds. Sometimes you're let down by the amount of people who come out." Even in Edmonton, where Clare Drake Arena is to CIS hockey what the Montreal Forum was to the NHL, a good regular-season crowd generally fills a quarter of the 4,000 seats.

UBC's AD Bob Philip just shakes his head at the situation. Granted, his Thunderbirds are anything but a powerhouse, but Vancouver is hockey crazy except for the university kind. "There is no reason why, and even the [WHL Vancouver] Giants would say, there's no reason why they should get 10,000 fans and we should get 200. The guys that are playing … it's good hockey. If you're a student here, it's two bucks to go and you're not going to walk across and watch it? People come to me and say, wow, that was a really good game. But we don't continue to push it, we don't make it important — we just don't make university sports important on our national landscape."

Philip and a few others tried to do just that a few decades back. And just guess which organization held them back? Turning back the clock to the mid-Sixties, Philip spins some good stories.

"The University of Toronto was really winning all the time in hockey. We had a senior league in football with the four Eastern teams, Queens, Western, Toronto and McGill, the Senior Intercollegiate Football League. We broke up the senior league and played everybody. And really, all we did was bring them down to everybody else's level.

"It didn't matter if you wanted to be better — you were all part of this thing. We used to call it the Ryerson Syndrome. How can we get everyone to Ryerson's level? And if Ryerson can't compete, then we can't have that rule. Bob Fullerton, I had a lot of time for Bob, he was the AD forever at Ryerson, the only one they'd ever had. A few years ago his men's basketball team made it to the national championships, the one and only time a Ryerson team had gone. We were in the washroom and I said to him, well, Bob, I see the OUAA has finally come down to your level, and he thought that was pretty funny, but in fact it really was the truth.

"In 1972 eight of us, representing eight schools, got together at a restaurant in Toronto to form a Super League in hockey. We had sponsorship, we were going to do it — Toronto, St. Mary's, Sir George Williams and Loyola College, and Alberta, among others. We had this planned. But the mistake we made was instead of just doing it we went and took it to the CIAU. Some of the dialogue with the other schools ... " Philip says, yes, rolling his eyes and shaking his head, "at one point I was standing there talking with Bob Fullerton and Tom Watt was coaching U of T then and Watt said to Fullerton, 'Why are you going to vote against us having this Super League,' and Fullerton said, 'Because we'll be second-class citizens' and Watt said, 'Well, that's a step up from where you're at!' They were third class.

"Toronto had beaten Ryerson, I think 19-0 and 13-0 in the two games they played that year. So the fact was, that was kind of counter-productive," was how Philip put trying to work with, through or around the let's sing playground-lullabies mentality of the then CIAU. Winning creates losing and everyone is oh-so-special and nobody deserves to lose because they will develop a complex and become dysfunctional and have to resort to therapists and huge daily doses of prescription drugs and beat their bosses and mothers and sell their wives and children to pirates and drink and smoke and gamble and lose their jobs and contribute to global warming and write rants — and the moon is made of cheese. Or, something like that.

If Philip and his cohorts had been successful, it would have meant the birth of Canada's own league for the many Canadian-born Hobey Baker Trophy winners.

Bob Hindmarch was the assistant coach for Father David Bauer's National Team that played out of UBC (and tied those Notre Dame Knights). That was then. Now? "You want to be on a winning team? Well, if you're really good you go to Alberta. The University of Alberta has a fantastic hockey team and I would say 80 per cent of them are former junior hockey players who were captains."

Hindmarch was long among those who applied pressure on the CHL to help provide for their players' education, post-Junior age eligibility. "I remember speaking up all the time about kids who go to play in the Western Hockey League and they're traveling all the time, they play 104 hockey games, and they're in Grade 12!" he says of the exact same situation today. "Where are they going to go? They're going to be pumping gas." Exaggeration intended and accepted because the point is, "How many hundreds of kids last year graduated from major junior hockey, how many who graduated were drafted, and let's just say of those, how many played in National Hockey League? About six," he says dismissively, but most effectively underlining the need to return for more schooling.

Over to Philip for another telling statistic, on those Canadians who opt for NCAA scholarships instead of Major Junior hockey, considered a more "sure" route to the pros. "I'll give you a stat. Now I don't know if it's still true but it was when I was with the CAHA several years ago. Of all the Canadian kids that went down to play sports in the US, 50 per cent stayed there after graduation," as the conservationists among us warn against sending gas down the pipeline.

McGill's Robert Dubeau was the longest-serving university AD in Canada before his retirement in August of 2005 with three decades of service. You might say he's seen it all. Seven months prior he shared his thoughts most freely, wryly chuckling at one point and asking, "Can you tell I'm retiring?"

The CIS might want to skip this. "The only sport we're Division One in is probably hockey but even then our top two or three teams might be able to compete with the best in the States, but after that it's a pretty big drop-off. Drafted players? Probably been a while, a few come to mind. But there's been some. Hockey in Canada comes up through the junior system, that's just the way it works. You're going to get the odd kid, he's probably not going to get drafted but he's going to get the chance to play. But if we ran Canadian university hockey exactly the same way as the Americans run US college hockey and if we had restrictions on junior players, age limits, etc., etc., we would develop. I guess what I am trying to say here is if we at the CIS decided that hockey was going to be a developmental program we would have a heckuva lot more people playing in the NHL.

"CIS hockey is Senior hockey, kids coming out of junior that were not good enough to play in the NHL. So you're not in the developmental stage. Our hockey players are quite old and they play the sport because they play hockey, that's it, there's nowhere else to go. That's for 95, 98 per cent of the players. But if we keep on having the current regulations with regards to no age limits and only taking players out of junior," Dubeau says with a shake of his head, "it's a retirement fund … a pension plan so you can go to university. If I was running a junior program, it's a very politically sound way of doing things, but not a whole lot of those kids get that, money, there are some, but not that many. And I find that half those kids, when they come to university out of junior they have lost, really, the desire of playing, their spirit is shot, they worked hard for how many years to make it to the NHL and they're not good enough. A lot of the kids that come to us through the junior program are problematic — because their desire is not there. All the kids would have desire if it was developmental hockey. It's something that the CIS is going have to, one of these centuries, deal with. Otherwise, hockey is going to remain Senior hockey with virtually no interest from the media or public."

Paul Carson, Executive Assistant to the Dean, Faculty of Physical Education and Health, University of Toronto, managed a few days later to explain away the CIAU's misgivings about scholarship hockey players, deflecting criticism from CIS restrictions and instead placing it on bumbling incompetence at other headquarters. "Hockey Canada started giving them out around 1970, a very well-intentioned program but not the best run. At our university they gave some scholarships to people who couldn't make the intercollegiate team so we had intramural hockey players on national scholarships because somebody in Hockey Canada thought they were good. It was experiences like that that soured a number of university people in Ontario to the scholarship system because they saw a program being so ineptly run and thought, my goodness, this is one sport, if this is a sample of what's going to happen, we're better off without them and plough the money into coaching development.

"The big argument in the early years in Ontario was that the route to develop better athletes was to develop better coaches and since there wasn't much money available their argument was spend the money on coaching, because you need fewer coaches than you need athletes and a limited amount of money, given to coaches, would probably both in the long term and short term produce better international-level athletes than any other system. And they pointed to the hockey debacle in the early '70s as Case Study A. Apparently we weren't the only case. A number of universities received money for people who either weren't students or had no idea why they were getting the money. This is the early years and of course none of those people are still around, but it was an absolute schmozzle.

"In our case there were people who couldn't make the team, yet they kept their money. In other cases there were people who didn't even go to school and presumably kept the money. Hockey Canada gave them the money without requiring proof they were in school and without proof they made the hockey team. So they had the money, and they cashed the cheque, I assure you. That created all sorts of bad vibes." As they would say in the rink, drop the gloves.

Common sense often competes with a tree falling in a forest to be heard, but it is out there. Luc Gelineau is the AD at the University of Ottawa, one of the few Ontario universities to give the maximum allowable athletic assistance to its athletes in CIS championship sports. "I'm not actually actively lobbying for it," he said in early 2005, "but take a sport like women's hockey, quite a new sport. You've got the presence of a national championship and the sport governing body sees the link with the universities. So with that there, we could probably use the reverse. We could say, in women's hockey, across the country, basically open our doors to the top student-athletes and be more liberal on awards. Let's try it. If we don't basically try, are not aggressive, I think all the good female hockey players will end up in the States and we will lose an opportunity." Hear, hear.

Hear, hear, CIS about a scholarship plan. "We could become basically the NCAA, under our rules, with our academics, in women's hockey. Each year right now you're adding four or five teams in the university system so it's time to basically do it. In Ontario as well, I think there might be some support for that. I think if you do it in women's hockey, the minute our athletes come from our university system then you're basically making a case and you could demonstrate that it's working. I think you have to focus on the discipline," Gelineau says. "In that regard, women's university hockey is part of Sport Canada's sport model. But we have to make sure at least that what we are offering our Canadians is a viable option, in certain sports right now it's not, in others it could probably become the best. In women's hockey it could become the best, for us to exercise leadership in partnership with Hockey Canada."

There is one good thing that can be said for CIAU hockey. It directly led to the formation of a foundation which bestows not only cold hard cash but merit to and acceptance of athletically talented students, openly and with favour. It's the Quebec Foundation for Athletic Excellence, and under the since-Day One stewardship of Monsieur Pierre Dube has evolved into the anti-thesis of the CIS, thus precisely what this country needs. Speaking at his office in the Big O in the middle of a typically frigid Montreal winter, but not so frigid to keep the locals off the outdoor rinks, Dube expounded on the history, development and of course, raison d'etre of the foundation, which on its website comes across as:

*ABOUT THE FONDATION DE L'ATHLÈTE D'EXCELLENCE DU QUÉBEC*

*The Foundation's mission is to financially help and support athletes-students in their pursuit of excellence and to contribute to providing role models for Quebec society at large. The Foundation will have given, by the end of 2005, a half-million dollars in bursaries through its various programs.*

"At the beginning it was not a foundation," Dube begins. "It's all because of a Quebecer who coached the Blue Eagles of Moncton and won two Canadian university championships with 14 francophone Quebecers — Jean Perron," taking us back to the early '80s. As the rest of the country, except it seems the philosophical hide-bounds who controlled CIAU policy, began to take notice of the exodus of our top high school seniors to the United States, certain concerned Quebecers obviously saw the problem in terms of migration south, west and east and wanted to keep their best student athletes home, from both the U.S. and the rest of Canada. When hockey speaks, all of Canada listens.

In June of 1983 the Quebec University Athletics Association created an advisory board, amply stocked with experts from the business world, to study the issue and begin handing out bursaries. Not a lot, no more than $28,000 a year between 1983-85, at which point the board recommended the establishment of the initial foundation. "We, the advisory board, became the directors of the new Quebec Foundation for University Athletics and decided to organize a campaign sufficient to raise capital of $1 million," says Dube of a target easily broken, with it sitting comfortably at $1.5 million by 1995, at which time the Foundation was distributing close to $100,000 annually.

"At that time, some members of the foundation and also some members of the business community wanted to create a new fund, to not only help university athletes to help Quebec in university competition, but also other athletes, perhaps some younger athletes, but also some athletes involved in study but not involved in university sports, some Olympic athletes studying at CEGEP or university."

Thus the Quebec Foundation for Athletic Excellence arrived on the scene. But with these guys, the more things change the more they stay the same: "So we decided to change the name of foundation, but the basis of the foundation is to help student-athletes, but not only at university and not only full-time students, with an open mind."

That fall, a second major fundraising effort, featuring Celine Dion, soon pushed the Foundation's capital to $4.5 million. It's now well over the $6 million mark, through which it allots around nearly a half millions dollars in bursaries and athletic awards.

Not done just yet, either, says Dube. "And so, we want to continue, we have a new plan, a five-year plan, we want to raise $5.5 million in the next five years to raise the capital from $6.6 million to $10 million — and also to give $800,000." And, non-Francophones need apply. "We support Quebec university sport, but not only Quebec athletes.

"And then we have what we call the recruitment bursary, or entry scholarship, to attract athletes to stay in Quebec, it's only for Quebecers, to stay in Quebec."

Because of Jean Perron? "Yes, that was the main goal. We have other scholarships. When you pass one year minimum at university, all student-athletes are eligible. If a guy from the United States is studying at McGill he would be eligible for a scholarship, or a guy from B.C."

The program works for all the predictable reasons. First off, it's arm-distance to the CIS. As Dube strategically notes, because of current CIS regulations on transfers, "recruitment is really important. We are a third-party scholarship because when we give recruitment bursaries, or recruitment scholarships, we select the athletes from CEGEP and we tell the athlete if you stay in Quebec you will receive bursaries, that's the amount of money you will receive, you can choose the university but you must be involved in sports. You can go to Sherbrooke, Laval, McGill, Montreal, Concordia, Bishops, we don't mind — if you stay in Quebec. It's impossible for a university to say you will receive a bursary from the foundation. They can if they want but they've got no say. When we approach the athletes, we say we will give it to you if you deserve it." And they deserve, whether from home or away. At the end of the day, "It's another tool to keep the student in Quebec," just long overdue considering that the pursuit of athletic excellence at the university level is relatively new to La Belle province.

Quebec was long five fingers up against the gun. French Roman Catholicism didn't follow their English cousins down the road of "Muscular Christianity," from which the Notre Dame universities emerged, and was rather more concerned with population explosion as a means of levelling a different playing field. The European tradition of sport delivery via the club system held way. The CIAU's "just say no" policy was in place. Every boy was playing hockey and girls were discouraged from donning athletic tights, much less personas. That, as historians should be wont to say, was then.

"I think there is in the past 20 years in Quebec a great change in mentality. In the last six or seven years, Quebec is really involved — and not only at the universities. The provincial government has made a lot of big moves to support Quebec athletes. The problem we have is to organize great competitions," Dube said, breaking out in laughter at the foibles then surrounding Montreal's on-again, off-again, on-again hosting of the 2005 World Swimming Championships. "From support to the athletes and to coaches, I think many athletes from all over Canada will tell you the best place to be in Canada, to receive support, is Quebec." And he's right.

Dube was quick to point out this doesn't hold true for everybody, say Cindy Klassen and her crew based at the Oval at the University of Calgary, but cited Olympians diver Blythe Hartley of B.C. and cyclist Sara Hughes of Manitoba as examples. "I think we realize we have to do a lot to help the athletes and so some athletes are coming to Quebec to train, they receive the support and they are Quebec members now and they come from Alberta, Saskatchewan," and become part of "Team Quebec"? "Yes, because we offer something interesting — not in all sports — but in judo, short-track speed skating, cycling, and some winter sports. The mentality in Quebec has changed a lot," repeated Dube, this time focusing his attention on the entire elite sport delivery system.

"There is a kind of cooperation, we try to work together and we influence also the provincial government. The history in Quebec is that the people involved in sport were fighting, yes, and we have changed that mentality and we work together to influence the government. Sometimes we don't agree about all the subjects, but when we focus on certain key points we have the same speech to the provincial government — a united front — and that's a great success to influence the provincial government because you know the money is there, with the provincial budget and you know, many billions of dollars are involved. Instead of looking at the pie only in sports ... we have to look at the pie in all the provincial budget so we try to have some money in health, in education, money for physical activity and sport. We have had a lot of success, more money for coaches, more money for athletes, Quebec athletes, and not only for the excellent athlete but both the elite and the hopeful athletes. The provincial government supports the foundation in its raising money from the private sector and they do their part, a good partnership, and we have a track record, so they are one of our partners."

There are many others. In September of 2005, the Montreal Alouettes donated $75,000 to their bursary program in conjunction with the Foundation. The bursaries are awarded "to highlight excellence in sports and academics, for perseverance in education, and for leadership and participation in the community." Five players from McGill, Laval and Montreal were among the 21 initial recipients, McGill's Ben Walsh, an offensive lineman from Vancouver among them. "Our objectives are to consistently encourage these young athletes to follow their dreams and to stay in school," said team president Larry Smith. "We believe football is one of the best ways of teaching the discipline needed to get through school and we're proud to be able to contribute in any way we can."

One month later the Montreal Impact of the WSL followed suit and donated $25,000 a year for three years to aspiring and promising young soccer players, boys and girls; the first year's 16 recipients ranging in age from 13 to 17. "The Impact's mission has always been to develop soccer in Quebec, but also to give back to the community," said Impact President Joey Saputo at the time. "Today, we are taking concrete action. In doing so, we wish to thank our fans by also doing our part to contribute to the success of our province's young soccer players."

Said Impact Head Coach Nick De Santis, "As a professional soccer team, it's our duty to mentor and encourage promising young players. The pro soccer players of tomorrow are the young kids of today who are playing their favourite sport all over Quebec. We have to give them the resources so they can succeed. I congratulate all the recipients for their accomplishments." Notably, since its re-launch in 2002, with the participation of major partners such as the Quebec Government, Hydro-Quebec and Saputo, the Montreal Impact has become a non-profit organization. Profits are reinvested in the development of soccer in Quebec.

In May of 2006, paper products company Cascades Inc. showed it had seen the bright light, announcing a three-year investment of $225,000 in the Foundation's game plan, leading up to the Beijing Summer Olympic Games. In announcing the 2006 bursary recipients, "We are convinced that offering Cascades Bursaries to some of the most promising athletes who represent the next generation of athletic excellence in the province of Quebec can make the difference, since they are remitted at a crucial moment in an athlete's career," said Monsieur Alain Lemaire, Cascades president and CEO. "Last year, certain recipients surprised us in the most agreeable manner by participating in the Torino Olympic Games. Alexandre Bilodeau and Audrey Robichaud are now among the best in the world. Cascades wishes to provide these athletes with a chance to focus on their training and studies without having to worry about the financial aspects of their career."

Added Foundation president Claude Chagnon, "Last year's Cascades bursary recipients emerged on the international scene and performed well beyond our expectations. It confirms the importance and credibility of the Cascades bursary program intended for young, unknown, promising athletes."

And you don't have to be an Inc. or a non-profit society to contribute to the cause. Sports agent Bob Sauve pushes his NHL clientele to support an amateur athlete through the Foundation. Olympian weightlifter Maryse Turcotte, sponsored by former New York Ranger Sylvain Lefebvre, says, "Sylvain has made it possible for me to get an education while I train. His support has completely changed my life."

Back onto the university track, the Foundation is a beacon of light. Robert Dubeau: "It's a wonderful program led by people who know what they are doing. They've given out a lot of dollars, they've got a lot of Montreal businesses and philanthropists involved, they've got Quebec corporations involved. I've got a lot of time for Pierre Dube, he's done a wonderful job with that organization. McGill student-athletes have done very well in receiving funding from that organization over the years, especially in the category athletics and academics together and we've always had kids that have been successful at school, super bright athletes, we've had more than our share. Our office is very aggressive in making sure the kids know."

Katie Sheahan, Recreation and Athletics Director at Concordia: "It offers student-athletes an opportunity to also shine in different circles, to be part of a larger network, and I think it's an excellent program. Pierre is committed to building and strengthening the program, he's just a tower of passion and is looked up to because of the fact he is so dedicated and devoted. He came and spent an afternoon with me to make sure I fully understood all the possible resources that we could tap into. I think our school, not unlike others, had been hot and cold on how actively we had promoted those resources over time. To make sure as a new athletic director I was aware of all its assets and merits, Pierre made sure I understood the program and that helped me to motivate our coaches to motivate their young people to apply."

Are the athletes well aware of it? "This is going to sound like an old woman speaking but one of our most difficult challenges with student/athletes is like anything else, they get so many messages passed in front of them that I'm not sure that it is a message that will stand out, among all the others. We try to make sure the ones about financial resources stand out a lot, but sometimes people are intimidated by applying for things. Sometimes you have to almost sit down and be writing with them to help them take that responsible step of sending something in on their own. We have mixed emotions here about sending everything in for people, not because you don't want to advocate for somebody but because you also want to help somebody take responsibility and pride and interest in their own situation. A student might not even consider themselves worthy unless they got a prompt from a university coach. They think they don't have a chance — or you get the ones that think they are entitled to everything."

Dube carries on, recalling that when the Foundation originally came into being, Quebec institutions "were in the middle, I think," when it came to supporting athletic excellence, some in favour, some opposed. "You must understand that in Quebec, the Anglophone institutions, McGill, Concordia and Bishops were really involved in athletics and some of the francophone [universities] were not involved," citing the biggest, Universite de Montreal, as the worst offender. That has changed. "Universite de Montreal is really involved in athletics, Universite de Laval right now is kind of a model for success with the business community, and also Sherbrooke is really involved, in many other sports."

Dube was quick to give the credit to new blood in much older buildings, as usual, it's the individuals who make the difference, and as usual, one institution's success spurs others to improve their own performance. A new rector who believes in the power of sport here, a rivalry there, and things can heat up quickly. "The University of Montreal is the biggest university in Quebec so it must be a leader, but in the past it was a leader — but a negative leader. Now it's Laval. Because of Laval the University of Montreal was really influenced and I think the key thing for the rector of the University of Montreal was in 1999 when [Laval] won the Vanier Cup and was across the media all over Canada and were superstars in Quebec. The University of Laval Rouge et Or were all over the place in Quebec and it was free publicity and you know, the rector said wow, I want a football team."

With a neat turn of phrase in his second tongue, Dube describes this evolution in his province's universities toward the pursuit of sport excellence as a "first reflex, first, but now they work to improve their programs, their recruitment, their marketing and they will have success."

But Pierre, the nay-sayers who thundered against the evils of athletic scholarships for so long? Directing his remarks through Laval, Dube points out: "If you're looking for excellence it's not OK to look at the bottom because you must look for the top. Go to Quebec City right now and turn on the radio, they will have big announcements of football, volleyball, basketball tournaments," luring in fans. "It's not only football now, it's all the sports, oh yes, good publicity. Well, they lost the Nordiques so university sports are filling the [media] gap. They have junior hockey but university sports is important right now in Quebec City so for Laval it's a great tool of recruitment, not only in athletics but publicity all across the country."

And Dube has zip, zero, nada fears that a Basket-weaving Major will ever appear in the Laval calendar. "There is a tradition of excellence in academics, they have a real good academic program to support the academics of athletes so they have a great graduation rate. And they know, the people involved, that if they want to have an excellence program, they have to have excellence also in academics because the administrators know exactly what would happen if they did not," which brings up the subject of academic abuses that long have and continue to taint the American system.

"In U.S. universities, how many programs do they have, 100,000? It's really hard to control that. In Canada, how many universities do we have? Fifty. It's really easy to control."

More pointedly, Dube's take on sports scholarships is reflective of what dozens of similar-minded administrators believe to be true. "I think it's a good thing, but the rules must be really strict, controls must be in place, but I am in favour because if we want to achieve excellence we must have the tools to do that: we must have good programs with good athletes," underlining his comments by noting if we continue to lose 2,500 athletes to American universities every year we won't have programs of excellence, simple as that.

Reflecting on the distance between Canadian universities and the national sport delivery system, Dube shakes his head. "It is shortsighted because I think the role of the university is to be involved in excellence in everything."

Dube proudly brings up the fact that Quebec topped the Canada Games medal podium for the first time in 18 years in 2003. "I think it is the result of what we did for young athletes in the past five or six years. When we see what's going on in Sherbrooke, in Montreal, from the government," it all adds up, if you start from the ground up and if you have excellence as the bull's eye in the middle of the target. The provincial education curriculum is adding an extra hour of physical education in primary schools, "In some places they will have two hours, in some places they will have three hours a week. It's not great but it's a start. But with the Quebec in Shape program they have another three hours a week plus the phys-ed hours."

Further up the ladder are a burgeoning number of high school sports academies. "If you look in diving, in figure skating, the success we have with the young people now is all the result of these schools," citing two Canadian figure skating champions, Joannie Rochette and Cynthia Phaneuf, as the primest of examples.

Add on the Quebec Provincial High-Performance Center, the Canadian Sport Centre Montreal, pick a sport, any sport. "It's a beginning, it's a change, another way to develop talent, so it's really popular in Quebec." Elitism or favouritism are not dirty words here. "I think in Quebec, the sports community, I think the sports community and the Quebec government have made a commitment to develop excellence and I'm sure you will see the results. If you look in some sports, we have 50 or 60 per cent of the national team, or the junior national team, in many sports, and that's a result of all the things we did in the past."

What is a problem in Quebec is the CEGEP years in the post-secondary process, which in essence requires two years of collegiate education prior to entering university. Dube notes Quebec is "the only place in the world" with such a system in place, and referring now to hockey states, "I can tell you that if we didn't have the CEGEP system in Quebec, with the philosophy we have right now in Quebec we would have a great university league with excellence development. With the CEGEP they enter the university at 20 years old and it's too late.

"The best ice hockey player is gone at 20 years old, they are professional, they are in the American league, the NHL, the EHL, the prospects are not there, the players are gone! But, I'm sure that the NHL would be really interested to draft 18 years old players and let them play and graduate at 21 years old. It would be less expensive. And if you are an 18-year-old player and you play against some players that are 20, 21, 22, it's really intensive and I'm sure that it [NHL] would be interested. As they are at university in the U.S., but that's an education system problem.

"Right now we have only three university teams, McGill, Concordia and Three Rivers," who are losing players to the semi-pro Ligue Nord-Americaine de Hockey. It's "a big show because they have some fights, it's like wrestling, but they attract many people and they pay their players and many university players who are playing in Three Rivers, Concordia or McGill drop [university hockey] to play for the [LNAH] team. They continue to go to university but they play and receive $300 to play one game."

So, let's get this straight: These players drop university hockey to play semi-pro hockey and drop their gloves to pay their way through university. "Yeah, they receive over $20,000 a season. And I can tell you that probably, this is a prediction, Three Rivers will quit their hockey program because they lost their best player the last three or four years, for money. In hockey, it's an education system problem so I think the future of Quebec university hockey isn't strong, no, not at all."

We rejoice until the cows come home from Victoria to St. John's at our Olympic, World and World Junior championships. We could care less about university hockey. But picture this: If it were developmental, a la the NCAA, and each organization were to hold simultaneous "Frozen Fours" to determine national champions, a subsequent match-up between our best and America's best would be nothing short of electrifying. But that's evolutionary in scope and unlikely to excite the deep-thinkers atop a certain food chain.

Dube is a builder of Quebec's fresh approach, and its Darwinian achievements. "In Quebec there's a big change in the last five years — the University of Laval, the University of Sherbrooke, and the University of Montreal. There is a kind of change of mentality. I think the sports community has done good lobbying, and we tried to work in partnership. I think there is an evolution."

Merci beaucoup to you personally, monsieur; vive le Quebec sports libre.

# Intermezzo
## Don't Just Take My Word For It

❝Sport is a way we should view society."
—Rick Hansen, 2004 B.C. Winter Games Opening
Ceremonies, Port Alberni
*

"No one says it's only a game when they're winning."
—George Carlin
*

"You are not even on the radar screen."
—Queen's University President Bill Leggatt, on the attention
Canadian university presidents pay to the concerns and issues of the
CIAU, as he addressed the body's 1988 AGM
*

"If athletes are prepared to commit the time and energy that is
necessary to compete at the international level, my guess would be that
in most cases they are not going to be able to satisfy academic
requirements and be full-time students at the same time."
—Dr. George Connell, University of Toronto, 1986
*

"How dumb is that?" Nancy Greene, to OUA concerns that if
the CIS offered scholarships some students might choose one
university over another due to their athletic interests. "I mean it really
is a form of snobbery to say we won't give athletic scholarships. I
think there's a huge case for athletic scholarships. We know we need
this, all the governments, from Iona Campagnolo, and the [1969] Task
Force, everybody says this, and if there is something called C I S that
is controlled by the presidents of universities and they are blocking
this thing, then we better hold their feet to the fire."
—Nancy Greene-Raine, 2005
*

"Exercise is man's best medicine."

—Hippocrate
*

"Any healthy sport has power to fulfill our desire to belong, at
the same time as building healthy minds and bodies. Sport instils into
those who take part, respect for authority, the spirit of fair play,
honesty, sacrifice, determination, patience, self-control and many other

values necessary for the development of good citizenship amongst free people. If we think of the great sacrifices others have undergone in order to make us better boys and girls, we ought to conclude that we should not so often ask, 'What can I get out of sport?' Rather our constant question should be, 'What can I return to sport that will help others enjoy a happier, healthier and richer life?'"

—Father David Bauer, in a speech "The Educational Value of Athletics", delivered to the Nelson Minor Hockey Association's year-end banquet, April 6, 1963

\*

"I have always believed that exercise is the key not only to physical health but to peace of mind. Many times in the old days I unleashed my anger and frustration on a punching bag rather than taking it out on a comrade or even a policeman. Exercise dissipates tension, and tension is the enemy of serenity. I found that I worked better and thought more clearly when I was in good physical condition, and so training became one of the inflexible disciplines of my life. In prison, having an outlet for my frustration was absolutely essential."

—Nelson Mandela, former freedom fighter and President of South Africa, in his autobiography *Long Walk to Freedom*

\*

"In fact, the existence of Olympic sports programs at the college level is what separates the U.S. Olympic Team from every other Olympic team in the world. The opportunity to participate in college athletics is a real motivating force for many high school athletes. Keeping talented athletes involved between the ages of 18-22 is critically important because so many athletes are maturing both physically and mentally during this period of their lives. It is especially noteworthy that colleges and universities employ many of our finest coaches, and this benefits the development of our Olympic sports in unquestionable ways. The simple fact is that those schools that employ professional coaches and offer varsity competition for Olympic sports are playing a vital role in the development of Olympians."

—Chuck Wielgus, Executive Director, USA Swimming, 2003

\*

"It's impossible to dig a field with a spoon."

—VANOC CEO John Furlong

\*

"On that last point, the universities must end their rather Victorian objection to athletic scholarships which have been the basis

of so much American athletic success. The system may be abused in some places in the U.S. but by and large it has given students who might otherwise miss out at least a chance for further education."
—Vancouver Province editorial, in response to Iona Campagnolo's 1977 Green Paper

\*

"Blessed is the man who by strength of hand and swiftness of foot, takes by skill and daring the highest of prizes."
—from Olympian ode, Pindar, 4th century, B.C.

\*

"Even as late as 1957, MP Doug Fisher commented in the House on "the very touchy field of sport and international sport", adding that many people saw this as being "a very frivolous thing on which to spend money."
—*Sport in Canadian Society*, Ann Hall, Trevor Slack, Garry Smith, David Whitson

\*

"A sound mind in a sound body is a short but full description of a happy state in this world."
—Philosopher John Locke

\*

"I'm amazed at how many people running our universities believe that academics and athletes are mutually exclusive. It's a shame so many of our young men and women have to head south to universities in order to pursue excellence in both academics and athletics. And I'm not talking about the sports factories. I'm speaking of outstanding institutions such as Yale, Notre Dame, Brown and Michigan, just to name a few. Why can't we keep our standouts in Canada? Remember, sports, like theatre and music, are part of a well-rounded education. In our country, we are still desperate for leaders in government, business and education."
—Brian Williams, CBC

\*

"If we can get enough schools together, I'd love to have a Canadian division in the NAIA, competing against schools like Alberta, Calgary and UBC. I don't like the CIS approach. My concern is that our students are being held back by the attitudes of the Ontario university administration and their athletic directors. We're over-legislated and rule-bound. I can live with the NAIA approach: give athletes the cost of going to university."

\*

"I think [scholarships are] a recognition that athletics is important to a university. To me, it's a debate that's not worth discussing anymore. It's just a waste of time arguing about it. We need to look for a solution."

—UBC AD Bob Philip

\*

"I was interested in playing the highest calibre of soccer I could find. The attitude here is totally different than in Canada. It's just so intense. People are more competitive and they make a bigger deal of their sports down here. They make more demands on their athletes. It was the best place for me to play against the best competition. Still, you can't escape the academics at Notre Dame. It's got to be your focus, too, or you're in real trouble."

—Katie Thorlakson, Canadian National Women's Soccer Team, Fighting Irish graduate and Sports Illustrated's 2004 player of the year for NCAA Division I women's soccer.

\*

"If you're ranked highly, people are going to want to come and watch you. We compete in front of 2,000-3,000 people for a gymnastics meet. At home, we competed in front of our parents. I'd heard of the intensity of U.S. college sports; if I'd stayed in Canada, I would never have experienced it, and [would have] sacrificed my athletic ability."

—Carly Dockendorf, Port Moody, B.C, two-sport star at the University of Washington

\*

"Would you cultivate your pupil's intelligence, cultivate the strength it is meant to control. Give his body constant exercise, make it strong and healthy, in order to make him good and wise."

—French philosopher Jean Jacques Rousseau, in *Emile*

\*

"Sport is an order of chivalry, a code of ethics and aesthetics, recruiting its members from all classes and all peoples. Sport is a truce: in an era of antagonisms and conflicts, it is the respite of the gods in which fair competition ends in respect and friendship. Sport is education, the truest kind of education — that of character. Sport is culture because it creates beauty, and, above all, for those who usually have the least opportunity to feast upon it."

—Rene Maheu, director general of UNESCO

*

"I will probably be even more busy than before, I find the lack of resources in health, youth and sports is inconceivable."
—Team Canada's Nancy Drolet on announcing her retirement, 2004

*

"An A-1 intelligence cannot function adequately in a C3 physique."
—Former UBC professor George Weir, in support of recommendations for a comprehensive program of physical education in a commissioned report on B.C. schools he had written in 1925

*

"They make me so aware of the impact I have on people, it scares me."
—Nancy Greene, on the throng at the Nancy Greene Day Parade in Vancouver on March 8, 1968

*

"It used to be that a skier could be a talented pair of feet and no brains. We want to turn them out with the talented pair of feet and the brains to go with them."
—Dave Jacobs, Canada's first national ski team head coach

*

"The scholarship athletes are good students. I find that the ones who work hardest at their sport also work hardest at their studies. I like conversing with these people. They have been around a lot more than the average student. They are more interested as a rule. And they have more an idea about what's going on."
—NDU history professor Walter Froese, 1966

*

"No one seems to have discovered a better way for producing fine adults than by making young men learn how to make creative use of rules which demand self-discipline, thoughtfulness and cooperation. Such rules govern athletic events. There may be better agencies for helping young men to mature, but no one seems to know what they are."
— *Sport: A Philosophic Inquiry*, Paul Weiss

*

"Canadians can be proud of their Olympians, even if they have little right to claim some of the credit for their achievements. A lot of them have had to [go] abroad to get the training and support they needed to make them world-class athletes – taking U.S. university scholarships, going abroad for coaches or training in other countries, like Australia where high performance is the focus. Every time we get close to an Olympic year we hear talk about doing better next time. We hear our political leaders – as Owen was doing this week [in his comments to not get "fixated" over the medal count] downplaying the importance of winning medals and stressing the need to increasing the overall health and fitness of Canadians, especially our young. Typically, we are unable to choose between producing world-class athletes or making universal fitness our priority, and we end up doing neither. We should let our Olympians show us the way. Even if their accomplishments are modest compared to those from other countries, we should build on them and nourish our elite athletes. For the higher, the faster and farther they go, they are sure to give other young athletes the inspiration they need to compete. Just talking about doing better next time just won't do anymore."

—Vancouver Sun editorial, during 2004 Athens Summer Games

\*

"She believed in the old-time way. Said it was a sin to play baseball for money, never did see me play."

—Satchel Paige, as quoted in *Invisible Men, Life in Baseball's Negro Leagues*, Donn Rogisin

\*

"I am struck by the enormous unifying power of sport. It is unquestionable. Here it is visible. Too often we lose the real strength of sport as a teacher. There are lessons of commitment and the power of focus, of fair play and of tolerance. And, most importantly, there is a willingness to recognize excellence in others."

—B.C. Premier Gordon Campbell in his last "Athens Olympic Diary" entry, Vancouver Sun

\*

"The whole idea of being on the national ski team came out of that era and is really, in many senses, the genesis of what the concept of what a national team is today. I'm not talking about just a ski team. I'm talking about the concept of a national team in any content. The national team back in the Sixties and the whole concept ... was pretty powerful. To me it was enormous.

"Those guys were heroes to me. Rod Hebron, Keith Shepherd, Gerry Rinaldi, Peter Duncan, Dave Irwin, Larry Nelles ... all those guys had enormous impact on young guys like me who were trying to figure out how to make it. Those guys were much bigger people and much bigger heroes than any have become since. Yes, the Crazy Canucks era is one that everybody points to and goes, 'Wow, what an incredible group of guys.' But that came from the concept of the national team ... from the fact Ken Read and I spent a lot of our time up on the glacier at Nelson with no distractions, with great coaching, and all you had to work on was the art of the arc turns."

—"Jungle" Jim Hunter

\*

"Yet of all the barbs directed against Greek athletics, the most common had to do with the glorification of physical strength to the detriment of mental and spiritual values. To the philosopher and satirist Xenophanes, it was "not right to honour strength above excellent wisdom." Ridicule was a favourite weapon of the critics. "You simpleton," exclaimed Aesop to a wrestler who boasted that he had beaten his opponent because he was the stronger of the two, "what honour have you earned if, being the stronger, you prevailed over a weaker man? You might be tolerated if you were telling us that by skill you overcame a man who was superior to you in physical strength." Milo of Croon was the butt of numerous jokes and slurs on the mindlessness of the muscle-bound athlete. "What surpassing witlessness," declared a moralist when he heard that Milo carried the entire carcass of a bull around the stadium at Olympia before [cooking] it up and devouring it. Before it was slaughtered, the bull carried its own body with much less exertion than did Milo. "Yet the bull's mind was not worth anything — just about like Milo's." The image of the dumb jock is as old as athletics."

"Whatever their religious beliefs, athletes compete to win, to prove their superiority over others, and thus to lay claim to a kind of primitive immortality. While the soul of Patroclus fought its own battles on the banks of the River Styx, his surviving comrades participated in a timeless athletic drama wherein patrons, spectators and athletes each played a part."

—*Sports in the Western World*, William J. Baker

\*

"France has first-rate coaching and excellent facilities, but the lack of a strongly supportive school physical-education feeder system has left them with few top-notch athletes. Britain, still bound to the nineteenth-century thought of sport as a noble hobby, leads the world in moralizing over the role of sport in society, while its athletes sink deeper and deeper in the world-class rankings. Australia and New Zealand, with the exception of Herculean individual efforts, have been following Britain's path. The United States has both the world's most extensive school sports system and, its first cousin complementing that, a professional-commercial sports system thanks to free enterprise.

"Canada, with a population of twenty-two million (comparable to the GDR's 16.8 million), has a life-style parallel to the United States in most everything except university sports. Canadian institutions of higher learning have steadfastly refused to follow the U.S. example of college sports scholarships, a course of action they readily defend by citing everything detrimental about commercial college sport and overlooking everything beneficial. They decry the fact that coaches wind up with reputations greater than professors, and cite the evils of high-pressured recruiting aimed at building winning teams, and the compromise of educational standards to help a star athlete stay eligible. They overlook the numbers of kids who otherwise could not receive an education at a good school, the alumni interest in sports and subsequent funding support, and the income from ticket sales that can be directed toward better programs. The also overlook the role of the universities in the national elite sports feeder system: the universities have not only the lion's share of the physical sports facilities, but also are the center for advanced research projects. All three levels of the Canadian government – federal, provincial, and municipal, do their well-meaning best. But the federal government, though now charged with developing a national plan for sport, has no control over schools and school policy. Education is a provincial responsibility. And the provinces have no direct control over the municipalities, which in turn are burdened with an ice hockey program, which has brought artificial ice surfaces to every town in the country, but which costs more than one billion dollars a year."

—*The Miracle Machine*, Doug Gilbert

*

"Canadians are hypocrites. We take such great pride in our world-class athletes, but only after they've climbed the mountain. Athletes from this country don't win because they are Canadian. They win despite the fact they are Canadian … What's lacking here is political will. But it's not lacking everywhere. Politicians in this country learned a long time ago that international sports, especially the Olympics, are their most valuable currency. It's why in the last 30 years this country bid on five separate Olympics. There are just 1,710 days to go until the 2010 Winter Olympics in Vancouver, and your federal government plans to spend $1.3 billion of your dollars to make you feel good about Canada. Add to that figure, $140 million a year for the next five years to support athletes and coaches through a program called "Own the Podium ... Where has the federal government been hiding this money all these years? Why in the past were our athletes denied all this support? Why is there no money promised beyond 2010? Canadians have allowed our sports heritage to be hijacked."

—David Pratt, The Province, 2005

*

"When I made up my mind to do that, I felt that we were really taking a bold step forward as a national team. This was a very unique program, one that really developed good athletes. I feel it was a large part of the reason for the success of Nancy Greene ... Nobody believed at that time that we could combine athletics with academics. [Today] I don't feel you can become a high-level athlete without an education. Sport has changed so much and athletes have to have every edge possible to succeed."

—Gerry Rinaldi on joining the National Ski Team at NDU, Nelson Daily News, 2004

*

"Perhaps this program will set a new trend in the field of Canadian amateur athletics and give new incentive to Canada's athletes, who should be second to none if given the proper chance to compete."

—Dave Jacobs, Nelson Daily News, November 10, 1965

*

"Most Canadians are still afraid of sport, regarding it as unpleasant medicine good for losing weight, disciplining children and rehabilitating cardiac patients. They agree with A. J. Liebling that *mens sana in corpore sano* is a contradiction in terms."

—*The Death of Hockey*, Kidd and MacFarlane

*

"In Europe they have the club system that's really strong, in the US they have a university system that for those sports is very strong. In Canada, we have taken a hybrid — kind of the worst of both and put them together."

"Our athletes likely over-perform, based on the support that we provide versus other countries."

—Dale Henwood, President/CEO of Canadian Sport Centre Calgary

\*

"I don't think we have valued or embraced what student-athletes represent. I think a lot of employers out there would tell you otherwise, that we want somebody who has come from a team into our team environment. We want somebody who's lived on the edge, we want someone who's been challenged, physically, mentally, emotionally, that has been there, who has lost and come back, these kinds of things, we don't want someone, you know, who's just been a bookworm for four years and then come out [into the workforce]. They understand there's a coach and there's a director and these kinds of things and there's a lot of people out there in the business world that say that's our ideal recruit for their employment situation. Heh, the value of athletics is immense.

"I think a lot of people that don't value athletics have no idea what athletics is all about. They have no sense of the character-building, they have no sense of the development, of commitment, work ethic, and these values and principles that we would espouse as being key in any venture."

—Mike Renney, 2004 Olympics softball coach

\*

"The idea of many universities, particularly in Ontario, is they think an elite program at their university is who are the best players at their university at the time they pick their team."

—Former UBC AD Bob Hindmarch

\*

"The CIS and scholarships? To those guys, it's anything but the S word."

—Wayne Kennedy, SIRC Sport Research, 2005

\*

"Every other kid on the university campus in Canada today has a part-time job. A student-athlete can't have a part-time job because physically they are not able to. What are we supposed to do? So, we create a situation where if there isn't that support from the university in the form of a sports scholarship, it turns into only the rich can play. If your Mom and Dad are real well-heeled and you can stay at home, no problem, you can play. But if you are a kid from inner city

Winnipeg and you're on your own, forget it. That is what is being forced upon us by the Ontario schools in my opinion."

—University of Winnipeg AD Bill Wedlake

# Chapter Six
## Timeline

With apologies to Dr. Stephen Hawking, a brief history of time is all about sport.

Spend but a few moments teaching children to know that play, and thus inherently competition, is one of our natural states. That little girl and boy inside all of us is only but a field, manicured or not, away. Still, almost all the power-mongers and social engineers among us have seldom given sport its due. There were always more important "achievements" to attend to, like rape and pillage, economic and political warfare, the fomenting of religious intolerance and infighting, virtually always for personal gain and dominance over others, although as today's catchphrase goes there is no I in team.

Sport pre-dates civilization as we know it and it isn't as if it was an invention. Pre-historic cave art on at least three continents contain the very basics of running/swimming and javelin/archery, no need to be an anthropologist to understand the why's and wherefore's of that. And you don't need to have ever actually witnessed two of man's best friends fighting over a bone to know their masters have themselves been wrestling since forever. But if you insist on an expert's opinion, American PhD David Sansone, in his book *Greek Athletics and the Genesis of Sport*, offers up this pause for thought: "Sport is the ritual sacrifice of physical energy."

Recoveries from China 6,000 years ago indicate a culture that includes sport, primarily gymnastics. From our discoveries of the lives of the Pharaohs of ancient Egypt, we first see fishing as a leisure activity as well as more recognizable sporting activities such as the high jump. As the ancient Greeks come into vogue, Socrates, Plato and Aristotle gave us the foundation of Western philosophy. They also were big boosters of the Olympics, and it was Aristotle who gave us the eternal if not always undertaken words of wisdom about a healthy body, healthy mind. The Games were named after Mount Olympus, which in Greek mythology was believed to be home to the "Twelve Olympians," their principal gods, and were held at Olympia in their honour. Generally believed to have first been held in the 9th Century, B.C., the first recorded Games date to 776 B.C. and bring to our competitive lexicon running, boxing, discus throwing and chariot racing (the marathon only became an event at the first of the modern Olympiads).

While the world's foremost acknowledged philosophers were no fans of professionalism in sport, they and their countrymen were simply put, sports fans. The Iliad details sporting competitions — Achilles held games during the funeral services for Patroclus during the Trojan War — and as they say, to the Olympic victor came the spoils, but only once they returned home, which more than made up for the simple olive-leave wreath they had placed on their heads in Olympia.

The 17th Century Briton Benjamin Farrington wrote: "Aristotle continually grows in stature in the sense that it is hard to find in any place or time a man who has succeeded in effecting a greater change in human thought." As for the man himself, he believed "what is true of the art of physical training is obviously no less true of medicine, or of shipbuilding, tailoring and all the other arts," recommended that physical education should last for a longer period than the instruction of all other subjects, and promoted physical exercise because "a beautiful, strong and healthy body is conducive to a sound mind." The bottom line? The intellectual abilities, Aristotle believed, are always influenced by the state of the body, a truism which shall prove of no small importance further on down this road.

Under the Romans, any high-brow notions of sport were discarded and the many Coliseums in their empire were but home to shamelessly bloody death spectacles. Sport had truly descended. Finally, upon Rome formally adopting Christianity, it first frowned upon and then banned "pagan" religious practices, such as the Olympic Games, which were abolished by Emperor Theodosius I near the end of the 4th Century AD.

As we traverse the trail of Red Letter Dates, they weren't named the Dark Ages for nothing. In the West, undeniably the home of sport as we know it today, sport then followed all else into the tunnel of malaise. As we come to the Medieval period games began to re-emerge, usually in conjunction with feast days — the original tailgate parties — and jousting meant more than acquiring elbow room at the local sports bar.

"The Renaissance (c1400-1600) began in Italy where city states bustled with trade and a money economy. Italian scholars and artists rejected the theological and ascetic pre-occupations of the late-medieval Church in favour of more humanistic concerns. As they looked to ancient Greece and Rome for a rebirth of European culture, there were especially attracted to the Greek ideal of the harmonious unit of body and mind. They extolled versatility. The ideal "Renaissance man" was socially adept, sensitive to aesthetic values, skilled in weaponry, strong of body, and learned in letters. No single virtuoso achieved the ideal of course, but many individuals excelled in sports as well as the arts. It was the day of the scholar athlete." — *Sports in the Western World*, William J. Baker

For those privileged few, humanists provided aristocratic sports with a philosophical basis, a rationale firmly planted in the soil of Renaissance thought. In the education of *L'uomo universale*, or whole man, physical as well as mental development was important.

"Games and exercises which develop the muscular activities and the general carriage of the person should be encouraged by every teacher," insisted one scribe in step with his times. "Serving as tutors in the courts of rich Italian nobles, fifteenth-century humanists … not only pored over classical manuscripts but also extolled swimming, running, horseback riding, acrobatics, archery, swordplay, and wrestling. They also wrote elaborate treatises declaring the complementary relation of sound minds and strong, healthy bodies." — Baker

One need only compete in sport once to know it's oftentimes the original stomping ground for one step forward, two steps back. The Reformation not only splintered the Christian church but dealt sport near-fatal death blows. As Protestantism gained strength across Europe, the enlightened humanism of Renaissance thought was eclipsed by religious zeal. If Calvin was dour, his biggest fans, the English Puritans, would have put a grin on his face with their outlandishness. During the late 16th and early 17th centuries, they thundered from their pulpits against "devilish pastimes," which were pretty much anything that turned the corners of one's mouth upwards.

To the Dutch scholar Erasmus (1466-1536), "We are not concerned with developing athletes, but scholars and men competent to affairs, for whom we desire adequate constitution indeed, but not the physique of a Milo." Healthy body, healthy mind be damned and yet the wicked sin of idleness was also a sure ticket to the fires of hell. A certain English Puritan, one William Perkins (1560-1602), expressed their fear of sport when he castigated the less-disciplined in life who "spend their time in eating, drinking, sleeping and sporting." As they say, God forbid, and of course his self-appointed minions did, even going so far as banning recreational and sporting activities on Sundays, which were, for the great majority who toiled in peasanthood six days a week for their daily bread, the only opportunity they had to partake in such activities.

But as physics teaches us, for every action there's a reaction and thus there's no small touch of irony to the fact the backlash to the English Puritans', well, Puritanical approach, was to result in the blossoming of sport pretty much as we've come to know it, from those very shores. Riding to the rescue was good King James, who in 1613 ordered his people be allowed to play. But so stiff was the Puritans' opposition to such heresy that 15 years later King Charles felt compelled to issue a re-declaration of his predecessor's edict.

In part, his "The King's Majesty's Declaration to His Subjects Concerning Lawful Sports to Be Used" read:

"Our pleasure likewise is, that the bishop of that diocese take the like strait order with all the Puritans and Precisians within the same, either constraining them to conform themselves or to leave the county, according to the laws of our kingdom and canons of our Church, and so to strike equally on both hands against the contemners of our authority and adversaries of our Church: and as for our good people's lawful recreation, our pleasure likewise is, that after the end of divine service our good people be not disturbed, letted or discouraged from any lawful recreation, such as dancing, either men or women; archery for men, leaping, vaulting, or any other such harmless recreation, nor from having of May-games, Whitsun-ales, and Morris-dances; and the setting up of May-poles and other sports therewith used: so as the same be had in due and convenient time, without impediment or neglect of divine service: and that women shall have leave to carry rushes to the church for the decorating of it, according to their old custom; but withal we do here account still as prohibited all unlawful games to be used upon Sundays only, as bear and bull-baitings, interludes, and at all times in the meaner sort of people by law prohibited, bowling." — Gee, Henry, and William John Hardy, ed., Documents Illustrative of English Church History (New York: Macmillan, 1896)

By the 1640s, the fight was on — literally — and King Charles was executed after losing a civil war to the Oliver Cromwell-lead Puritans, who then made fun-seeking criminal. They were in opposition to "horse racing, cockfighting, bearbaiting, dancing, the stage, gambling, and desecration of the Sabbath. They banned maypoles, abolished Dover's Cotswold Games, and declared null and void the Declaration on Lawful Sports. In three successive Parliaments, they prohibited Sunday amusements." — Baker

The theologians' attempts to eradicate those dastardly, forbidden fruits were not altogether successful. Maypoles appeared periodically as acts of defiance against Puritan rule. In 1656 some citizens of Maidstone reported boys and men playing football in the main street "to the disquiet and disturbance of the good people of this Commonwealth." Two years later, an official at Westminster School complained that studies were languishing because schoolboys were playing too much at games. Rigid prohibitions apparently provoked outright insubordination. According to one contemporary, in a village in Essex "where the Book of Common Prayer was read the people did usually go out of church to play football, and to the alehouse and there continued till they were drunk, and it was no matter if they were hanged." — Baker.

Tip one to sport's martyrs.

Germaine to all this was that it was Puritans who filled the Mayflower and brought with them their other-worldly mentalities on using our muscles for reasons other than propping up their self-designed image of a creator. In America's first settlements in New England, idleness was as wicked as ever in the eyes of Church officials, whose grip on public life was stronger than in England. Idleness was in fact unlawful, which taken to the extreme meant the act of falling asleep could land one in the same hot water that bouncing a ball could, the penalty at the time for that crime against heaven (or more precisely the minds of its guardians) included being flogged, locked up in the stocks or, if one were lucky, rich or connected enough, just paying a fine.

The path of an extremist of any stripe leads only to one climax, a raised middle finger back. The British flicked enough of them at their Puritanical rulers and under the Stuart Restoration returned with joy to sport, but not only those of their past. As English rulers eventually swam with the tide and in fact became patrons of sport, often with an eye to gambling, sport was off to the races. In Victorian England, and in lockstep with a growing, prosperous middle class demanding more rights, the granting of Saturday afternoons off work lifted the final nail from the coffin in which the Puritans had hoped to bury sport. Not only was there now more time to play, there were also vast numbers free to watch, which was of course the first step to, uh-oh, professionalism, and soon to assume the role of bogeyman the entirety of sport had held for the Puritans.

"Although games and, thus, embryonic sports, have existed since primitive times throughout the world, there is no denying the pivotal role played by Britain, and more specifically England, in laying the foundations during the eighteenth and nineteenth centuries of the modern sports culture. Above all, it was in the English public schools that many games were first regulated. It was also in England that the notion of national sporting administrative bodies first emerged. In no way, however, can this be said to have remained a parochial matter. The British approach to playing and organizing sport was rapidly exported to the various parts of the expanding British Empire, along with Christianity and the English language. Of these it can be argued that the role of sport was of equal worth and some might feel that in the long term, the sporting legacy was to prove even more durable than those other "gifts" of imperialism." — *Sport, Nationalism and Globalization*, Alan Bairner

Given England's pioneering role in this area, it is scarcely surprising that sport came to assume a high profile throughout the global British Empire.

"The formation of character was the essential purpose of Victorian elitist education — at home and overseas," and for the export of character, it was necessary to have "trainers of character, mostly from public school and ancient university who used the games field as the medium of moral indoctrination." — Bairner

One of the first definitions of an amateur ever published by an athletic organization included the mechanics clause. According to the definition issued by the Amateur Athletic Club of England in 1866, an amateur was "any gentleman who has never competed in an open competition, or for any public money, or for admission money, or with professionals for a prize, public money or admission money and has never in a period of his life taught or assisted in the pursuit of athletic exercises as a means of livelihood; not as a mechanic, artisan, or labourer." Reads like justification for an unfair advantage for those who played at life instead of working at it.

Soon a new term appears. "Muscular Christians" held that sport builds character, which is true, but professionalism soon became a devil incarnate. The young colony of Canada's first sports organization was the Montreal Curling Club, born in Gillies Tavern in Montreal on January 22, 1807. It was no exception to the "professionals be damned" rule, and from that point on play for fun, not for pay, ruled the day.

"The predominantly Protestant middle class that controlled sport rejected the ideology of professional sport because it was seen to debase play, to emphasize ends rather than means, to involve passion rather than restraint, and to encourage gambling, drinking, and frivolity. Those who controlled amateur sport maintained a strong ideological belief in the amateur ethos, which meant competing for the love of sport rather than for material gain.

"While Canadians of every region and background engaged in these practices, it was a very narrow group — urban, middle-class males of British background — that succeeded in controlling the emergence of what became Canadian sports, steering adaptation of British sports to Canada and turning their favourite games into the sports everyone played. If Canadian sports were segregated by gender, they were also divided by ideology and organization. The men who created and promoted the new sports initially clothed them in the aristocratic mantle of British amateurism. The earlier 'amateur codes' restricted participation on the basis of class and race, reflecting the upper classes' desire to reproduce the social hierarchies of Victorian England and the British Empire and to maintain the primacy of sports as an expression of manly honour and elegant display.

"For the strict amateur, the idea of hiring an athlete to represent one's club was as repugnant as the idea of taking performance-enhancing drugs has been among the Olympic circles in our own time; it undermined the sacred tenet of 'fair play' and distorted the identifications between athletes and their followers. Many denounced 'pay for play' as a form of prostitution. For them, it debased sports and the character formation it make possible." — *Sport in Canadian Society*, Ann Hall, Trevor Slack, Garry Smith, David Whitson

No less an expert than historian Bruce Kidd, with an eye to the forming of the CAUU in 1910, wrote:

"The outpouring of Canadianism during the trials of the CAUU fired the nation-building imagination of both leaders and members alike. In 1910, Norton Crow held discussions about the possibility of a pan-Canadian sports festival along the lines of today's Canada Games. Others dreamed about sports-focused physical education in the schools. Henceforth, the aspirations of Canadian amateurism and English-Canadian nationalism would ever be intertwined." — *The Struggle for Canadian Sport*, Bruce Kidd

---

Be that as it may, we must now take a slight step back in time because as the end of the British Empire politically began to dawn the rise of the American sports powerhouse began. Most pertinent is that it began in America's bastions of higher learning. In the middle of the 19th Century, student numbers fell amid a generally-held belief American universities were catering to the privileged few. To combat this, "charity funds" came into existence to assist the poor and those funds soon became known as scholarships.

"Wealthy industrialists tended to support a practical curriculum, one that prepared students for careers in commerce or industry. Many were not entirely convinced that college was even necessary. For such men, the highly skilled athlete testing his courage, endurance, and native intelligence on a playing field was learning more about life than the poet and the scholar." — *College Athletes for Hire*, Allen L. Sack, Ellen J. Stuarowsky

And, even though it wasn't the first college sport in the U.S., it soon became all about football.

"According to Gorn and Goldstein (1993), College football, as a consuming phenomenon in institutions of higher learning, stood at the center of the cultural transformations of the late nineteenth and early twentieth centuries." — Bairner

That transformation has been defined by many as the professionalization of university sport. As American universities tied more of their prestige and thus recruiting power to their football programs, no one was fooled into thinking the viewing public would pay to watch amateur sport, where theoretically at least, according to its proponents, winning and losing was irrelevant. In that there was and still is no doubt. We ourselves recreate, we don't pay to watch others do so.

"The social climate of the late nineteenth century was hostile toward the amateur spirit. And that hostility was as much anti-intellectual and anti-female as it was anti-elitist. The University of Chicago provides a clear illustration of how far college sport had drifted since Yale's first rowing meet with Harvard in 1852. William Rainey Harper, Chicago's newly elected president in 1892, was no anti-intellectual, but his philosophy of higher education had a decidedly utilitarian cast. As the first president of this newly founded institution, Harper consciously integrated sport into the university's marketing plan. One of his faculty appointments was Amos Alonzo Stagg, a former football star at Yale. Harper's instructions to his new coach were to "develop teams which we can send around the country and knock out all the colleges. We will give them a palace car and a vacation too."

Commenting on Harper's sometimes unorthodox methods for promoting the university, one of its professors quipped that Harper was the "the P.T. Barnum of Higher Education." This marketing strategy appears to have worked. Between 1986 and 1909, the university's enrolment increased from 1,815 to 5,500 students. Harper's university had risen to considerable prominence in a fairly short period of time, and winning football teams, in addition to generous support from John D. Rockefeller, had contributed to that rise.

"Given football's strategic importance, it had to be brought under a university's control, and highly talented athletes had to be recruited and subsidized in a fairly systematic fashion. Alumni played a vital role in athletic subsidization and recruitment, but universities themselves were finding innovating ways to fuse financial aid funds to procure athletes. Although both Harper and Stagg swore allegiance to the time-honoured amateur ideal, the demands of the university as they saw them required high-performance spectator sport. Hypocrisy became rampant."

"College alumni were often at the center of nationwide efforts to procure athletic talent. Cash payments, jobs, and loans that were invariably forgiven were just a few of the inducements.

"By the turn of the century, athletes were receiving scholarships, sinecure jobs, gifts from alumni and citizens, and a hundred other types of financial compensation." — Sack, Stuarowsky

Backlash was certain, vocal and vociferous. Academia, if not the growing number of university presidents with eyes more focused on increasingly blacker bottom lines, continued to espouse critical views of the slippage from sport's first role as a purely recreational activity into what was fast developing as a career path. It was only a matter of time before things came to a head, and it can be easily pinpointed: In the 1904 season, as the "Flying Wedge" was "perfected," 21 college football players were killed, more than 200 severely injured.

The resulting backlash resulted in the formation of the National Collegiate Athletics Association in 1905, and while a few simple rule changes immediately eradicated the threat of fatalities, attitudes died harder. Philosophical debates on amateurism and eligibility quickly came to the fore. The only problem then, as today, as it will be again tomorrow, is that there is no turning back the clock.

"The NCAA's position on amateurism, as it appears in Articles VI and VII of its 1906 bylaws, is unequivocal, uncompromising, and virtually indistinguishable from the position taken by British universities such as Oxford and Cambridge. According to Article VI, each member institution was to enforce measures to prevent violations of amateur principles. Included among these violations was "the offering of inducements to players to enter colleges for universities because of their athletic abilities or supporting or maintaining players while student on account of their athletic abilities, either by athletic organizations, individual alumni, or otherwise, directly or indirectly. This principle clearly forbade scholarships or financial aid based on athletic rather than academic ability. In true British fashion, the enforcement of this principle was left to each institution, the assumption being that gentlemen do not need outside agencies to enforce a code of honour.

"Die-hard advocates of amateurism (including elitist anglophiles as well as some faculty and college presidents) fought against athletic recruiting, athletic scholarships, under-the-table payments, lowered admission standards and the other trappings of professionalism. Their efforts were futile. By 1905, the year in which the NCAA was created, rampant professionalism had spun out of control." — Sack, Stuarowsky

Sport worked wonders for many American universities: profiles and enrolments increased, and coffers were filled. The nagging thought and belief it was on the back of intellectually impoverished but physically rich youth wouldn't go away, however. The Big Ten in 1927 felt compelled to reaffirm its stated provision that "no scholarships, loans or remissions of tuition were to be awarded on the basis of athletic skill." The legislation of enforced amateurism wasn't worth the paper it was wasted on. In 1929, the Carnegie Foundation of the Advancement of Teaching published a report on collegiate sport, which stated subsidization in some form or another occurred in 81 of the 112 colleges and universities it had studied. Does prohibition and the consumption of bootleg liquor ring a bell?

In the 1930s, most southern universities simply began ignoring the NCAA restrictions on scholarships. Powerless, or perhaps just leaderless, the NCAA could do little else but acquiesce and in 1948 agreed that financial assistance for tuition only could be granted if the need for aid was shown, further aid being allowed if superior academic achievement was shown. When in 1957, an NCAA "Official Interpretation" defined education expenses to include tuition and fees, room and board, books, and $15 for laundry, the full-ride scholarship, as it is known today, was officially on the books.

That definition of professionalism, as maintained not only by Sack and Stuarowsky but critics of athletic scholarships in general, is, in the first place, such overblown hyperbole that the so-called intellectuals who espouse such should forever abandon all claim to fully using their minds, and secondly is based on the assumption that there should be absolutely no remuneration in any way, shape or form for athletic endeavours performed on a university campus. This, despite the fact that athletes perform a service to their institutions; this, despite the fact the public vote with their wallets in favour of such service — but only if it is performed at a high level. The critics also argue that the admission of athletically-talented individuals onto university campuses endangers the intellectual standing of those institutions. If true, it says volumes of the validity of that intellectual standing, and, if not true, belies a smokescreen composed of unfounded and unethical elitism, bigotry, academic racism — and a healthy dose of petty snobbery and jealousy.

Canadian university sport's first umbrella organization, the forerunner of today's CIS, was founded in 1906, and included only Ontario and Quebec institutions. The Canadian Intercollegiate Athletic Union Central lasted more than five decades before eventually morphing into the heart and soul of the CIAU. From the outset amateurism was the path, and, it must be sardonically noted, is to this day. Any individual tainted whatsoever by the professional brush was banned from Canadian university sport, the definition of an amateur being "a person who has not competed in any competition for a stake bet, monies, private or public, or gate receipts, or competed with or against a professional for a prize or where gate receipts are charged; who has never taught or assisted in the pursuit of any athletic exercise or sport by means of a livelihood; who has never, directly or indirectly, received any bonus or payment or consideration whatever for any service as an athlete."

In other words, lily-whites only need apply. In other words, sport, which entails the pursuit of winning, became a dirty word. Recreation, which developed character, made the person, and preferably one qualified to rule over the natives. This sentiment was strongest in Toronto, a bastion of British loyalty, and although there were dissenting voices in both Quebec and the West on the restrictive nature of this policy, pure numbers ruled the day then as now.

Sanctimonious numbers, it must be added, because to this day defenders of their status quo have always upheld the Canadian approach because it wasn't the dreaded win-at-all-costs American approach, but a kinder, gentler understanding, one in which the powers that be would drum into us underlings that it was all about play, really, really, it is, old chap! That's a good boy, run along now. From late in the 18th Century, leaders of Canadian sport saw it as a vehicle to promote the values of character that only blue-blooded WASP males could command. They even gave a name to it: rational recreation, which meant things like "the game first and victory second" and "play for play's sake," actual utterings, rather mutterings, from two presidents of the Amateur Athletic Union in the 1920s. Such was nothing but and in effect an utterly absurd attempt to remove real competition from the field of play. As a support mechanism it was Ode to Joy to the ears of the CIAUC, which looked with horror upon the burgeoning state of the "evil" scholarships south of the border. Just imagine their chagrin, following the 1932 Los Angeles Olympics, when every single one of Canada's male track and field medalists, including gold-medal high jumper Duncan McNaughton, was a product of an American university.

Being right of course means never being wrong: The CIAUC, 1933: "Unquestionably, intensive competition, the desire to win and gate receipts are assuming proportions which are masking our vision as to the more important functions which this Union should serve ... This Union reaffirms its faith in the aims and objectives outlined in the forward of the handbook which declares in part, that 'through the medium of competitive athletics, it seems to promote health, character and citizenship'. That a renewed emphasis be placed upon these objectives so that 'the highest ideals and traditions of British sportsmanship and fair play be maintained and developed.'" These words were obviously written with a view to the explosive growth of "big-time" sports south of the border.

Our Canada of the time was guilty of a form of crime of history that today is a dirty word: colonialism, but ours was worse, it was sycophantic self-colonialism. We have long had a difficult task coming to grips with the fact our only neighbour is a behemoth, a rather brash young behemoth which strode to its own, new tune, and seemed to only want one thing from us, hockey players, which we were only too happy to provide.

But we were better and more than just that, weren't we, especially if viewed from our own self-described if completely laughable Center of the Universe, Toronto. Really, how many places nicknames themselves The Good? What other local citizenry would tolerate that one? Canada could, and eagerly did, readily imbibe the British notion that we were on top of a nation of louts, easily and righteously looked down upon as our moral inferiors. We would become benignly, even embarrassingly, if not downright insufferable, in our anti-Americanism, soft-pedaled in our "we're the nice guys here" Canadian way.

Once the United States pushed the envelope on financial aid to university athletes, our Eastern "brain trust" by their very misplaced idealism had to disavow there was any merit in supporting our young, talented, intelligent achievers, and instead of striding forward on a continent which we, like our neighbours, had plucked like a ripe red apple just because historically it was there for the taking, retreated inward to a safe and soft landing upon our stuffy British heritage with its joyless streak of Puritanism and dark vision of life and sealed that envelope for good.

The CIAU as we know it today as a pan-Canadian organization came into formation in 1961 through the union of the original Ontario-Quebec bloc with those of Atlantic (formed in 1910) and Western Canada (1920), largely through the efforts and persistence of the West. These regional associations maintained a surprisingly strong base of independence, but differences were inevitable. Ontario balked at the West's proposal for national championships, because that meant someone had to win. The West had also long viewed with distaste Ontario's rigid view that providing financial assistance was professionalizing their little darlings and when it went ahead and approved small tokens of assistance to athletes on campus, through third-party funds and university bursaries as opposed to outright scholarships, the Empire struck back.

In the mid-Sixties, a special committee was established to examine the scholarships issue under Ivor Wynne, then President of the CIAU and athletic director at Hamilton's McMaster University. Only the West was in favour, so the CIAU re-laid down the law and in 1967 issued:

"The Canadian Intercollegiate Athletic Union realizes that:

1. Some students in Canadian universities who happen to be outstanding athletes do receive financial assistance from sources outside of and not directly associated with a particular university.
2. Some Canadian students attend United States universities upon receipt of financial assistance from these universities based upon their athletic talents and not necessarily relating to academic ability.

Not withstanding the above, the CIAU:
1. Accepts only the principal of academic scholarships.
2. Opposes the principle of any form of financial assistance to a student based solely on athletic ability. The CIAU wishes to preclude individuals or institutions from using financial assistance as a system for soliciting or bargaining for outstanding athletes."
— "The Controversy About Athletic Scholarships in Canadian Universities: A Historical Pespective", Patrick J. Harrigan, Professor and Chair of History, The University of Waterloo

"Whatever," was basically the response outside the heartland, and both the Atlantic and Western organizations simply reworded their constitutions to make financial aid to athletes allowable under the stipulation they were "administered by the awards office of the university". By the early 1970s, the split was essentially outright, with some even having the temerity to suggest that since there were so many under-the-table payments to athletes, why not be honest about it? The CIAU, dominated by Ontario through its sheer numbers, officially rapped the knuckles of its recalcitrant members in the hinterlands. Didn't they, after all, know better?

In 1970 the federal government released "A Proposed Sport Policy for Canadians" and in it promised to provide $5 million to fund 45 scholarships of $2,000 annually, based on students' athletic ability. Ottawa's big mistake was that it acted unilaterally, without consulting the CIAU, and the result was predictable and immediate: the CIAU was not going to have scholarships "forced" on it in the words of Carl Totzke, athletic director at Waterloo, and a hurriedly amended CIAU constitution reiterated that any student who received any athletic scholarship was "ineligible for competition." In 1971, a Canadian Association of Health, Physical Education and Recreation (CAHPER) meeting at Waterloo poured scorn on athletic assistance, even dredging up the 40-year-old Carnegie Report with its view of the professionalization of university sport in the United States. In 1973, the CIAU AGM yet once again reiterated its "A student who is receiving an athletic scholarship or subsidy shall not be eligible to compete in any union contest" thunder from the mountaintop, but curiously its final report also contained this statement: "If all universities could offer identical financial support to the student, scholarships based on academic and athletic performance would be acceptable." All of a sudden it's all about money? What's going on here?

In 1974, the CIAU and the Association of the Universities and Colleges of Canada (AAUC) commissioned The Matthews Report and predictably got exactly what it wanted: clear and present condemnation of the American approach and absolute rejection of any notion of athletic scholarships having any value in Canadian universities.

How could it have been otherwise?

Almost immediately, Matthews sees fit to comment: "The rather wide divergences of opinion regarding intercollegiate athletics, in particular, undoubtedly is an outgrowth of differing educational philosophies underlying our educational system. However, it is very evident that many persons see in U.S. college sport today much that they consider to be undesirable and foreign to the purpose of a university and see our intercollegiates inevitably being tarred with the same brush."

Yes, we wouldn't want to be tarred with that Stanford brush, now would we? The nay-sayers then and now never mention the fact there are American universities with higher educational standards than some of ours, despite letting knuckle-dragging Neanderthals roam freely around campus. For them, it's always been what we won't do rather than doing what we are actually capable of. And if there was one constant the CIAU leadership harped on, it was that by actually encouraging competition as opposed to letting Johnnie and Joannie make happy playing in the sandbox, there would be financial abuses by the unscrupulous.

Matthews, on the state of affairs in Canadian universities, post World War II: "Although there were those on the athletic councils, particularly continuing faculty representatives, who continued to carry the torch of amateurism, it was a broader concept of amateurism and it was widely conceded that in the immediate pre-war years many of the universities had been tolerating some form of aid to their athletes. The hope was freely expressed, however, that such unsound and unethical practices would be discouraged now that a more or less fresh start was being made."

Such was not only unlikely, but impossible, as long as Ontario's amateur torchbearers held sway.

Even then, abuses were occurring within its own crystalline borders, but no matter, ground in stone policy was ground in stone policy and the reality of the situation had to be ignored because it would have been too painful to admit it and be damned as hypocrites, which is what they were, since in 1974 Ontario actually threatened to pull out of the CIAU championships over the issue of athletic aid, insinuating only that others cheated. Sheer and absolute pretentious gall carried their day, but must have also made for some sleepless nights, hopefully.

Matthews took verbal whacks at the Canadian media's limited grasp of the moral issues involved in prohibiting athletic assistance, citing as an example a Globe and Mail editorial (June 17, 1974): "Our Canadian universities refuse to recognize the value of financial aid to a student who is clever outside the classroom as well as in ...." In discussing the gushing flow of our top university-aged athletes to American universities for scholarship reasons, the Globe was referring to, Matthews wrote: "To suggest that Canadian universities should become involved in this type of program is to propose that they enter into the kind of ruinous competition in which institutions in the United States have been involved for the past 50 years and which now apparently has brought them face to face with an explosive situation." Yeah, it's done blown right up in their face, yuk, yuk.

Carrying on, he even had the effrontery to insinuate climate conditions had "more than a little" to do with track and field athletes accepting scholarships to southern American universities. Well, yes, it is more fun for most of us to run in the sun than it is to snowshoe around Lake Ontario.

But he wasn't done dissing; the value of sport on its own was soon in his high-beam headlights: "In assessing the need for financial assistance to enable an athlete to obtain a university education while at the same time developing his/her athletic skills, we recognize the objective as desirable but question that a significant need exists."

Upon noting the existence or "talent" awards being given to athletes, he impaled sport on the Puritanical alter of sport as frivolity: "Perhaps a more valid objection to a talent award is that, like the above mentioned athletic award, it implies a reward for a service performed, or that can be performed, in the interest of the institution. It is this service aspect, together with the subjective judgment involved in assessing which student is the more meritorious, that constitutes our primary objection to athletic awards."

Recruiting? See the horned one's hand at work. "It would be wrong to view the recruiting of athletes by Canadian universities as a fairly recent development. However, it can be said that recruiting and commercialization of university sport appears to go hand in hand. While references to developments in college sport in the United States are perhaps too frequently made, nevertheless it would be folly to ignore the evidence that these two forces have combined to make a monster south of the border and to assume that this cannot happen here." Bash the monster mash.

Matthews proceeds to quote brother-in-arms Maury Van Vliet, who at the 1971 CAHPER meeting offered this homily: "Ninety percent of the problems which we normally consider objectionable are directly attributable to recruiting. If there is no money involved between athlete and coach or athlete and athletic director, then recruiting policies are usually wholesome and based on such positive things as academic program, staff capabilities, campus atmosphere, facilities, equipment and athletic program. What our boys in Canada really want is excellence of coaching, equipment, facilities and program, with particular emphasis on program."

Apparently not, judging by the fact that the cream of our crop of boys were just as busy then as they are today accepting American scholarship offers, with the cream of the crop of our girls now also south of the border. But Matthews was right there to back Van Vliet up, with a line that perhaps is most reflective of his views on this subject: "It may also be observed that in asking why universities recruit athletes, the conclusion likely to be reached is that the motivation is to develop a winning team."

You don't say? We certainly wouldn't want that, now would we, and Matthews makes certain we get his point when he writes:

"Having given consideration to the many aspects of this involved matter, we recommend as a general guideline, that the soliciting of student athletes, either by letter or visitation, by any member of the university athletic department, not extend beyond the methods and the geographic boundaries of the institution's usual secondary school contacts. It is further recommended that any exchanges with athletes who reside outside such boundaries be by mail, not by visitation, and only occur if and when initiated by the prospective applicant for admission to the university." It only emphasizes the dream-world Matthews envisioned to note that in the 1973 CIAU men's basketball final, nine of the 10 starters were Americans. The championship team, incidentally, was from Guelph, Ontario.

Enough! Sorry, but no. In 1986, academics and sports administrators gathered at the University of Western Ontario to examine the issue, high-brow style, in a day-long gabfest. In his summary of the day's proceedings in The Role of Interuniversity Athletics: A Canadian Perspective, which was essentially another endorsement of the status quo, editor A. J. Taylor, PhD, returned to the Canadian tribal drumbeat of anti-Americanism when he declared: "Today, as is obvious from the situations at Georgia, TCU, Clemson and Alabama, we must guarantee that the role of interuniversity athletics in Canada does not follow the NCAA pathway to its present destination. We must guarantee an academic stability to athletics, an integrity based upon moral and ethical and academic standards."

Note that these are four southern universities, and thus the image is conjured up of exploited black athletes enrolled in Basket-weaving 101, and less than stellar graduation rates, the very evil Simon Fraser's Davies had been tarnished with without a second thought by supposedly lucid minds 20 years earlier. The purveyors of this continual condemnation for reason of exclusion never asked the question, who is exploiting who? In segregationist America, much of the Negro community was totally cognizant of the fact that aside from education, which was stressed, sport was one of the few avenues available for social mobility to a more equal standing in society.

— "It was almost as if the traditional black commitment to education, epitomized by the creating of the Negro colleges, and the missionary role of education in the black community had spilled over into baseball, an arena where such aims could prosper and pay dividends."

— "For John "Buck" O'Neill, a future manager of the Kansas City Monarchs, entering a Negro college's high school department was the decisive event of his life."

— "As the Gray's Cum Posey wrote, "Regardless of opinions concerning the owners of the clubs it is helping the Negro Race morally and financially."

— "Robinson [Mr. Bojangles] developed lasting friendships with most of the key Negro league personalities, and indeed, virtually his dying act was to summon Jackie Robinson and Roy Campanella to

his death bed. Wheezing in his oxygen tent, Bill Robinson held their hands and offered a prayer for their success in the major leagues."
— *Invisible Men, Life in Baseball's Negro Leagues*, Donn Rogosin

Undoubtedly, black scholarship students in American universities wholeheartedly welcomed the opinion of the white, well-educated, upper-class Canadian elite who would have denied them the opportunity to better themselves in a country where that every option was limited, in many cases by laws eventually struck down in the Supreme Court, especially if they'd thought to gaze north to see how Canada was doing such a slam-bang job of equalling the playing field of opportunity for its First People.

UBC's Bob Philip: "There's abuses in a lot of things in life, there's a lot of things that aren't fair. If you want to correct things, then you've got to have tougher penalties, you do this or that. I went to a NCAA meeting where they were kind of beating themselves over the head about the number of athletes, especially from low income families, who had arrived in school and weren't doing well. So I listened to it for a while and I said well, what is the problem? 'You know, we are getting these kids in, we're letting them in and half of them are failing.' I said, yeah, but half of them are passing and if you didn't let them in, if they didn't have the opportunity to get into your school to play sports, none of them would be going through. You could see the wheels turning. If you go to a ghetto area in some city in the States and you get 20 or 30 kids out of that ghetto that get into school somewhere and they play sports and 10 of them pass and 10 of them fail, well, you know what, that's 10 more than would have passed than if you hadn't let them in. And you've got to start somewhere. Now start working with them. There are abuses because it's all up to some schools. You think there are abuses at Stanford? I don't think so and yet Stanford is one of the better schools athletically. So there is no direct correlation. A lot of times, too, they float these numbers in men's basketball about the graduation rate. What they don't realize is that a lot of these kids turn pro and don't finish school. But there are over 1,000 universities down there and if you take a look at the number of abuses, there's not that many. And you know what, just because there's abuses down there doesn't mean there has to be abuses up here."

American university sports scholarships, so detested by people of power in Canada, broke ground in the just battle for racial equality in the United States and in a very real sense kept leading the way, while at the same time our universities held themselves separate and aloof from cultural developments in mainstream society. People were beginning to take notice and asking the hard questions following Canada's go for anything but gold showing in Montreal in 1976.

Sport Canada, wanting national leagues in which to develop our athletes, told the CIAU it had "better get with it." Upon assuming her portfolio shortly after the Games, Sports Minister Campagnolo turned her sights squarely on our universities. From the preliminary Green Paper:

"Canadian Universities possess all the resources necessary to produce good athletes. They have professional coaches, youth athletes, excellent facilities, dormitories and food services, support staff and the services of physiotherapists, doctors, sports scientists and librarians. Extensive intercollegiate programs are, however, expensive. At many universities, a shortage of funds has held back the development of intercollegiate sport. We propose that the universities be given assistance to subsidize the salaries of coaches contributing significantly to national team programs. In return for this financial assistance, we would ask that the universities commit themselves to excellence in their sports programs, coordinating them with those of the community, and expand training and competitive opportunities. We would also ask that coaching be year-round, that provision be made for testing athletes and there be a close liaison among the university physical education and coaching staffs, the national sport governing bodies and the Coaching Association of Canada."

And, from the subsequent White Paper: "Canadian universities can play a decisive part in the pursuit of athletic excellence in our country. They have the capacity to relate advanced research to sports situations where that research can be directly applied. They could be translators of research and applied experimentation, bridging the gap between theoretical concepts and the programs of sports organizations. In themselves, they constitute an important pool of athletic potential, one that might be further enhanced were the universities to accept the principle of athletic scholarships. The facilities, training expertise and systems of talent identification they possess are, in terms of the national sport effort, largely unexploited assets. It is to be hoped that in the years ahead our universities will find the means and the inclination to participate more fully in a national sports partnership."

From the Speech from The Throne, October 18, 1977: "The goal of this government is to ensure that the athlete, at whatever level of competition, is regarded as a full-functioning, productive member of society. The goal of this government is to see that sport, fitness and recreation is acknowledged by one and all as a full-functioning part of that culture which is Canada. No more the sweaty athlete syndrome. No more the denigration of the athletic scholarship. No more the culture which is divided between artists and athletes. Athletes are artists and some artists are athletes."

In February of 1978, in a Parliamentary report, Campagnolo went further, stating, "A certain righteousness has arisen in Canadian universities which negate all the favourable aspects of the scholarships as a vehicle to encourage both academic and athletic pursuits," adding that scholarships "should be an acceptable, if not laudable, avenue for student hockey players within the CIAU." In a subsequent speech in The Bahamas, she hammered home her point: "The [Canadian] universities, especially — as a countrywide network of splendid facilities and excellent personnel — remain sorely unexploited as a national training and competitive resource."

In 1979, Campagnolo entered the dragon's den and at that year's CIAU AGM bluntly called for a revision of the scholarship policy. Wasted breath. Two years later, another federal government paper stated, "The [CIAU's] very objectives and programs it has fostered (with substantial federal funding) towards the pursuit of amateur excellence are being severely undermined through this exodus of highly qualified young Canadians who envisioned a better educational-athletic experience in the U.S. ... The CIAU is very cognizant of this unfavourable trend and is actively working to resolve the problem. Unfortunately, a consensus as to its resolution is not apparent within the union in the foreseeable future. But unless this trend can be reversed, government intervention, through some form of 'third party' student-athlete assistance program may now become a necessity," which prompted The Globe and Mail to editorialize: "This may well mean that the federal government would withhold financial assistance from universities that refuse to install athletic-scholarship programs."

The silence of the bullheaded ones remained deafening. But in the early 1980s, with the B.C. and Alberta governments taking the proverbial bull by the horns and providing those "third-party" scholarships in an attempt to stem the flow of our top high school athletes to the United States, with the Maritime universities lobbying for athletic assistance to recruit in order to remain competitive with larger Canadian universities, and with statements such as "The CIAU is sticking it's head in the sand. There are all sorts of financial awards being given right now, by schools all over the country," coming from the University of Calgary's Dennis Kadatz, the resolve of the philistines finally broke. Albeit over their near-dead bodies, and with a caveat that showed the true pettiness of their character. At the CIAU's AGM in June of 1980, and after three votes were required to achieve the necessary two-thirds majority, Resolution No. 24 was passed:

"Be it resolved that all financial awards which recognize athletic participation and are administered through the Awards Office of a member institution shall not be in violation of regulation C-3 provided the following criteria are met:

a) The awards may be granted only to continuing students who have completed at least one year of fulltime university study at the donor institutions.

b) There must be no obligation for the student to participate in inter-collegiate athletics.

c) The academic success of the recipient must be a major component of the awards criteria."

Read b) again. Read it again.

In February of 2005, the late Mark Lowry, Executive Director Sport for the COC until his death from cancer later that year at age 51, and another past president of the CIAU, expounded on the change in direction a quarter century ago.

"I've always been in favour of scholarships. When I was with the CIAU [early 1990s] I was in favour of scholarships and was in favour of moving towards anything that was going to provide talented student athletes with additional support to participate in sport as well as participate in academics. It's by no way a statement that would suggest for a moment that academics are not the primary reason why athletes should be going to Canadian universities, full stop. You know, it's just got to be there. So, for me, there was never an issue with this, from the perspective of what I believe is important. The value that I think student athletes bring to a Canadian university is huge. I don't think, very, very few of them, particularly in Canada, are essentially looking to become fulltime, paid professional athletes. That's not the reason they are there. They're there because there is a genuine effort to receive some academic credentials to be able to be employed in the future. So for me, it was never an issue because we had in the CIAU all sorts of support in other ways, for continuing student-athletes —

sports scholarships have always been in place in the CIAU, so long as you're in second, third or fourth year. It was the entering sports scholarship [that was the problem]. There's always been money in place for any continuing student-athletes.

"The big issue all along is entering student-athletes, which, the debate was the rich would basically attract the entering student-athletes over the smaller universities who did not have the resources, or the capacity to compete. In the case of Ontario, the Ontario universities' presidents were opposed to the concept of entering sports scholarships, so really told their directors of athletics that this was something they simply couldn't support. So you have the West going very strong toward the principle of having sports scholarships, entering sports scholarships through to continuing student-athletes. The East were back and forth, Quebec was very much moving toward supporting the notion of entering sports scholarships and really Ontario, with 22 universities, was not supportive of it and there was continuously votes that would end up in an impasse because you needed 75 per cent.

"And that's the reality of the six years that I was with the CIAU, that this debate was on. What would happen is that there would be some tinkering and some adjustment and some small variations. But the overall principle was that nobody disagrees with the idea, including the universities in Ontario, with the idea that a student-athlete could receive financial support, and they did, from second year on in many Ontario universities, but it was the entering student-athlete who there was opposition to providing sports scholarships for and that is still the case today. So what you have is, really, in my mind, a principle that suggests that the concept of providing financial support to the student athlete is, as a basic principle, acceptable. But when you apply it, what you find is that there seems to be an aberration with the value when you approach it on a first-year student. That to me was the contradiction that I felt was not really something that I could personally support.

"In other words, it's OK for any other students as long as it wasn't first year so why is the first-year student, in effect, discriminated against? There's equally, in my mind, a rationale for supporting them, as much as there is from second year on. So for me, it was very much a philosophical argument, not based on money or anything else. If you're saying it's OK on the one hand to support academic, student-athletes, then why would you not be allowing first-year, entering students to have the same benefit – full stop. That being said, I've always felt there should be an effort to try and change that. The argument continues today."

Another issue that stuck in Lowry's craw was the fact that student-athletes could receive "an academic award of any amount, which is another interesting anomaly. It seems if you are receiving a sports scholarship or bursary because of your athletic prowess, somebody somewhere has determined that there needs to be a limit on that, whereas if it's academic, there's no limit. I'm not sure if I've ever sort of agreed with that principle either."

Continuing students only? Why? That pettiness of character, cloaked in the guise of anti-elitism.

And just to make sure that everyone knew Ontario did not agree with the 1980 — discriminatory by their insistence — change in direction by the CIAU, Waterloo's Trotzke read into the minutes this declaration:

"In consideration of the action taken and drawing our attention to the legislation that exists in the OUAA constitution relating to athletic scholarships, please be advised that the OUAA wishes to re-emphasize its strong opposition to any legislation that opens the route to the awarding of athletic scholarships. It is our intention to retain this stance. Further, we will review our position on future participation in CIAU championships should this legislation remain in force. We will also pursue alternate competitions with other universities and conferences which share a similar philosophy."

In playgrounds there is a well-know term that describes the behaviour of such types: cry babies. The rest of the CIAU should simply have said, good, go, hope you like playing on outdoor rinks, gyms and fields in Outer Oblivia. Instead, the resolution was put on hold for a year and in that time inflammatory statements confirmed Ontario's pigheadedness, as if it alone were right and the rest of the provincials from sea to shining sea were misguided, if not downright crass simpletons.

From Marge Prpich, University of Windsor's Director of Women's Sport, to her university president: "One of the strengths of the Ontario universities is the dominance of integrated programs where decisions are made in the best interests of the academic development of the student-athlete and the academic reputation of the university. In contrast, within non-integrated programs, decisions are made for the athletic departments by athletic personnel based upon the promotion of business-like, semi-professional programs with the athlete-student, not student-athlete, being exploited for superficial and financial gains."

Dick Moriarty, Windsor AD: "Big-time university athletes and serious academic studies are incompatible." From the Report of the Special Committee of Intercollegiate Athletics to the Council of Ontario Universities: "The situation of university athletics in Ontario universities is substantially better in every way than it appears to be in the United States ... Ontario universities are foremost academic institutions ... the principles governing [athletics] should be clearly developed in accordance with the academic mission." OUA presidents voted to uphold a 1973 statute banning post-season games against schools that offered athletic scholarships.

Despite all of Ontario's bluster, the CIAU held firm and in its 1981 mid-summer AGM refused to rescind Proposition 24. The OUA again threatened to withdraw from national competition, drawing the public ire of Ontario Premier William Davis, and finally that fall the OUA swallowed all the egg on its face and agreed to remain in the CIAU and compete with other universities. But — and there had to be a but, didn't there — its university presidents voted 14-2 to ban sports scholarships. And proceeded to get downright ridiculous — and not for the last time. In 1982, the Council of Ontario Universities allowed what they termed "recognition awards", but only for students in their last two years of studies, only if they were administered by the awards office, pointedly not the athletic department, and only to 10 percent of athletes per sport. Cluck cluck, squawk squawk, they went, we need something to hide behind.

The CIAU scholarship for continuing students was capped at $1,500. Ontario fought on. In the mid-1980s, after efforts were made to grant athletic awards to first-year students died a much deliberated death, Federal Sports Minister Otto Jelinek addressed the CIAU and asked for a "Canadian Athletic Awards Foundation for highly-skilled athletes" because, as anybody honest enough to look in a mirror could have predicted in 1981, Canada's most athletically talented high school seniors naturally saw no merit in the CIAU's new approach and continued to pack their bags and belongings and start new lives in the United States.

In 1997, Ontario voted as a bloc to defeat a proposal to raise the ceiling to $3,000 and allow first-year students to receive awards, and now it was the West's turn to vent its indignation. Canada West announced it would begin implementing first-year awards beginning in

1999. Ian Read, Athletic Director at the University of Alberta: "I don't care whether Ontario supports scholarships. All we're telling them is to get the hell out of the way so we can offer them. We want to compete for our [Canadian] athletes," nearly 2,000 of whom were then on U.S. scholarships.

Prior to the AGM of 1998, the University of Toronto, Canada's biggest post-secondary education institution, fired these volleys, upon presenting its position paper on sports scholarships: "All admission awards have to be primarily based on academic criteria," said Liz Hoffman, associate director of the Faculty of Physical Education and Health and past-president of the CIAU.

"I believe in the student-athlete and am totally opposed to any scholarship which allows admission below standards," said Bruce Bowden, registrar of Trinity College. "Any scholarship has to be based upon academic ability."

"In an ideal world universities should not be giving out scholarships," said University of Toronto Blues swimming coach, Byron MacDonald. "A student will choose [which school to attend] based on money, not whatever school is best for them."

And to top it off: "This is one of those issues U of T must think in terms of their own students, province and the country," said Bruce Kidd, while reinforcing the point that the university always opposed athletic scholarships, viewing them incompatible with its academic mission. This is one of those issues: Canada doesn't belong to Ontario, a concept which viewed from afar sometimes appears to confuse an entire province.

Patricia Pickard, director of athletics at Laurentian University, felt compelled to point out that, "There are a number of schools from out West that come and take away Ontario kids by offering them both athletic and leadership awards. Over the last year and a half it has been discovered that a number of these leadership awards have been distributed to undeserving first-year students based on athletic prowess."

In June, the West's motion to legalize first-year awards was defeated at the CIAU's annual general meeting by a vote of 43-37, guess which bloc vote won that day?

Canada West and the Great Plains Athletic conferences immediately announced they would flout the foolishness and provide entry awards anyway. Yet once again, several Ontario ADs responded that if the malcontents followed through on this threat they would either seek their expulsion or themselves leave the Canadian university athletic union.

Heading into the CIAU AGM of 2000, the battle lines hadn't budged an inch, the West pushing for scholarship sanity, Ontario unwilling to see the light of day. Kim Gordon, inter-university athletics coordinator at UBC: "We want to keep the best kids in Canada, and we want to raise the level of sports in Canada. The recruiters from American institutions are just stealing our kids because we can't offer them anything." Don Wilson, Athletic Director at the University of Alberta (Calgary): "It's ridiculous. I don't think it's appropriate. Why should we lose student athletes to the States? We should award people in the first year, second year, third year or fourth year. Period."

Tut, tut, was Ontario's response, according to one report from the Carleton University website: "But Bruce Kidd, dean of the faculty of physical education and health at the University of Toronto, says giving money to students solely on the basis of athletic talent would lower academic standards. Such awards would simply result in an expensive recruiting war between universities when funding is already scarce. The money, he says, would be better-spent on academic priorities." More Kidd: "It's in this vein that Ontario institutions take a unanimous stand against athletic awards. We will always be opposed to giving an award that's primarily based on athletic ability. Pure and simple. Even if we vote yes for the package, U of T will not give entering athletic awards to student athletes in the future."

What does he know? But we will deal with Dr. Kidd and more of his blarney baloney in due course.

In 2002, the now CIS once again rejected entry-level athletic awards, Ontario's numbers once again holding sway, but did agree to raise the cap to cover tuition and auxiliary fees. The latter was a significant step forward, admittedly, but of course did nothing to alter the opinion of Canadian high school seniors there was no athletic scholarship available to them upon graduation. Still, Ontario glowered. Noting that the West distributed more in scholarship money than the East, Queen's President William Leggatt said that these circumstances make a "level playing field" impossible and floated the idea that Ontario withdraw from CIS and confine itself to competition within the province. Add. Nauseum. A CIS survey at this time showed how little support, on average, varsity athletes competing in CIS championships received: Canada West (at about $550) and the Atlantic conference (about $300) led in the awards dollars available per registered student athlete; Ontario (about $90) and Quebec ($100) trailed far behind.

Two years later, we were still hearing the bleating: "We didn't want to get into bidding wars over these students," says Ontario University Athletics president Drew Love. "They should make the decision on where they go based on the academic strengths of the school." Which beggars the questions of why even build gymnasiums?

In 2004, with the help of Maritime universities facing harsh economic times, the OUA managed to restrict the awards to 70% per varsity team. So, while we push for gender equality on the one hand, we demasculate all 18-22-year-old university athletes on the other. That's one kind of progress, but in today's world we can't discriminate against progress even if it's backwards.

At the 2004 CIS AGM, the decision was taken to put the kibosh on the organization's decades-long debate over the rules for "Athletic Financial Awards", as they were now referred to. Time out, children. If you don't know which end of the wagon to hitch the horses to …

Finally, drum roll, please, late in 2005, a voice of opposition was raised from within, and an OUA president called his peers' bluff.

*Vancouver Sun, December 12, 2005*

*HEADLINE: How Canadian*

*Blurb: Universities, unsure of their role in developing athletes, and put off by the unseemly American example, skimp on athletic scholarships to the detriment of all*

*By David Atkinson, Carleton University*

*Since my own days as a student-athlete, the question has been asked: Why can't Canadian universities offer athletic scholarships as occurs in the United States?*

*In more recent days, we have expressed concern that many good university-age Canadian athletes are heading to NCAA Division 1 and Division 2 universities and colleges, resulting in an erosion of quality in university athletes in Canada.*

*Granted, Canadian universities do offer athletic awards, but they are modest compared to what is offered at many U.S. schools. There are those who wish things were otherwise, and certainly the issue of athletic awards has proven divisive for Canadian Interuniversity Sport, the governing body for university sport in Canada. Some schools want a more generous policy, while others, notably a majority of Ontario universities, hold out for more stringent rules.*

*Why this opposition to athletic scholarships? What one hears most often is that we simply do not want to be like U.S. college sport, with all its extravaganzas and abuses. This ignores, of course, that U.S. college sport is part of a larger cultural matrix that we in Canada both love and hate. How many of us watch the Bowl games or get taken with March Madness? More to the point, the NCAA oversees thousands of teams, of which only a handful are ever found guilty of any offence.*

*Inevitably, too, we are quick to assume that placing prominence on university athletics erodes academic standards – that athletes are not good students and would not otherwise be at university if they were not playing a sport.*

*The very reverse is the case. The academic average of athletes playing at Canadian universities is inevitably higher than the overall academic average for all students. And athletics has proven to be an important recruitment device for attracting good students to a university. Look to the number of Academic All-Canadians at any Canadian university if you want proof. The self-discipline, focus and motivation that make good athletes also make good students.*

*Canadian universities have not come to grips with one simple question: What is their role in the development of elite athletes? In the United States, the question has been asked and answered; in Canada, we are simply not sure. The result has not been an altogether good one. While there is consistent competitiveness among the marquee sports – football, hockey, basketball – this is not the case with "minor" sports. There are a handful of competitive teams and the rest are just also-rans. That Brock University has won the CIS men's wrestling championship for six years running is the direct consequence of having two national-level coaches, something no other university has. The same situation exists in volleyball, swimming, lacrosse and rowing.*

*A big issue for Canadian universities is cost. For Ontario University Athletics, this is especially a concern, as the Ontario universities have, to their credit, many more sports than do schools in other conferences. For cash-strapped universities needing to buy books for the libraries, one can understand how athletic awards are hardly a priority. If universities did, in fact, have a role in the development of elite athletes, then perhaps we could have a serious discussion about funding, rather than just concentrating on the scholarship issue alone. And this, too, might legitimize university efforts to raise support from the public sector.*

*At Canadian universities, athletes give back much more than they get. They give of their time and energy, and more often than not they are great university citizens. To represent their universities, they forgo working to finance their university education. At the same time, the universities benefit from the public profile that having a successful team brings. Carleton University likely gets more coverage from its sports teams than any other activity. While we may not have the craziness of American university sport, athletics does contribute to institutional identity and community. How often do we hear that Carleton is a three-time CIS men's basketball champion? All this contributes to a university's competitive advantage. Surely supporting our student athletes is not so outrageous.*

*We need to have a serious discussion about this. It is time to take our head out of the sand. This requires the leaders of Canada's universities to step up and be involved. It is not something to be decided by the OUA or the CIS alone. Canadian university sport is both great sport and great entertainment. It is too bad that most Canadians don't know it.*

*—David W. Atkinson is president of Carleton University, and chair of the Ontario Commission on Interuniversity Sport*

David W. Atkinson, our newest Canadian hero. Finally, an insider who would step up to the drawn battle line.

In 2005-06, both the University of Ottawa and Carleton took steps to opt out of the OUA, the only conference in Canada to refuse first-year students AFAs, the only conference in the country to restrict AFAs to a maximum of $3,500 per student. Outside Smallville, first-year students who carry an 80% average are eligible, the maximum is each institution's and mandatory fees.

Blinkers exposed, the OUA addressed the subject at its semi-annual meeting in January and prepared a report for the OUA council of university presidents for a decision on the matter at the OUA AGM in May. Said Western University's Mike Lysko, "This will be decided at the presidential level. We're losing as a conference if we don't move forward. I know we're compromised nationally in competing for student athletes. I just think we have to paint a bigger picture of this conference. But it doesn't matter what I think, it's what the presidents think." Added Lysko, "There are people around the table who don't

166

believe this is in the best interest of the OUA and I respect that opinion, but I've lived under U.S. college athletics and it's not always as evil as people try and make it out to be."

Atkinson made a presentation in Hamilton in favour of scholarships and told the Ottawa Citizen, "The OUA must emerge from the dark ages and give student athletes their due for the mileage that universities get out of their athletic endeavours." Emerge from petrification it did, and no-one cared, the tree did fall silently in the forest.

From the OUA's website:

*OUA BOARD VOTES IN FAVOUR OF OFFERING ATHLETIC FINANCIAL AWARDS TO FIRST-YEAR STUDENT-ATHLETES*

*May 10, 2006 - HUNTSVILLE – First-year student-athletes at Ontario University Athletics institutions will be getting some more help on the financial front when the 2007/08 season commences. The OUA's Board of Directors voted 16-3 in favour of the league providing Athletic Financial Awards (AFAs) to entering student-athletes (individuals who have yet to complete two full semesters of study in one academic year at the Canadian Interuniversity Sport school they are attending). Entering students with an average of at least 80 per cent are eligible to receive up to $3,500 annually from their university to help with expenses for the school year.*

*"This is a significant day in OUA history," said outgoing President David Dubois. "As a conference, we have always tried to attract the best and the brightest student-athletes out there and with the implementation of this new policy on the granting of Athletic Financial Awards, I believe we will see more of Canada's best at the doorsteps of our 19 member schools."*

*At the OUA's Semi-Annual General Meeting held in Hamilton this past January, a motion was unanimously passed to strike a Task Force to investigate what has long been a contentious issue throughout the league. A survey of OUA member schools determined that the granting of awards to eligible entering student-athletes was the highest priority, prompting the Task Force to offer guidance on a new model.*

*"Though this debate has been going on for years, the Task Force was very aggressive in terms of proposing a new model for AFAs," said Dubois. "We have had the support of the university presidents to examine this issue. It's rewarding to know that in just four short months, we have made a proactive and positive change to*

*our model. What this means is that some of our finest young student-athletes will see the OUA as a great option to help them advance from an academic and athletic standpoint."*

*The OUA has traditionally had a higher academic standard for returning student-athletes to meet in order to obtain an AFA. Returning students must maintain a 70 per cent average to be eligible. While the OUA Board of Directors felt there was a need to open up opportunities to entering students, it was imperative that the standards remain high, hence the 80 per cent minimum for those in their first year of university, which is also the standard requirement for entering students in the other regional associations.*

*In September of 2001, the OUA increased the maximum level of AFAs from $1,500 to $2,500. Last September, that figure was upped again to $3,500. The Task Force will continue to examine the maximum amount of AFAs and will report back to the Board of Directors at the January 2007 Semi-Annual General Meeting.*

*"For years, there was a stance among OUA members that offering too much in the way of AFAs would foster an athlete-first environment that is the norm at various American institutions," said Dubois. "But it is clear that our student-athletes are intelligent, hard-working individuals in both the classroom and on the playing field.*

*"If first-year students can receive academic awards, then it only makes sense that those athletes who meet the strict requirements of our universities be rewarded for their achievements, as well.*

*"Given the time our entering student-athletes commit to both their school work and competing for a varsity program, they should be eligible to receive financial assistance."*

The news, a reversal of 100 years of policy, received the scantest of attention across Canada. Why should it? This whole university scholarship issue has always received scant attention across Canada. More to the point, Ontario universities have always said they don't have the financial means to actually provide athletic assistance, and that hasn't changed — yet. Three Dinosaur U's can be expected to remain taint-free, so it seems we don't need global warming for more free hot air. With oversize righteous blinkers as its signposts, the OUA has neutered itself, and in this grand scheme of things has rendered itself irrelevant, or at best an afterthought, to the courageous and talented. As compared to those few ivory offices primarily in Ontario that demeaned sport, our neighbour took it and the rest of the world along with it to the undreamed of height of cultural phenomenon, nea, force. We've looked at it with askance; when that happens from the intellectual top down the mentality diffuses like pollen in the breeze with the result that sport, real sport, becomes somewhat of a national allergy. In our anti-scholarship stance, our best effort to be the un-Americans, sport as a utilizable national force for healthy growth has always been given a slightly bemused reception. More's the pity.

Atkinson's gumption to try to beat down a brick wall simply by using his head cannot be over-applauded, even if we had four arms instead of two. The CIAU's stance began when only amateurism existed, it's time to move on, boys and girls.

Lowry very much wanted any remarks he made about the issue to be countered with his personal belief: "I think my final comment would really be that there is an underestimated value, in my mind, within many sports federations about the role of the CIAU in the development of athletes. If there was not the range of programs being offered in CIAU institutions there would be many athletes who would have no place to play. CIAU sport for many athletes is really a springboard to continue on further in their athletic careers if they have the potential, or, if they don't, it's a wonderful pinnacle of success. I would hate to have any representations from me suggesting for a moment that I don't value and believe that there is a huge role for CIAU sport in this country. What I really want to get across is the fact I think it's unreasonable to expect CIAU institutions and directors of athletics to be responsible for creating and being the developers and the entire programming support for Olympic athletes. That's just not reasonable."

Which is true — if our status quo is the favoured one.

# Chapter Seven
## You've Got To Be Kidding Me

Just like those who brook no tolerance of a differing opinion, anti-sports scholarships types deserve professional scorn. And, just as the truism that any news is goods news is recognizably false, so, too, is their stance, based as it is on fallacies and misconceptions, even outright deception. That scorn is shared.

Fuelled by a couple of pots of coffee after lunch, and in the middle of a discussion regarding Notre Dame University, the state of Canadian sport, university and otherwise, Peter Webster, multiple Canadian sports hall of fame inductee, let loose with a barrage — and I'm sure he'd be the first to say pardon the language, fully aware as he was that the tape was rolling:

"I'd rather accent the positive side of what Notre Dame did, not what the stupidity of the system didn't do. Why not just celebrate our successes and let them all scratch their heads, have people wonder, 'Why did you screw it up? Look at what you've done to our kids.' But everybody knows. Put it this way, I would put it in about six paragraphs, all the crappy things we didn't do, and say to all you guys in the decision-making process, look at how you screwed up our youth. It would be the smallest chapter in the book. It might be the most provocative because it would make everybody think. You just don't mention them at all, the guys that were involved in the decision-making process from 1960 until today that screwed up our youth. You're not naming anybody, you're not doing anything, and I'll tell you! Then you have the positive side of things and you cite all sorts of examples.

"And you know what? Everybody will turn around and say, 'Who were these bastards who buggered us around, look at what these guys from Notre Dame did.' You put in a short, concise, very provocative two pages and it hits them between the eyes. I think it would be a brilliant idea. Just forget about all these screw-ups. Just put it concisely and neatly: 'You guys screwed up a whole generation of people!' Rather than citing all these guys that are stupid. You will have 17 books of that!"

Uh sir, there is Bruce Kidd.

Well, that stopped him in his tracks for a split second.

"That guy had a huge opportunity to do outstanding stuff for the Canadian sports system. He was recognized for his athletic prowess, he was outstanding. He then went across the line and went into the academic side, way off the radar screen, and they still quote him today. In fact, you know what, his might be the only name I might put in that last paragraph, you know, Bruce Kidd and his cohorts."

Kidd's many allegations in support of the fraudulent misconception that granting athletic scholarships will lower a university's academic standing is, first, a leaky defence of bad administration practices, and 1-A just a joke, full stop. A bad one played on all of us. I considered Webster's mini-rant in the vein of sage advice, indeed. Kidd, by default or choice, is the figurehead of the opposition to sports scholarships. What makes it surreal is that in his own words he also puts the very lie to his and their so-called position.

The minute one starts looking into the debate over Canadian athletic scholarships, or lack thereof, his is the one name that appears most frequently for a number of reasons, the obvious one being the fact he controls the largest university sports "franchise" in the country from the centre of "the centre" — downtown Toronto. Use his name as a foil to represent the opposition to, and the discredit, denial and belittling of athletic scholarships and you save a lot of breath trying to explain yourself.

He has long seen fit to support Ontario's simple but effective, and these are his words, "traditional no", to them, and at the turn of the century was still promoting the party line that people can't think well and run well at the same time. In 2000, from a Carleton University website, "But Bruce Kidd, dean of the faculty of physical education and health at the University of Toronto, says giving money to students solely on the basis of athletic talent would lower academic standards. Such awards would simply result in an expensive recruiting war between universities when funding is already scarce. The money, he says, would be better spent on academic priorities."

Whoever said a sports scholarship was solely in exchange for athletic talent? The facts always present a problem when manufacturing a smokescreen.

It's a thoughtless dismissal of character development and the entirety of sport to deny students their choice of university because of an individual athletic concern. That, in essence, relegates sport to the realm of pre-schoolers on Monkey Bars in the playground and there is no forgiving that nonsense. If this is the learned tripe that emanates when deciding money is better spent on academic priorities that better part remains to be seen.

Webster is far from alone in his heartfelt criticism of Kidd — and all the rest of those bastards who buggered up our youth.

Currie Chapman, former head coach, women's alpine team: "There are a lot of people that don't believe him. He is the leader in keeping mediocrity within our performance. The other thing I'd like to figure out, there are thousands of Canadian athletes on American scholarships ... and they're our best. But I'm sure that a lot of them would say 'I'm not going to take a part scholarship at, you know, University of Toronto, and be put down by people like Bruce Kidd all the time, and get a little scholarship and play in this league where I'm never going to develop. I'm going to take that University of Memphis scholarship and get that full ride.' When I was teaching I got some girls scholarships; it wasn't hard."

Bob Hindmarch, former UBC AD: "Many universities, particularly in Ontario, think an elite program at their university is who the best players are at their university at the time they pick their team. Yeah, I saw the article where Bruce Kidd is talking about their programs keeping Canadians in Canada, and he votes against scholarships," he says softly, gently combining rhetoric, incredulousness, and downright indignation, "the same guy that has no problem taking money from the federal government with a grant when he was a runner? I like Bruce and he's a hard-working guy at something he does — but they all vote for the government of Canada, or the government of Ontario, to give money to athletes. Call them government grants, government assistance, and that's OK, if they get $5,000, that's OK.

"I worked with Bruce with the Canadian Olympic Committee, he was head of our education committee and frankly he did a fantastic job. He brought that whole aspect into perspective, the education program for the Canadian Olympic Committee, and in fact, then also worked it out so that we re-connected with Greece and now the education aspect of that program is really in a very solid position because of Bruce.

"Having said that, I don't agree with Bruce's philosophy in regards to sport in Canada, and particularly university sports. And I think one of the things we need to do is go to the next level where we have people who are prepared to put up scholarships for young athletes to go to school. Actually, I'm opposed to the government kind of scholarships, and private scholarships for athletics, I think that's where the abuses started in the United States. I would like to see the universities be responsible. Most universities in Canada have very responsible Senates and wouldn't allow the kind of abuses that occur in the United States. I think we have an excellent athletic program and we should take it to the next level. Unfortunately, voting against the idea of scholarships, to my way of thinking, is just telling every young kid in Canada to go the United States.

"And, one of the things I guess I am really opposed to is the idea you can't recruit a young boy or girl to come to university for athletics. I mean, the math departments do it, the physics departments do it, all the top departments in the university are encouraging and trying to get the very best. Why shouldn't we in athletics? We live in a community which is dedicated to excellence. Why wouldn't we want to do the same thing and why wouldn't we make it attractive for young people to accept those things? And I think that if you don't agree with that, then we should have a two-tier system in Canada where we have those who want to do those, and those that don't want to do that, that's fine. They continue to do what they do."

Robert Dubeau, retiring McGill AD: "You could say that Bruce, for all his positive points and all the good things he has done, I am not on the same wavelength as him as regards to sports in Canada. He tends to look on them a little more on the socialist side, intramural side, mass participation and that's good, but I think we've gone beyond that now and I think the student-athletes, the coaches, and I believe the public to some extent, and definitely the media, are clamouring for something other than what Ontario has to offer at this particular time. And unless the changes in aid with regards to athletic awards changes, it won't change. That is changing in Toronto. They realize they can't continue. They have one of the worst athletic programs on the competitive side in Ontario. It's not only football, in all sports they have a difficult time. They have very stringent regulations regarding equity, which hinders them a little bit. They have a policy which hinders [scholarships] and don't give out enough of them. They live in a city which is very apathetic towards intercollegiate sport, they live on a campus which is worse than apathetic when it comes to intercollegiate sport, in a very expensive city to live in if you are a student athlete, so they've got a lot of things going against them. And they haven't won for a long time and when you don't win recruiting is 10 times harder. They've got themselves into a little bit of a mess but they can get themselves out of it if they want to, it's just a question of how much desire there is to getting themselves out of that situation."

Bob Philip, current UBC AD and former CIS president: "Yeah, well, I don't want to talk about him." Would you then care to expound on some of your earlier Ontario rants I've seen in print? "I would put it in this context: I did feel that way and I do feel that way, but not so much because of what they believe or don't believe in, because I don't want to get into what I think they should do. But I think where they're really holding back is not working with us to say we need two systems in Canada. It's one thing to say we don't believe in that. And that's fine, you don't believe in it, I believe in it. But if you want to have a system that allows us to go to our level — and you do what you want — then you have to accommodate it within that structure. If you're not prepared to do that, if you're just going to simply say we can stop you from moving ahead because we have got more votes, that to me is totally counterproductive. So I don't necessarily think that we would like to try and convince Ontario. I'm fed up trying to do that — I don't want to convince the U of T, Bruce Kidd that he should do this or that but I want Bruce Kidd to say to me, 'Hey, you know what, this is the level we want to play at. If you want to go and be the NCAA model then you go for it and we'll accommodate you within Canada.' Because, I'll tell you, there are enough schools in Canada that think we should be taking it to the next level and one of the ways you go to the next level is by keeping Canadians in Canada and one of the ways you do that is being competitive scholarship-wise."

Wilf Wedmann, SFU AD, former head of Sport Canada: "Even he has undermined it, right? I guess I would argue that if you think to be an athlete you need to be a fulltime athlete, and that you should be an employee of the state, which is what he advocates, that all those carded athletes are employees of the state, then why are you having an athletic program at the U of T? Unless you're trying to say, well that's nice, it's not really serious athletics. Then call it what it is, recreation, and let them have a good time, just spend a heckuva lot money on your recreation program, as opposed to on serious athletics." Why field an 0-8 football team that in the 2005 season scores something like 60 points and gives up 600? Why do that? "That's crazy. And it doesn't help the image of the University of Toronto Blues, or the institution.

"Bruce had a perfect chance to implement Nirvana, I mean, if he's got the vision. U of T, I don't think, represents Nirvana. I thought they were onto something with that new stadium proposal at Bloor. That was the site to be. That Varsity Stadium was a beautiful place and to put that stadium there would have been brilliant but they couldn't even manage that. Tragic. So, I'm not quite buying into this idea, this Bruce Kidd idea of these fulltime employees of the state. He's actually one of those interesting characters that I think hold us back, from my perspective he straddles the line. So he's part of all the solutions and everything, but he's really not. His U of T, he's responsible for that."

Kidd, of course, and his cohorts, of course, are as entitled to personal opinions and beliefs as the rest of us 33 million. According to his executive assistant Paul Carson, "Easily without question, Bruce's major interest is the philosophy debate. And in Ontario the two big issues, one was the intrinsic philosophy and the other is the money. What are universities here for, how much are you going to water down your academic standards by having scholarships? Once you put an academic component on a scholarship, if the university really wants that athlete are they going to fudge? Is that the slippery slope to the American system? The critics said that the only difference between what would happen here and in the States is the Americans have more money. We will have all the corruption but at simply a lower scale. They argued that it was simply inevitable that once you start throwing money around that schools would want to win, on the theory that winning programs generate more alumni money. And recognition and everything else and it would simply be a slippery slope.

"Bruce was part of that, he certainly is very concerned about the abuses, but on the other hand he is very concerned with equity and saw the scholarship dynamic as one way to get money especially to women's programs that otherwise wouldn't be able to get their hands on any. To him, he could live with scholarships provided there was equity. And it turned out that in the end that became the price. Ontario would sort of grudgingly support it, or agree that it could happen even if they didn't do it, provided there was legitimate sport and gender equity. The debates at some of the meetings over the years have been incredibly fascinating because you could have someone like Bruce who comes at it from essentially a philosophical, ethical point of view and the very next speaker basically saying 'I don't give a hoot about philosophy, I want to know, show me the rule that makes my team competitive and I'll vote for it.'"

Kidd's philosophy emerged from fertile feeding ground. George E. Connell, who by the turn of the century was Professor

Emeritus of the university, in 1986 delivered a paper: "The Role and Place of University Athletics in a Large Canadian University" at a day-long confab at the neutral site of the University of Western Ontario. Read it and weep.

*"At the University of Toronto, intercollegiate sport is part of a comprehensive, broad-based athletic program. This program is the largest extracurricular activity on campus and is viewed by the university as an important aspect of the educational experience it offers its students. While much of the program is essentially recreational, the intercollegiate program is designed for students with a serious interest in sport excellence. Intercollegiate athletes are encouraged to make a commitment to both academic and athletic excellence. However, our firm view is that students are, first and foremost, students and their academic commitments must take priority. This principle underlies the whole of the universities [sic] educational program, including athletics. It is reflected in the reporting structure for athletics, which is through the University's academic vice-president. So as to ensure that there are no institutional inducements to place sport commitments before academic ones, participation is completely voluntary. No scholarships or financial incentives are offered. No concessions in terms of admission, academic or degree requirements are made. Recruiting practices by athletic staff are carefully monitored.*

*"While the University is proud of its excellent athletic program and wants prospective students to be aware of its quality when the [sic] consider attending the University of Toronto, the emphasis in recruiting is on the provision of information. Coaches are firmly discouraged from trying to persuade prospective students to attend the University for mainly athletic reasons.*

*"The University recognizes that student athletes may need assistance in maintaining both their academic and athletic commitments, and that the University has a responsibility in this area. An orientation program is mounted for intercollegiate athletes, along with special study skills programs offered by the staff of the University's Counselling and Learning Skills Service and the University Library. A senior member of the Department is responsible for counselling intercollegiate athletes regarding their academic progress. This is monitored through direct access to the University's academic records system. The need for special test and examination arrangements is recognized, but these are carefully controlled. Only*

*the coordinator of intercollegiate athletics is authorized to make such arrangements with academic departments. Individual coaches may not do so.*

*"And, finally, the University's coaching staff are selected on the basis of their commitment to the University's philosophy regarding the place of athletics in the student experience at the University of Toronto, as well as their ability to develop the athletic skills of student athletes. It is expected that in all their interactions with students, they will reflect the educational emphasis of the University's athletic program.*

*"Inter-university athletics involves a relationship with other universities for athletic competition purposes, and we believe that the nature of these relationships is an important factor in the quality of our athletic program and its fulfillment of its educational purposes. In the University's view, the most appropriate competitive relationships are with other institutions that share our academic and athletic philosophy, and are committed to athletic programs of comparable breadth and quality.*

*"We see no educational value in having our student athletes beat, or be beaten by, competitors whose skill level is radically different from theirs because of differential academic standards or athletic program quality. In fact, such competitive discrepancies may be an inducement to compromise the principles to which we are committed. Competitive alignments are also important because of their impact on schedules, which should be compatible with student athletes' academic priorities.*

*"In the past, intercollegiate sport was a major force at the University of Toronto in terms of campus spirit and alumni loyalty. This is less true today, and to some extent this is regrettable. While we are endeavouring to revive interest in intercollegiate sport on campus because of its capacity to support a sense of community, this will not be done at the expense of intercollegiate athletes. Similarly, revenue generation is not a major issue in our intercollegiate program. Current gate receipts cover only a fraction of the cost of the intercollegiate program itself. We would welcome additional revenue but are not prepared to compromise our view that the major beneficiaries of the intercollegiate program should be the student athletes themselves. Corporate support is another area with which we are prepared to become involved up to a point, but not if it becomes exploitive of our program or the interests of our student athletes.*

---

*"The role of high performance sport is another area of concern. The benefits to student athletes who are interested in international competition as well as the spill-over benefits to our athletic program in general that can occur as a result of collaboration with Sport Canada and the sport governing bodies are apparent. At the same time, just as with our intercollegiate competitive relationships, we are concerned that our involvement with high performance sport not distort the priorities of our athletic program or our student athletes. Therefore, we are monitoring our involvement in this area with great care."*

Kidd has been the protector of this fear, indeed, has been the public face of its advocacy. And today, varsity sports at U of T is no Nirvana, no, indeedy not, and will long be playing catch-up. The bluest chip program in today's CIS is football and the Sing The Blues are winless since the 2001 season. Which is, nice.

Akin to the Canadian university presidents who voted for rules establishing academics as having paramount importance over athletics all those decades ago, the selectors of the Order of Canada voted for Kidd's approach to sports. In 2005, he was awarded Canada's highest civilian honour, joining roughly 5,000 others "who exemplify the Order's Latin motto: Desiderantes meliorem patriam, or "Desiring a better country." From the Order's website: "An athlete, administrator, educator and scholar, Bruce Kidd has devoted his life to eradicating sexism and racism in sporting communities around the world. As director of the International Campaign Against Apartheid Sport, he built bridges of cooperation between diverse groups and cultures. His great love of sport has made him a powerful advocate, as he successfully lobbied government to promote the value of physical activity in our daily lives. He has also shared his vast knowledge with students at the University of Toronto, where he serves as dean of the Faculty of Physical Education and Health."

Fair enough. Olympian and Commonwealth Games competitor, Dean of the biggest and most diverse university sports program in the biggest city in the biggest province in the country, a recipient of the Order of Canada. A life well lived. Twice he very politely agreed to be interviewed, twice it never happened. He surely had neither the need nor the responsibility to undergo cross-examination by little old me. So it was left to reading his writings, and he left in his wake some curious words for a man who has staked out his position so bluntly on the academic potential of athletes.

In his 1972 book *The Death of Hockey*, co-written with John MacFarlane, an anti-big business diatribe against the evil influences of money on the original game of pond hockey with cover art showing a fist squeezing blood out of a puck: "My generation grew up dreaming of emulating heroes who were forced to leave home at an early age in order to practice their craft, hardly circumstances that encouraged us to develop a strong commitment to our own society." Today, under policies Kidd and his cohorts defend, 2,500 Canadians attend American universities on sports scholarships, hardly circumstances that encourage them to make a strong commitment to our society.

The co-authors direct much attention to the National Team pioneered by Father David Bauer who originated a fresh approach to the international game that the CAHA adopted in 1962.

"Father Bauer's idea was to collect the best graduating juniors and Canadian college players in Canada and the United States, and assemble them at a university where they could play hockey and continue their education. Father Bauer had four objectives for this national team.

"1. To establish an organization that would enable Canada to compete effectively in international competition with the increasingly skilful teams of other countries.

"2. To create a new ideal for Canadian youth by associating excellence in hockey with excellent opportunities for personal education and technical development.

"3. To help increase awareness of the significance of amateur hockey and to give support thereby to the CAHA in arranging an agreement with professional hockey that would guarantee to the amateur body true independence of operation.

"4. To provide a focus for Canadian unity on the level of athletics that could bring together, for a truly national effort, all parts of this country.

"Father Bauer proposed that his team begin practices in the summer of 1963 and first represent Canada at the 1964 Olympic Games in Innsbruck, Austria. The CAHA's acceptance of his plan came just in time. The following winter, in Stockholm, the Trail Smoke-Eaters [sic], the last Allan Cup champions to represent Canada overseas, placed fourth in the world tournament, Canada's worst showing since the Winnipeg Falcons' victory in Antwerp in 1920."

The marriage of hockey and education was important to Father Bauer. A former Memorial Cup player himself, he had turned down an offer to turn professional with the Boston Bruins in 1946, "because when the world is in turmoil, the mind wants to know why. I wanted to get an education, not as an alternative means of getting the financial benefits I could get as a pro hockey player, but because it was important for me to see what one could learn about truth." He accepted religious orders and became a priest. Ever since Father Henry Carr led St. Michael's College to the Allan Cup in 1910, there has been a powerful sporting tradition among Canadian Basilians, the order to which Father Bauer belonged. So it was inevitable he would coach hockey and bring to it his conviction that it should be part of a broader education.

In the late 1950s, when Conn Smythe was telling national television audiences that too much schooling ruined hockey players (because it gave them what Smythe derided as a "jellyfish handshake"), Coach Bauer of the St. Michaels College Majors conducted fewer practices and carried six extra players so that every player had as much time as possible for his books. No St. Michael's player was required to dress for all 54 games of the regular OHA Junior A schedule. In 1961, St. Michael's won the Memorial Cup.

In analyzing Canada's fourth-place finish at the 1964 Innsbruck Winter Olympics, the National Team's first Games under the guidance of Father Bauer, Kidd and MacFarlane wrote: "Not quite the beginning Canadians had hoped for, but a victory for the National Team concept, nevertheless. The Nats had demonstrated to Canada what the rest of the world had known for some time; namely that competitive athletics and scholarship are compatible." Excuse me, gentlemen, Mr. Kidd? What did you just say? "The Nats had demonstrated to Canada what the rest of the world had known for some time; namely that competitive athletics and scholarship are compatible."

After reviewing Father Bauer's seven years at the helm, the pair opine: "The team's best record was in the classroom: 31 of 82 players received university degrees and 42 others, many of whom played for the team only a year, earned degree credits."

Best record, Mr. Anti-athletic scholarships? Most of the players on the National Team received an athletic scholarship, which interestingly were then verboten by Olympic eligibility rules. Ken Dryden had turned down a $75,000 offer from the Montreal Canadiens to sign with the National Team for $10,000 a year. The National Team lasted seven years, before Canada withdrew from Olympic competition to protest the professionalization of the Russian game. Kidd here takes another pot-shot at big business before stumbling again in his role of protectorate of an athletic award-free landscape.

"The beneficiary of Canada's withdrawal from international hockey was the NHL. Among the members of what Charles Hay called our thirty-first team were Ken Dryden, Danny O'Shea, Gerry Pinder, Billy MacMillan, Denis Dupere, Brian Glennie and Ab DeMarco, all of whom later went to the NHL. The loser, of course, was Canadian hockey. With the National Team gone, the NHL was free to continue skimming off the cream of Canada's young hockey players and sending them off to the United States to make money for the likes of Weston Adams. In a sense, it hurt all Canadian sport. Canada has been the National Team's point of reference. If it had survived, it might have encouraged other Canadian sportsmen, who all too frequently look to the United States for leadership, to find Canadian solutions to the Canadian problems.

"The death of the National Team was also the death of an idea: the marriage of sport and career. It is difficult to identify with the NHL player who devotes his life to hockey and nothing else. The members of the National Team taught school and studied law and played hockey as well. They could have shown us that sport can be a part of a normal life and responsibilities. So bang the drum slowly. The National Team was a noble experiment that got it in the neck."

And we won't go down that dreaded scholarship route? Is that bee's wax or bull's, er, poop, in my ears?

We encounter Kidd's flip, flop or fly philosophy next in a scathing retort to Iona Campagnolo's 1977 Green Paper. He and fellow Canadian Olympian Abby Hoffman co-authored a 47-page so-called brief which reads throughout like that tired old whine "you didn't ask me." Obviously attempting to sound thunderous, they demanded the whole Green Paper process be torn up, thrown away, re-done. Properly this time — read, as they'd see fit, beginning right with their introduction:

"If the publication of the Green Paper on Sport, "Towards a National Policy on Amateur Sport", was intended to encourage full public discussion of the many issues facing the Canadian sports community, the process has been a dismal failure. The Paper was made available to but a small fraction of those Canadians interested in sport who could be expected to contribute to such a discussion. The few public meetings were so hurried along, that even some of the specialized sports bodies which did receive the Paper were unable to prepare properly to give their response. The document itself was written to obscure rather than clarify major problems and differences of opinion; it provided no data by which one could evaluate existing programs, it made no attempt to define or redefine objectives, and it failed completely to spell out alternatives or options for action. If a genuine and responsible public discussion of sports policy is to occur, therefore, the whole process must be conducted all over again. This is the most important point to be made to the Green Paper: the process must be done again – properly."

Their brief was cruel, their belief in their credentials and views overbearing.

The Green Paper made no attempt to define or redefine objectives?

*The Federal Role in the Development of Amateur Sport*

*Only as recently as 1961, with the passing of the Fitness and Amateur Sport Act, did the federal government commit itself to an ongoing involvement in sport. Through most of the 60's, however, its role remained ill-defined. As a consequence, organizations were created and patterns of spending established which caused dissatisfaction among politicians, sports people and the permanent officials. However, during this period, one theme did emerge: "Do something about the sorry performance of most Canadians in international competitions.*

It failed completely to spell out alternatives or options for actions?

*Intercollegiate Sport*

*Canadian Universities possess all the resources necessary to produce good athletes. They have professional coaches, youth athletes, excellent facilities, dormitories and food services, support staff and the services of physiotherapists, doctors, sports scientists and librarians. Extensive intercollegiate programs are, however, expensive. At many universities, a shortage of funds has held back the development of intercollegiate sport. We propose that the universities be given assistance to subsidize the salaries of coaches contributing significantly to national team programs. In return for this financial assistance, we would ask that the universities commit themselves to excellence in their sports programs, coordinating them with those of the community, and expand training and competitive opportunities. We would also ask that coaching be year-round, that provision be made for testing athletes and there be a close liaison among the university physical education and coaching staffs, the national sport governing bodies and the Coaching Association of Canada.*

Yes, that part about our universities committing to excellence would have been an alternative, but according to our co-authors not a viable one as it elicited virtually zero attention from them. They blithely went about attacking everything else in sight even while making statements like "The success of U.S. teams in international competition is a result of a sophisticated college sports structure." You don't say? And though over half of their report was devoted to "Excellence as a Goal of National Sport Policy" the role of Canadian universities in their proposed national sport policy theoretically connected with excellence warranted nary a mention. Wonder why that was?

Their brief was so Messianic in its devotion to the platitude of "sport for all," they temporarily went insane, forgot they were once elite athletes on the world stage and dropped this turkey of a line, delivered in ultimatum style:

"We believe in the importance of providing opportunities for Canadians to reach world-class levels of performance, but if forced into a choice between "high performance" and "sport for all," our choice is clear: until Canada is fully democratized, until every citizen in every community has ready access to opportunities, not a penny of public funds should be spent on high performance sport."

One can only assume that upon publication the two authors had their personal cheques in the mail returning any and all financial support they'd received in their careers as Canadian internationals to any and all levels of any government or organizations or communities which had supported them. That would be the democratic thing to do, it would seem to me. Suddenly this brief turns into a shallow show of political grandstanding worthy only of an insidious career move.

Having survived this invective-laced facing-down, Campagnolo wasn't, let's say, as gentle on the universities in her subsequent White Paper in the spring of 1978. In February, she began laying the groundwork for attack. A special parliamentary committee report she tabled in the Commons said that government-financed hockey scholarships should be made available at Canadian universities and recommended that scholarships "should be an acceptable, if not laudable, avenue for student hockey players within the CIAU. A certain righteousness has arisen in Canadian universities which negate all the favourable aspects of the scholarships as a vehicle to encourage both academic and athletic pursuits. The federal government should make available increased funds for the purpose of providing financial assistance to deserving students players at Canadian educational institutions."

Finally, to the point in the White Paper: "Canadian universities can play a decisive part in the pursuit of athletic excellence in our country. They have the capacity to relate advanced research to sports situations where that research can be directly applied. They could be translators of research and applied experimentation, bridging the gap between theoretical concepts and the programs of sports organizations. In themselves, they constitute an important pool of athletic potential, one that might be further enhanced were the universities to accept the principle of athletic scholarships. The facilities, training expertise and systems of talent identification they possess are, in terms of the national sport effort, largely unexploited assets. It is to be hoped that in the years ahead our universities will find the means and the inclination to participate more fully in a national sports partnership." Campagnolo's vision and efforts never received the opportunity to bear fruit as her government was defeated several months later. She never received a reply from the CIAU. Subsequent federal appeals and efforts went similarly unrecognized.

But Kidd was at his hypocritical best in his 1996 offering, *The Struggle for Canadian Sport*, which won the Book Prize of the North American Society for Sport History in 1997. Mr. Equity trips up big-time over a certain issue known as "girls rules," which were in effect in the 1930s and 1940s in NCAA institutions that restricted the amount of physical exertion women could put forth. Imagine today having a basketball court divided into thirds, and being restricted to just one. That would be laughable. But what follows is lamentable and may just be the biggest catch in a two-faced Kidd's approach to self-promotion and came from reading this "long live the Marxists of this world" tome: "US advocates of 'girls rules' were largely successful in eliminating interscholastic and intercollegiate competition, thus depriving women in those institutions of the training and competition necessary to reach international levels of skills."

So what you're saying, if I read you right Mr. Order of Canada holder, is that even though we recognize a university career is a necessary part of an elite American athlete's development, it's not something Canadian universities can, in good conscience, support both scholastically and athletically through to the elite level here at home. You've got to be kidding me.

This "stance" is "what's wrong with the picture." Our universities earn A-Plus for their disconnect from the national sports delivery system. Actually, Kidd and his cohorts established and managed disconnection at two levels, primarily at the university sports level, but also by purposely playing a head game the result of which they never foresaw.

# Chapter Eight
## 100 Years To Get To This?

*" There's no question that it has coloured the history of the CIS, really the last 30 years, because it's coloured their marketing programs and it's coloured their image and it's coloured their media coverage, and most people 30 years ago predicted this is exactly what is going to happen. Even 30 years ago you had people saying if you don't get this settled and get it behind you, you will suffer in marketing, you will suffer in media coverage, you will have no end of problems. Come up with a system, get it in place and get on with life and it's been a major struggle to get a system that people can live with and get it in place and get on with life – for a variety of reasons, they haven't been able to do it. They're trying to, they're trying very hard. And certainly the tone, if you go on their website, certainly the tone of their release last week, because they've done their annual review of scholarships, is we've got a system in place and life is great and we're moving on. They're trying very hard to position themselves, yes, we have a scholarship program, we are progressive, we are student-centred, we're avoiding the problems of the States. We have vastly higher graduation rates, which is true. We have lots of great and good things. What they don't have is massive media coverage, massive corporate sponsorship and arguably massive competitive success. "* — Paul Carson, 2005

What a difference a century doesn't make. I'd say well done, but nobody would believe I was serious. This foisted upon us planetary distance between our universities and the big-picture sports system irks, particularly when focusing on excellence, for which one should not have to make the sign of the cross.

One, however, does need an extremely thorough examination of Canada's existing national sports policy to run across the word university. That being said, this is a great document. From its introduction:

"The Policy is unique in comparison to the many previous studies and policies on sport in Canada because it:

Represents the shared vision and goals of 14 governmental jurisdictions for sport for the period 2002 to 2012 and challenges the sport community to share in their achievement.

Reflects the involvement in the policy development process of stakeholders not previously included.

Emphasizes increased communication and collaboration amongst all the stakeholders.

Commits all governments to setting targets for enhanced participation and enhanced high performance sport in collaboration with their respective sport communities.

Commits governments to strengthening their regular and formal communication with their respective sports communities on issues affecting sport.

Will be implemented by complementary Action Plans developed by the government collectively and individually, bi-laterally and multi-laterally, and by the sport community."

By my count, that makes it really unique.

"THE BROAD DIRECTIONS:

The Vision of the Canadian Sport Policy is to have by 2012:

A dynamic and leading-edge sport environment that enables all Canadians to experience and enjoy involvement in sport to the extent of their abilities and interests and, for increasing numbers, to perform consistently and successfully at the highest competitive levels."

The Goals of the Canadian Sport Policy are:

ENHANCED PARTICIPATION

A significantly higher proportion of Canadians from all segments of society are involved in quality sport activities at all levels and in all forms of participation.

ENHANCED EXCELLENCE

The pool of talented athletes has expanded and Canadian athletes and teams are systematically achieving world-class results at the highest levels of international competition through fair and ethical means.

ENHANCED CAPACITY

The essential components of an ethically based, athlete/participant-centred development system are in place and are continually modernized and strengthened as required.

ENCHANCED INTERACTION

The components of the sport system are more connected and coordinated as a result of the committed collaboration and communication amongst the stakeholders."

If all that isn't the most admirable of stuff, then shiver me' timbers. But, as for sighting the dirty university word? Try twice in the

22-page report. First, in a listing of international games Canada participates in, via the scarcely heard of World University Games, and last, under the subhead Federal-Provincial/Territorial Governments, page 15: "Within each province and territory, municipal and community administrations and school authorities from the elementary to the university level support community-based participation through programming, building, maintenance, and upgrading of sport and recreation facilities, and hosting of sport events."

Under the subhead Sport Community, page 14, there is nary a mention. The word search process results in post-secondary just once, as well: Under the subhead Sport is focused on development: "Sport is best developed at the local level where participation is provided through sport organizations, school settings, post-secondary institutions, municipal recreation centres, and other community-based organizations." Colleges make a single appearance.

If separation of the Church of Canadian Society and the State of Sport Excellence was the goal of the nefarious CIS power block all along then it must be said job well done. And they get a bonus point. Besides making the entire CIS essentially irrelevant, Canada, which pays this power bloc's way, grades D on its youth health report card. The mind-numbing pollen so long disbursed by the anti-sports scholarship lobby, primarily based in Ontario, has raced on the breeze like a golden and green summer's dandelion seeds to both coasts, up to the Arctic Circle and eventually seeped into our minds. We need a coast-to-coast-to-postal-code HOHOHO good Q-Tipping to remove its spread.

Athens did have one positive effect. A year after those results-challenged Games, the federal government released its "Sport Excellence Strategy" in which it officially buried ex-Minister Owen's speechwriters' platitudes by pledging to make Canada a leading, repeat, leading, medal- and world championship-winning sports nation; medals and trophies the bottom line at long last. In the same breath it reinforced the fact Canadian university sport floats around in a sphere of its own.

The 3,000-word report describes the Federal Government's commitment to high performance sport in Canada. "The Excellence Strategy is designed to address a segment of the sport system that is focused primarily on podium results at Olympic and Paralympic Games; results that are essential in defining Canada as a leading sport nation."

Word search for university results? Nadda. Arghh. Word search for post-secondary and bingo, you finally hit pay-dirt, twice as a matter of fact, on page six of the 10, under the subhead Athlete Assistance, which opens the Appendix: "There will be a continued focus on providing direct financial support to athletes via the Athlete Assistance Program to support the living, training and post-secondary tuition (where applicable) costs of Canada's leading international level athletes and those with the greatest potential to achieve that level of performance. The monthly stipend provided to each athlete (for both senior and development levels) enhances their ability to train and compete, thereby contributing to raising Canada's international sport ranking. In addition, providing support for post-secondary education assists athletes to prepare for life after sport."

Not to be impertinent but, well, duh. It also still delivers bureaucratese like this in its final few paragraphs before the Appendix: "Progress on the Excellence Strategy's objectives in the areas of collaborative leadership, sustainable funding, and sport system performance will be monitored regularly and objectively through ongoing performance measurement and program evaluation activities. Athlete performance and sport system targets and indicators will augment those contained in the Umbrella Results-based Management and Accountability Framework for Canadian Heritage's three sport programs. Essential to the collection of these data will be collaborative relationships with provincial and territorial governments, National Sport Organizations and Multi-sport Service Organizations, including Canadian Sport Centres. The development, collection and dissemination of this performance information will be carried out in a collaborative and transparent manner, permitting the Government of Canada, stakeholder organizations, elected officials and the public to track and evaluate the achievement of sport excellence in Canada."

The train could be a long time coming.

Then again, then again, in the spring of 2006, a triumphant, oh-so-polite, and in-your face declaration that winning is important, the "Road to Excellence Business Plan For The Summer Olympic and Paralympic Sports" a 50,000-word opus, finally gives the word university its due: 24 times in fact, and post-secondary chips in with an additional one. Could this be the proverbial light at the end of the tunnel? Keep the faith, university sport fans, but don't hold your breath, it was published after all, as a proposed business plan, the tricky part being the tens of millions of dollars that needs to be sliced from that proverbial sports pie in the sky over the next decade for it to be implemented.

The report is authored by Dr. Roger Jackson and the late Mark Lowry, to whom we return. Speaking in the COC's Ottawa offices in early 2005, Lowry was coolly blunt when asked what the CIS needs to take its game to the next step. "I think it's totally a business model. The reality of the universities right now is that without exception every one of them is identifying how "poor" they are. There aren't the resources to have enough teachers, there's not enough capacity to build new facilities for schooling. It's an economic quagmire."

How did it all come to this is not the immediate question, because who wants to unravel a ball of twine that could roll all the way to Tierra del Fuego. The calls have been made before, Lowry and Jackson's Business Plan is but the latest to say our universities should play a bigger role in the sports delivery system.

Lowry says it's not an academics vs. jocks thing, however. "If you talk to the academic people, they're saying you are asking us to help an elite athlete to be the best in the world, what can I do? How can I do it? They are extraordinarily interested in that. There's a Canadian patriotism within, I think, most Canadian universities. If you ask a sports psyche person for a physiologist, or a bio-mechanist, or people who do research and testing, they'd love to work on this. This is exciting, this is fun — but who's going to pay for it? Who's going to give them the time off work from their normal jobs in terms of being a professor, who's going to be in a position where all the different ancillary costs around that kind of research and time commitment are going to be taken care of?" Canada, because it wants to, I venture.

"That's the model that's working at the University of Calgary, where we get those types of people, and it's happening as well with what Roger's [Skillings, CEO of PacificSport, Victoria] doing with the University of Victoria, and at the University of British Columbia and to a degree at the University of Montreal. We're getting those people because we are paying for them, it's that simple. There has to be a business model so the universities can say this is a good investment because we are getting these services purchased. That's part of what we've said as part of the COC's Own the Podium program. One of our biggest weaknesses is that we're not doing enough research and testing and development, and we don't have the expertise in the performance-enhancement teams around our athletes, which make up those people we're talking about.

"To get them, we need money to partner with universities to provide the support financially to free these people up as well as train a new generation of young people. But universities right now are not doing any of these kinds of efforts through the goodness of their heart. They simply have taken the position we can't afford to, so it's a business model strictly [to start]." Lowry pointedly noted it is unreasonable to expect a sudden focus on athletics from any university administration, "because we are, in their minds, no more important than culture, arts, all the different programs. But I think we know that and I think we'll make strides with that knowledge, that we will go forward. You will see in the five years, as we move to 2010, a significant increase in activity with partnerships of this type with Canadian universities. But we will not be asking, because I don't think it's reasonable for the CIS to be the brokers of that activity, for it to be responsible for setting that up. It's not just their business."

Not their business, I ponder, but surely a fresh, proactive partnership in the process wouldn't be too much too ask?

"I think they would be very supportive of the concept but I think the business model of what we need is really a sport-to-sport, program-to-program, scenario that really again would be more geared toward the high-performance side."

In the business plan, co-authors Jackson and Lowry proclaim that in the CIS "Only men's ice hockey realistically achieves the technical requirements required for excellence," then offer this analysis on "Strengthening the Canadian university (CIS) and college (CCAA) team sport programs: Canadian university and college sport programs often provide the highest quality of team sport competition in the country. Other than professional teams, they are usually the best in basketball, volleyball, field hockey, soccer, hockey, field hockey, swimming and other sports. They are the most immediate feeder system to national teams. Their coaches are often fully paid, and are often the national team coaches. Thus, there should be a review with the colleges and universities as to how their programs and coaches could be strengthened for national team purposes. Such a review should also consider how to extract more value from the American university and college systems."

Even when solutions, also known as scholarship programs, see NDU and SFU, read north instead of south of the border, are right under our noses, we don't always see them, or is that certain individuals don't want to.

In this perfect, politically-correct era, we can't go about damaging anybody's self-esteem, as over-burdened as the mental health care system is. Given that there must be government involvement in both education and sport, a pair of comments from SFU AD Wilf Wedmann bear repeating: "I came here four years ago and I realized what a gold mine I have here," and "Then I looked around and thought why isn't this part of the sports system?" while 2,500 Canadians are on sports scholarships in the U S of A.

Cue his crosstown "rival," UBC AD Bob Philip, who, as we know, is as pro-scholarship as they come. "It's a lot of work. We run that Millenium Breakfast that raises $600,000 but we don't just snap our fingers and do it. We work hard at it. We've raised a lot of money and other people can do that. But if you don't want to do it, don't tell me I can't. That's not how you get better. If universities in this country want to be part of the sport delivery system, then they've got to do their part. And part of what they [scholarships] do is to keep Canadians in Canada."

Asked if Canadian universities want to be part of the sport delivery system, Philip delivers a double-edged sword. "Well, I am not all that sure whether they want to be and I'm not at all sure whether the sport delivery system wants them involved. I think that what the sports delivery system wants is some of what the universities have to offer in terms of research, and the medical component, sports science, and so on. We tend to get caught up in basketball and hockey all the time, but for the lesser-known sports it really helps if the good athletes play at Canadian universities so they can bring them together for training camps and so on. When they're down in the NCAA, it's very, very difficult to get them back. If you don't think the [scholarship] model works, look at our most successful sport, swimming. We never lose a swimmer to the U.S. because we have a good scholarship program, good coaching, a good facility — and you can do that in Canada.

"What they do in the United States has happened over a long period of time. They give scholarships, they've now got it set up so that it's a multi-million dollar, gazillion dollar industry with TV and all that. Everybody has bought into it. There's no reason why in Canada you couldn't create a similar situation. Like, tell me, what is wrong with trying to keep a Canadian athlete in Canada!"

I don't know, I don't know, I don't know, so I ask Philip what his critics say? "I've never heard a response from the president of

Laurier, for example, who is always saying what he's saying, that makes sense to me. The argument in Ontario is that the schools are close together for example, and if we're out there trying to recruit, get money, we're stepping on each other's toes and all that. Well, they do that for students, that's the reality. You've also got 6-7 million people [in Ontario]. We don't have the same thing here.

"What's wrong with going out into the community and trying to get money? One of the arguments is, well the money that would go to athletics scholarships could go somewhere else. So now you're saying this is not only a low priority but it's not even a priority at all!"

Ludicrous, bizarre.

"It is discouraging," Philip responds with a major league touch of understatement. He relates how Canada West asked him to address a meeting on why UBC was moving some of its sports programs into the NAIA, and what that said about UBC's relationship with its governing body this side of the border. "My question to Canada West is: What's your commitment to taking it to the next level? We'll commit to Canada West if you're committed to taking it to the next level. Are we going to be dictated to forever by Ontario, or are we going to take it to the next level? If you're prepared to do that, we're committed."

Having yet to receive that commitment, Philip made national news because of the following column, written by Ed Willes of The Province in August 2006:

*Headline: UBC tantalizingly close to NCAA nod*

*Subhead: U.S. college giant considers accepting its first Canadian school*

*Ed Willes, The Province*

*It's all heady stuff if you've been one of the lonely few who's supported Canadian varsity athletics over the years, but let's stop for a moment and consider the full impact of UBC's application to the National Collegiate Athletic Association.*

*Try to envision the UBC men's basketball team and a starting five composed largely of Canadian kids playing North Carolina in March Madness. Or imagine the men's and women's hockey teams playing in the Frozen Four. Or the baseball team in the College World Series. Or the golf team teeing it up against Arizona and Arizona State.*

*Now, can you imagine the excitement that would generate in our town? Can you imagine the incredible energy it would create at the UBC campus? There was a time when it was all a wild fantasy, as likely to occur as man cloning a sheep.*

*But it's right there now, so close that the university can see it and taste it. "I think [the NCAA] is going to come back and say, 'The door will be open for a Canadian school or UBC,'" said UBC athletic director Bob Philip. "The question is, when will that opportunity occur? I think the NCAA is looking at this from a different angle now.*

*"Everything we've heard has been so far, so good. On the other hand, there are a lot of issues."*

*Oh, maybe a few minor details, but when you've come this far, you begin to believe any obstacle is insurmountable. Against all odds, the Point Grey school is awaiting a decision that would fundamentally alter its future even as it changes the course of Canadian university athletics. When this process started it seemed to have the same chance as Mel Gibson playing the lead in the remake of Exodus.*

*But now, as the NCAA contemplates UBC's application, the whole concept isn't quite as far-fetched. Philip and his colleagues have been told they'll hear from the governing body of U.S. college athletics by the end of the summer. Thus far, the message from NCAA headquarters has been encouraging.*

*Add it up and, virtually any day, an announcement could be made. But where will that lead the university and its athletic department? And how will they begin to answer the hundreds of questions raised by their acceptance into the NCAA?*

*As Philip mentioned, there are issues. And he doesn't lie. "Right now we're not sure what the process would be," Philip said. "We'd want to go slowly. If you're the first school [let into the NCAA from outside of the States], you want to do it right."*

*But the school didn't decide to apply to the NCAA on a whim. Marty Zlotnik, the chair of the Thunderbird Council and one of the athletic department's more significant boosters, has been working on this for the better part of a decade and he's had company. The money, reportedly, is manageable.*

*The university has also earmarked sports in which it believes it can be competitive right away.*

*They like their chances in volleyball, baseball, rowing, hockey and golf. They'll have to build a tennis program. Basketball will be the marquee attraction and football does present challenges.*

*But there are a few others. For starters, the NCAA has to amend its constitution to let in a non-American school. Then, they have to find a conference which will accept the interlopers. Then there's the whole question of Division II versus Division I.*

*Philip was originally focused on Division I and, while that's still the aim, he said Wednesday his school would accept Division II membership while they worked their way inside the velvet ropes. While in Division II, the school could also take part in two Division-I sports.*

*"We want to give our athletes the opportunity to compete at the highest level and that's the NCAA," Philip said. "It has its critics but no one has ever said the NCAA doesn't offer the best competition in collegiate sports."*

*No, there are more than a few uncertainties surrounding this story. But that's not one of them.*

Lest we forget, there were those in the OUA who not so long ago said if scholarships were ever offered to CIS athletes, the only option would be to withdraw from CIS competition, to take their play-dough ball and go home. Well, nefarious Ontario power bloc? Your bluff has been called, again — and thank you again David Atkinson.

Take this last bit of Philip's mind. "I was president of the CIS for two-and-a-half years. I'd just like to say that all I've ever tried to do is take university sports in this country to the next level, and [show] how I believed it should be done. My argument with people is that it's not about the method, there are many different ways you can do it. But if you are not prepared to say that's what you want to do … if everybody got in a room and said we want to take it to the next level, make it the best we can be, how could we do that, I'd even accept that. But people who just want to play in the sandbox, you know, I have no time for that."

Elite recreation, what a concept, thank you OUA.

University of Winnipeg AD Bill Wedlake, CIS elegibility chairman, chimes in on the OUA's fears of resistance to AFAs: "I think it should be based on facts, not fears. It should be based on information, not emotion. I don't know what the fear is, that they can't compete?"

Fear of recruiting?

"Recruiting is recruiting. But they always get out-recruited. I recruited in Ontario and got a lot of great kids. That's where I see the irony, they're the ones losing the most kids to the States."

Our best young athletes go south as we bicker up north.

"It's a very divisive issue in Canada right now and it's basically an East against West issue. There's a whole lot of unhappiness, I'll tell you and there certainly is a wall that's being developed on the Ontario-Manitoba border because the Canada West schools are very solid."

Across Canada's newest border, Nancy Greene's one-time national team barrier, just what is the OUA's problem, Mr. Wedlake? "My opinion? They don't have the money. They have a lot of philosophical problems."

The abuses? "The abuses. They don't want to have kids that are academically not doing well playing sport, fair enough, nobody wants that."

Is this an example of academia looking down its nose at sports? "Oh, of course it is."

If the OUA says they don't have the money, then they are holding back the rest of the country for paternal, selfish reasons. Can I say that? "I would say that. The programs in Canada West are funded very well by the university. We still have to raise the money but the rest of the program is covered by the university — our salaries, our travel expense, our equipment expenses, everything, the building. But in many Ontario universities, they're fundraising to operate the program. That's why they don't have the money. They haven't got the ability to fundraise for scholarships because they are fundraising to operate. We don't have to fundraise to operate and we can put all our energies into fundraising for scholarships."

Philosophical differences from university presidents or ADs?

"Both. There are some that are sure, OK, I understand, but there are some that I think are just out of touch."

ADs or presidents? "Both."

In tune with Philip's elite tier aspirations, but walking an adjacent path through the forest, Wedlake is completely unapologetic when stating: "Our approach here is we do basketball, we do volleyball, we don't do anything else," and judging by the championships banners hanging from the rafters, "We do it as well as anybody in the country. The difference is it is called specialization. As opposed to, how many times do I get phone calls: Are you opening a curling team, are you going to have a golf team, are you going to have a women's hockey team, are you going to have a baseball team, are you going to have a football team … no," the gregarious Wedlake says to the accompaniment of his own laughter.

"And do you know why? Because we haven't got the money and we want to win, not just be mediocre and offer a whole bunch of stuff. You look at some of the universities, I think Queen's has got 35 teams, 35 programs!" The University of Toronto "prides" itself on providing even more. "That's why they never win. But nobody wants to make a decision."

The discussion turns to the new outdoor stadium project in Toronto which played dodo during pit stops at U of T and York.

"It's somewhat typical of the Ontario situation, maybe mass mediocrity is their goal, maybe that's their motto and that doesn't wash. This is all about excellence. Not cheating and not win at all costs, but excellence. That is why the kids that are coming out of this system, they come out of here with a degree and they've participated [athletically] for five years, they are gobbled up by employers. They are gobbled up."

In 2004, the CIS agreed to shelve debate on the scholarship front for two years in order for "the organization to dedicate more time and attention to other issues beyond athletic awards," CEO Marg McGregor said at the time. "It's time for us to be focusing on issues of marketing and promotion and advocacy, and raising the profile of university sports."

OK, but then this is what you get. In the 2006 Pre-AGM Report, a discussion on bias is 2,400 words long. In the subsequent AGM Report, there are 9,000 mind-numbingly words of eligibility issues of interest to participants and navel-gazers only. Reporting on AFAs, there are 3,000 words on much ado about nothing, merely the technical management of the current near-nonexistent system.

There is a hole in the middle of the CIS doughnut, and it knows it but because of a face issue versus a belief issue the Canadian university sports system remains running on much less than a full tank of gas.

During this legislated interim of see no evil, hear no evil, speak no evil, enter the: Canadian Interuniversity Sport Strategic Plan 2005-2009.

*CIS Mission:*

*To enrich the educational experience of the athlete through a national sport program that fosters excellence.*

*Vision:*

*CIS is the destination of choice for Canadian student-athletes to pursue excellence in academics and athletics. CIS is recognized as one of the influential leaders in sport in Canada.*

*Values:*

*1. Quality educational and athletic experience.*

*2. Unity of purpose, respect for autonomy.*

*3. Integrity and fair play.*

*4. Trust and mutual respect.*

*5. Equity and equality.*

*Strategic Directions:*

*Sport Development Objectives*

*Work with universities and NSO partners to develop and deliver quality competitions and programs, such that Canada is the destination of choice for student-athletes and coaches.*

*Contribute to the Canadian sport system and the achievement of the vision of the Canadian Sport Policy.*

*Develop and implement programs and activities that assist in developing coaches and recognizing their valuable contribution to student-athletes, CIS, and the Canadian sport system.*

*Marketing / Branding / Communication Objectives*

*Generate television coverage and financial resources to sustain and grow the operations of Canadian Interuniversity Sport.*

*Promote and celebrate the values and achievements of student-athletes and university sport heroes.*

*Raise the profile of CIS such that it is recognized as a destination of choice for student-athletes.*

*Tell the story of the impact and contribution of university sport to the sport community and the university community.*

*Undertake initiatives to get more fans in the stands.*

*Governance and Operations Objectives*

*Ensure policy making and operations are informed by accurate and up to date research, and contribute to CIS becoming a destination of choice.*

*Review and improve upon business processes to ensure that CIS operates in an efficient and effective manner consistent with its values.*

*Create a shift in culture so that CIS can more efficiently and effectively deliver on its strategic plan, and can become a destination of choice.*

*Review all aspects of the organization's spending to see where savings can be derived.*

*Develop and strengthen strategic partnerships with key organizations to advance CIS objectives.*

Fair enough, CIS, go to it. But this is one organization that has its work cut out for it and its hands tied ass-backwards. As regards its Mission statement, fostering excellence is a far cry from perpetrating perpetual mediocrity; as regards its Vision statement, it should surely be the pursuit of athletics and academics, not the other way around. The latter is the university president's responsibility, especially given a number of them disdain the top level of breaking sweat. The student-athletes are your responsibility, the young charges whose development you are supposed to be assisting. As for the CIS being recognized as one of the influential leaders in sport in Canada? You be the judge.

In search of its big picture, back to perusing simultaneously the drippings from the 2006 pre- and post-AGM reports. Under Communications, "In a promising signal, the Globe and Mail created an "On Campus" weekly column. This was a major statement by a national media outlet." A weekly column, in the biggest city in the country is a major statement? The word grasping comes to mind.

Under CIS as a Destination of Choice: "Over 750 responses were received to the CIS survey conducted in March/April relating to Keeping Talented Student-Athletes in Canada. The survey results will be used in the design of resources and tools to help high school/CEGEP aged athletes make informed decisions about where to pursue their university academics and athletics. The costs of education and the financial support available in Canada was identified as the top factor in retaining talent." Make informed decisions? Maybe if you hypnotize them first. And there they go backwards again, their university academics and athletics. Costs and the pool of money is the top factor in retaining talent? Ya think? Can you say scholarships without grimacing and excreting? Apparently not, and the buffoonery continues.

"For the first time ever, CIS collected data on graduation rates. While the final results have not been released, preliminary responses illustrate that student-athletes are graduating faster than their non-athletic peers and with higher marks. Something to be very proud of!"

Ya don't say.

"In December 2005, CIS expressed concerns that CB [Canada Basketball] had not been doing enough in the past to promote CIS and celebrate student-athletes who chose to stay in Canada." Such gall. What do you mean, *chose*? Ah, yes, but then please do tell, why have you put Canadian high school seniors in that position in the first place?

"CIS partnered with Swimming Canada to launch "Canada First", a joint initiative to retain top swimmers in Canada. SC and CIS plan to increase awareness of the advantages of pursuing athletics and university academics in Canada. Research was done to poll swimmers on what factors influenced their choice of universities. Next steps are being developed with Swimming Canada. The plan is to translate learnings from this pilot to other CIS sports over time."

A flash of light at the end of the tunnel, it must be admitted. They did say top and did get the athletics academics sequence right. Another flash of that light: "The implementation of "destination of choice" projects with Swimming Canada and other NSOs is an important priority for us."

Just as we're starting to sound connected, a nasty short-circuit occurs. While most people watch a lot of big-screen television these days the stats show you nearly need an electron microscope to catch a glimpse of CIS action. In the 2005-2006 CIS season, there were 77 hours of live coverage, spread over four networks, with a total audience of 2.4 millions viewer, the CIS fronting a big part of the costs. What that says about the entire Canadian sports system, given that the CIS is a self-declared leader of such, should not be considered by the faint of heart.

Under Branding: "In December of this past year, the board and Marketing Committee coordinated a branding session hosted by Jim Albanese, a branding guru of Albanese Branding and Communications. It was a very eye-opening event and allowed many the opportunity to receive feedback on our brand, in a very constructive and open manner. Some key elements we looked at from a CIS perspective was the aspect of "Brand Personality", which determine the brand expression, the feel and the tone – something we need to work on. We also looked at the CIS brand, what it needed, what it lacked. It is the mandate of the Marketing Committee to recommend next steps and create a plan of action for further integration of the CIS brand within the organization as a whole." There is no brand. What we're talking about here is something we're really not actually talking about, remember, mum's the word.

This item brings Wilf Wedmann to mind: "Upwards of $200 million was invested by members in facility development and upgrades."

This one brings dusty archives to mind. "27 Develop materials to show the contribution that athletics makes to universities. Not done yet." It must be quite some task. "28 Influence public policy through Sport Matters involvement and other activities. Participated in meetings and advocacy activities related to the federal election, the speech from the throne and the budget." Get outta here.

At the 2006 CIS AGM, scholarship eligibility and regulations were the last and biggest two issues on the agenda, even as they were officially observing zipped lips on amount. They should be concerned. Myopically, the report also trumpeted the OUA's one-month-old decision to, for the first time in 100 years, allow financial assistance based on an athletic component to a first-year student, saying the move will "deliver a clearer message about the availability of financial support in Canada." When you wish upon a star, as this news did, it makes no ripples in the national consciousness, not even a U-turn after a century of stagnation. That's today's CIS.

The value of university sport to Canadian society has been smeared by an extremely influential small circle for far too long. That our universities did this to themselves is anti-consolation matter, because as a whole they can never be held accountable. Its most polluting effect was to raise a country suffering from that dreaded general malaise of wanting it for free when it comes to funding for sport – except from grown-up John and Joan and their kids paying through the teeth for certain NHL, MLB and NBA tickets. We're so far behind the ball that if Canadian universities were allowed to grant AFAs as they saw fit, by far the vast majority couldn't fund the move to a full-ride approach. If the gates were opened, it would result in one of the CIS's biggest fears and the thrust of Bob Philip's argument: a two-tiered system. That, to the fear-mongers, would of course lead to a multi-tiered system which belies the every-one-is-equal-and-totally-deserving argument that's so popular these days.

Witness: Quebec is in the midst of a failing attempt to eradicate grading students from its elementary curriculum with 80% of its teachers with at least 10 years experience in the classroom playing Caesar and going thumbs down. The fact we won't grade people smacks suspiciously of a failed and decried political ism once in vogue last century. Any further attempt to suppress the pursuit of excellence of any kind ought to be regarded as a crime against justice.

The average age of an Olympian in Athens was 27. Being 19th in the world begins here at home. The hole in the CIS is the lack of financial support for our student-athletes. The hole in the Canadian elite sports delivery system is the CIS itself.

From the end of the last appendix in the Business Plan for Sports Excellence:

In 2002, the Ethics Strategy, a partnership between governments and the sport sector, was adopted by all 14 federal, provincial and territorial governments. It has since become known as the True Sport Strategy. Among other things, the Strategy is founded on the belief that no one owns sport. It is a public trust which Canadians view as second only to the family in its role of transferring values to young people, and as an important part of our culture. The pursuit of athletic excellence is an expression of our collective pursuit of human excellence.

Sport loses its way when it artificially distinguishes between sport for all and sporting excellence. As so clearly argued fifteen years ago in the Dubin Report, the pursuit of excellence (winning) without an ethical foundation does not work. But we also know that ethical sport devoid of the pursuit of excellence does not work either. Winning is a measure of our sporting excellence. Ethical conduct is also a measure of our sporting excellence. Indeed, it is the combination of the two that produces human excellence; it is the combination of the two that we call True Sport.

Canadians know what it is to win and how to do it well. There is a uniquely Canadian kind of sport that is rooted in our values of inclusion, fairness, respect and excellence – where Canadians win when we experience the joy of community sport and physical activity, where we win when sport contributes to the physical and moral development of youth, and where we win when we excel in international arenas.

Canada is a sophisticated enough society to be able to participate on the world stage, and excel. Doing so in sport reminds us of our ability to do these sorts of things in other areas. It reminds us of who we are as we display our national values, our character, to the rest of the world.

Is it important that we should have world-class athletes? Yes, in the same way that it is important that we should have world-class doctors, educators, artists and public leaders.

We have education systems within which we include the pursuit of post-graduate studies and world-class research. Indeed, education can also be seen as a public trust, there for the good of all Canadians, within which we can excel.

We have health care systems within which we include the pursuit of optimal health, medical discoveries and world-class *practitioners. Indeed, universal health care is a public trust, there for the well-being of all Canadians within which medical excellence is pursued.*

*The same applies to sport. We have a sport system within which we include the ambition to do well. As world-class researchers are part of our education system, and as highly-trained medical specialists are part of our health system, high-performance athletes are part of our sport system. True Sport is for all Canadians, including those who wear medals of excellence from sport competitions, and those who participate simply for the joy of it. Let us do well, and let us do it well.*

*Victor Lachance*

Mr. Lachance, the CEO of the Sport Matters group, did not use the word university once. When you break down disconnect into syllables, the middle one is what's been pulled on us.

# Chapter Nine
## It's Elementary

8 a.m., Canada Day, Vancouver Island, 2005: our nation was 138 years old and 350 days removed from the medal drought in Athens.

It's also a pleasant if less than perfect morning at the Legislature Building in Victoria, one of seven sites across the country staging a charity run to promote unity and health sponsored by the Hudson's Bay Company, one of the first major Canadian companies to step to the fore in sponsorship of Vancouver's 2010 Winter Games. One of the recipients of share the wealth is The Mustard Seed Food Bank, the necessity of which is pan-Canadian and which in one of the richest countries in the world either amply or merely demonstrates the scope of modern society: there will always be the less fortunate among us.

Another recipient is PacificSport-Victoria, which was home sweet home to a sixth of those Canadian Olympians those 350 days ago.

I walked around the morning's festivities once again asking myself, "What's wrong with this picture?" Now our best athletes are charity cases? Sport, the healthy marriage of exercise and play, is deadly serious, despite what others may have you think. Just because they make you think it, though, doesn't mean you have to believe it.

The A-Plus in Disconnect is awarded to those who thunder the absolute importance of academics and undermine the significance of sport because they manage to link sport to another Canadian institution, Trivial Pursuit, thus making the term "serious sport" a serious oxymoron. Because of this, Canada has yet to embrace the totality of sport's offerings. That's the crime. Book 'em, Danno. Considering it's been going on for 100 years, book 'em in a comfy jail, Danno, and only occasionally use the key. Let them out for a new statutory National Sports Day, let's say the third Monday in February. Put their power in actual true believers' hands.

One of the biggest believers, and there are many in Canada, is George Heller. A PacSport employee provided this bio of the man: "George, President and CEO of HBC, is a huge corporate fan and supporter of performance athletes. He was CEO of the 1994 Victoria Commonwealth Games, now pushing the federal government for better support of the Melbourne Commonwealth Games and is pushing the Canadian government, VANOC, and Corporate Canada to support PacificSport and the PSI [PacificSport Institute, Camosun College] ... plus he's the main force behind HBC's $100 million 2010 Olympic sponsorship. We are pleased that he is an advocate for PacificSport."

So, you can be sure, is Roger Skillings, President and CEO of charity case PacificSport, which produced all those Canadian Olympians for the Athens Games and in the run-up aired disturbing TV ads claiming some Canadian Olympians live below the poverty line. So we will let him have his platform.

"The PacificSport Institute is really about combining education, health, wellness, sport, to all different levels of athletes. It's a really, truly innovative design. The best way to think about it is you can have a Simon Whitfield in the middle of a picture, and on the left hand side of Simon is a college student, and on the left hand side of that is a six-year-old because there will be protocols for elementary schools that will be developed through the sport education side. And on the other side of Simon will be a Masters athlete, people that still think they can, somebody like me who wants to be a weekend warrior, and on the right side of that it will be seniors and there's no reason why seniors shouldn't have protocols for them. This institute is really going to lead the way in terms of providing programs for our high-performance athlete, through sports science and sports medicine and also for all various ages of individuals, right across the spectrum," says Skillings.

Anyone want to argue the points?

"The culture in Canada often, outside of hockey, is not really trying to pursue excellence. I think a lot of people want to have a sort of mentality that we're all equal, we should all be given the same type of resources, and really what we need to do in high-performance sport is have centralized athletes, centralized situations. We need to have a lot of resources going to them if they are going to take on the world, everything from sports science, sports medicine, sport technology, the best coaches in the world, the training opportunities, facilities, access to the facilities at a subsidized rate, and if we don't have that, then we're in trouble.

"If we're going to be a country that doesn't aspire to produce the best doctors, the best lawyers, or the best teachers, or the best artists and sculptors and painters, and I think also athletes, then we're not going to become the country that we can become," said Skillings shortly after the Athens Games. "This whole sort of sense that we shouldn't really be trying to be the best in the world in the 100 meters dash, or we shouldn't be the best in the world at snow-jumping, I just can't ascribe to that type of thinking. I think it diminishes what we are, and diminishes what we can be and I think it's very sad," suggesting we need a mechanism to make everybody realize that excellence is something that in itself we should be striving for.

"One of the things we do need to realize, though, is that Canada is a winter sports nation. And when you think about Canada, our culture is a hockey culture, we are a hockey nation, so every community in the country has its hockey rink and in fairness, our best athletes go to hockey because its part of our cultural identity. Given that, there's a recognition that obviously we can be number one in the world at 2010 in a winter sports environment, we can, and I think John Furlong and VANOC are doing everything they can, through Own the Podium and other programs, to achieve that. We don't want to forget that some Olympic sports, the mass participation sports, basketball, volleyball, soccer, field hockey, are tremendously important for the health and well-being of our kids. And adults. There are more and more of our generation that are physically active. I'm 55 years old and I don't want to stop being physically active."

Skillings is a tennis player, but just look at the growth numbers of adult recreational hockey participants in the past 20 years.

"Yes! All that's really good. Dreams may start at 10 but they don't stop at 60, you can still become better and do things wiser.

"In the world today, the bottom line of high-performance athletics, for me, is what it does to the next generation of kids, to get them to aspire to physical literacy, physical activity and understanding that physicality. You may be playing a game of squash today because you enjoy it, but what it does to you and your body and your mind is substantive and it reduces health care costs down the road and look at the generation of kids now with obesity and Type 2 diabetes."

Yes look, it's not a pretty sight, as I remind him of one of his favourite people, Iona Campagnolo, and her belief that it is a personal responsibility of all Canadian citizens to not use, preferably need, the health care system for the longest portions of their lives.

"Absolutely it should be a personal responsibility, and one of the aspects of that is kids have to have physical literacy trained into them, because physical things are important — rather than just sitting here with my computer game or watching TV and going to the fast food place, and the mall, if we're on exactly the same page. For me, the pursuit of excellence is helpful to everybody. I think if you look anew at the podium, the podium is not athletes on the podium but concepts. On one side of the podium you've got participation, all the recreation, and the investment in recreation, which I think is phenomenal.

"If you think that 30 years ago people didn't believe in investment in recreation, they thought, geez, there's money being taken away from police and fire, now everybody agrees in the investment in recreation services that is going on. So the participation base is pretty solid, thank you. We're spending billions in this country if you think of all the recreation departments and so on. And on the other side [of the podium] you've got performance athletes, and some people are saying why fund them. What I'm saying is they are a part of this ingredient, if they are both working together."

Hold on there, Roger, that sounds suspiciously like a leap in faith, but then again that's what concepts usually start out as. But this is his soapbox, and he makes his point. "On top of the podium is health care, is reduced health care costs."

We'll get to the arguers of that point shortly, but Skillings quickly plays devil's advocate and then proposes yet another leap in faith. "You can't say all the money we have put into recreation has increased the physical activity of kids, we know it hasn't. So, let's put another blend in that, let's spend a little bit more money," meaning a lot, "maybe spend $150-$180 million on Sport Canada, what's that, one percent of health care? It's nothing, it's not even on the radar screen." The radar screen of disconnect of course. "One percent of the health budget is $180 million. The federal government, in its wisdom, is now giving sport — Sport Canada — $140 million. So we're still not one per cent of the health budget. And sport, in many ways, can be viewed as preventative medicine, the role model, the inspiration it gives to kids. Now it's more important than ever with what's happening with kids. Kids are now spending their time in front of computers, in front of Game Boys. We know that diabetes rates are getting higher, we know that obesity rates are getting higher."

One thing does tend to lead to another, but it is difficult to convince some it can work in reverse, witness the crowd that still disputes the value of elite performances being performed in front of our youth as an inspirational tool of major significance. Still, there are those that do fight the good fight, and Skillings bridges the spectrum.

It's all about "getting both sides of this equation working, physical activity/physical literacy for the young ones, and performance athletes. I use the term performance advisedly, I don't like the word elite, because of what that conjures up, but they are elite. Allison Sydor was once just a 10-year-old kid who was on a bike."

They are elite, but they are not elitists?

"That's exactly right, that's why I like the term performance athletes because they are performing, and you can perform as an athlete in elementary school, in junior high, in high school, in colleges, universities, in national championships, internationally, world championships, Olympic Games, and I just think, we need everything we can do so that both kids become more active and seniors can become more active and I think performance athletes, their shine goes in both directions. I'm sort of a little bit passionate about it. I hope I'm not sounding like a wacko! But I really, really believe in that."

Don't go changing, you're lots of people's kind of wacko, in fact their conscience, we just need to convert that into consciousness. Putting beliefs into action is often the tricky part; PacificSport is working hard at it and quelle surprise, producing.

Six months later, I share a quick conversation with Skillings again, this time putting the high beams on the university scene. He starts right in.

"One of the things that I think is really extremely important is to determine precisely how universities fit into the high-performance development path. Because all these facilities, these coaches, these athletes, sports science, they're all there, so we have to really tap into them in a more creative and innovative way."

Why the current disconnect?

"Well, I think universities have been founded on the premise that academic achievement and academic/scholastic research is what university is all about and my view of the world is that we should be supporting our best athletes, our best scholars, our best painters, our best sculptors, our best writers. If we don't have the pursuit of excellence in all fields, then we're not going to have the society we can have. So, athletic scholarships to me? It's one of those areas, we just need them, it's a benefit to the system. [The Olympics are] not just once every four years, or every two years for two weeks.

"We have to make sure these athletes are supported. Athletic scholarships is something," he says meaning money, "that would be going to keeping a greater number of athletes in our country. Kids can see them, and kids can see great sport. Right now we're losing too many of them."

What they are seeing is U.S. stars in their eyes, witness the burgeoning number of high school sports academies across the country, home to many Canadian youth with no ambition of entering a Canadian university.

"We're losing them. We're in a situation where when you get to be 18, 19 years old and you want to pursue academics and athletics, in order to do that you've got to have some resources. The United States offers scholarships and we don't. There is a real disconnect with that."

Talk to a sports scientist about it, suggested Skillings, and as it happens, right down the PacSport hallway from his office is that of Dr. Gord Sleivert, PacSport's resident, officially the Director, Sport Science and Medicine.

"I guess, number one, financial support of athletes so that they can train and not have to spend so much time trying to find their next meal, or pay for their accommodation, etc., is something that I'm sure you are finding that has relatively universal support. I think the thing that people are debating, to some extent, is well, what level of financial support is required," says Sleivert.

The good doctor literally has a well-rounded background for comment on such matters, having spent seven years in the development of high-performance sport in New Zealand, much of that time establishing three national sports academies. Back home, and when it's his turn on today's soapbox:

"As you know, the amount of money from the federal government has gone up, the Athletes Assistance Program, but we are still not funding our athletes very adequately, so by and large, I would suggest yeah, that a scholarship program is a phenomenal idea — to allow more athletes to become full-time athletes. The fact we have very many athletes that are training part-time, not full-time, is often I think reflected in how those athletes actually compete, their results." How they perform after the starting gun goes off? "Yeah, exactly, and sometimes athletes aren't willing to train fulltime, they don't want to, that's another issue. The level of commitment to be an elite athlete is something that I think is hugely misunderstood by the public — and a lot of athletes don't even realize what it takes. So we have to create an environment where they become fully committed to what I guess we might call the lofty goal of being the best they can be.

"So myself, being a sport scientist, of course I come into this with some baggage," which is nothing too new to any of us. "We all have our own bags, and biases, and so we can talk about sport science support from a variety of perspectives. In addition, one of the big things in terms of Own The Podium, it's really looking at how we support our athletes and coaches? Can we give them more expertise in areas like sport physiology, sport nutrition, sport psychology, biomechanics, video analysis, technology? That's a big investment and some places," read Down Under, have used scholarships to provide athletes with access to those services.

"When we talk about full-time commitment, what does it take to be the best? It's more than a full-time job. So, defining scholarship, loosely, may be necessary, in some cases, at some phases of an athlete's career. I mean really, if you think about, it's not really a scholarship in the strictest sense, it's providing them with support. Do you understand what I mean by that?" as I begin to come around.

"See, it's not necessarily linked to academics, necessarily," as I grasp that it is possible to define scholarship in terms of total support of athletics, a right just as significant as academic, and even given that the percentage of those who get to step up on an athletic podium is extremely small, a right just as essential to our aspiring such youth.

Sleivert and his wife both attended UVic on athletic scholarships, so small to be of next to no importance, read true assistance.

"It was enough to cover most of our tuition at that point, but that was it, right? So really, what did it achieve? You either have to get a student loan or you have parents that help you, or you work part-time, or full-time. I think it really did very little to allow athletes to be athletes and to focus on sport and school."

More of a gesture?

"Yeah, and by and large, I don't think it has changed that much. I think Canada has lacked vision and leadership, by and large," he laughs when I ask if he could please be a bit more blunt.

"It's true, we have a very fractionated system. People use geography as an excuse, but I don't buy it."

Call me a scoundrel or a scalawag but it was very easy to coax words like disconnect and fractionated from PacSport. They're smack dab in the middle of the top of it.

"Look at, for example, our Canadian sports center network, we are one of eight centers," says Sleivert as he ticks them off coast to coast. "Well it's not a true network, these are independent centres that receive some funding from Sport Canada — except Victoria doesn't receive any because we have a legacy fund left over from the Commonwealth Games. Mind you, Calgary has one left over from the Olympics, and Winnipeg has one from the Pan-Am Games, but for whatever reason, I'm hoping that will change."

Say again, PacSport receives no funding from Sport Canada?

"The only one of all the centres that doesn't get any federal support, that may change this year," as I mistakenly at the time refer to that as another subject entirely. "We've applied, I'm hoping."

Another issue. "Now you have eight centres that are sort of the applied service wing of sport that are not centrally coordinated, and so you know what Calgary does and Victoria and Montreal, could be completely disjointed. Sport Canada, I guess is the governing body, from a national perspective. They obviously have to be accountable for the funding they deliver and the centres are accountable, but that doesn't mean there's coordinated leadership of the centres, it means they have separate contracts with each of the centres to do what it is that they do."

Say again, Sport Canada doesn't provide centralized leadership?

"That's what I'm getting at."

Ignore my shaking head, carry on.

"The Canadian Olympic Committee is another organization that until now has not been involved in developing athletes, they've been involved in running Games, and making sure that athletes are taken care of," getting them to and fro, "yes, exactly, and they've done a great job of that. Their mandate is changing and now they are seeing themselves playing more of a role in developing performance. You now have the Vancouver Olympic Games, and so you have VANOC and Own The Podium, and VANOC has, in a sense, revolutionized how they [COC] see their role in terms of taking a certain percentage of their revenues and putting that into sport development and now funding Own The Podium, which is having to work with Sport Canada and the Canadian Olympic Committee, it has been a great thing, because what's it's actually doing is forcing these different bodies to work together.

"What they have not yet done is formed a central leadership team that actually has power and can coordinate things across the country. Then you also have to recognize that not only do you have all these national sporting organizations, you have the CIS system and you have the college system," and does the word disconnect ring again, "yeah, where's the connection? But there is a disconnect, there is no doubt about it, and you think about the number of varsity athletes that we have, and the age gap that they're in and they're knocking on the door often, so a scholarship program you know is a really viable way of supporting those athletes — and of preventing the talent drain south to the U.S., keeping them in Canada. But there is a disconnect.

"I worked as a professor at universities for 10 years, and I made the case that it is very difficult for us to partner with the universities because if we are hiring experts that work in universities they're spending most of their time teaching, doing research and academic type work. What time can they actually spend doing applied work with sport? Now, the flip side of the argument is that universities are public institutions that are funded by public money and we should be accessing the expertise and the resources that are there. It is a very difficult argument to counter, but I strongly believe that we need people who are working full-time in sport, not fractionated with the university. Maybe [today] there are some exceptions to that."

Through coaching, purely coaching, of varsity and outside elites?

"That may work better, because they are focused on coaching whereas as an academic I need to publish, I have to run my grad students, I have to run my undergraduate course. Then I would do a little bit of work on the side, work with sport, but it was on the side, in my spare time, maybe a contract or two, you know? You're not making much money, you don't have much time, so you don't put your heart and soul into it. You can't. So it's separate from the scholarship issue.

"But you talked about a leadership role and how we use our institutions and when you think about scholarships from a university perspective, we want university athletes to access the kind of services our athletes here access, well, our universities aren't providing it, they aren't," to be fair, they never set out to do it. "They didn't and it's not in their mandate either," it could be, "it could be," depending on who has the hammer. "I guess that's true," as I end an interview with a most learned one and retreat back into my own little dream world.

Across town in the offices of The B.C. Games later that day, President Kelly Mann shifts our gears, slightly. "I see a fundamental shift in the minds of politicians about the recognition of equating Kyle

Shewfelt to more participation in six- and seven-year-old kids, who develop a healthy lifestyle, and who move on to live healthy and productive adults."

Really, they've finally cottoned on?

"I think the light has finally come on. I was in a conference in Alberta about four years ago in Red Deer and I was pretty much a new CEO, and I asked their sports minister, a man who was in his sixties, a farmer as I understood later on, and I said Mr. Minister, and I asked that very question, why haven't politicians gained that recognition that an investment in sport and recreation is an investment, in a pro-active way, into the health care system? 'Well, let me tell you, my friend from B.C.,' he said, 'a little thing called Participaction,' and he went on to talk about Participaction, and how people who got involved in sport because of Participaction meant more knee replacements and more hip replacements and more broken ankles because they were out exercising.

"And it's just like ..." as my incredulousness boils over, I've heard rumours of this before, but you've got to be kidding me. "Honestly. Honestly. I was sitting next to one of the other MLAs from Alberta, and of course I'm with my other friends at the table who are all in sport and recreation and they're just gasping themselves and the MLAs are apologizing. I said look, that's what he believes, the problem is that the people who work for him have not told him the truth. Yes, somebody might have needed a knee replaced but the thousand other people who aren't in for cardiovascular surgery more than make up for that."

Given the near-miraculous advances science is delivering us, our ability to "do" more about our health, once afflicted with an illness or disease, is only going to happen, that much should be already obvious. It seems we could spend our entire GDP on the health care system, the stats of how unhealthy we are and how much more we need to spend get gloomier by the day. Iona Campagnolo says, repeat after me, it's every citizen's duty to stay off the health care plan, and if that doesn't read like play plus exercise = sports to me than I'm a monkey's uncle.

If it's too late for most of us, which recent studies such as the one that says even a few pounds of belly fat is as or more dangerous than current obesity alarmists indicate is so, we need an about-face in our national psyche so as to not similarly afflict our apparently sports-disaffected youth. As for the argument that the Americans are the most obese people on the earth and the most sports oriented, they are also the richest society ever on the face of the earth and massive consumers, as are we. The Canadian university establishment fear-mongers rejected sports scholarships because of the American failures, mostly minor until self-magnified a million-fold for argument purposes, blissfully dismissing all its successes.

Quite frankly, who cares what the Americans do? If they want to adopt a national mentality that says sports is as much fun as eating and watching other people play, let them. Sport is often sublime entertainment, the original reality TV. It also is so much more than that, which must become the accepted norm north of the 49th. As an added bonus, we will throw in a few dozen more medals every Games and close the gap with the most successful sports country on the face of this round ball in the sky.

Changing a national mind-set, especially about something as unhallowed as sports, needs to come from the top down, but won't be as easy as lopping off a few heads, as is often the case of rearranging national psyches. However, infinitesimal steps, in the big picture, are not always just small ones. It will take money, and lots of it, and let's let it be said loud and clear, verily trumpeted into our collective mind, we are rich, rich, rich, and we can pay for this if we want. Health-care spending dictates we should indeed want, that ream of scary headlines and statistics and increased payments and waiting times bombards us daily. There's already dozens of books on the subject and they don't make for pleasant reading.

Desire a convincing display of total health in action? Log on to the COC's website and read about the "Role of COC" to find an A-1 blueprint on how to achieve it. But now read this, from the COC's website in the recent past, an even more passionate argument:
*COC on value of sport*

*The Canadian Olympic Committee also advocates on behalf of its partners in the sport community for improvements to the structure of the sport system in Canada and increased government funding for amateur sport. Following is the COC position on increasing investment for sport in Canada.*

*1. Sport is not separate and distinct from other cultural activities but is as much a part of Canadian cultural life as any of the arts. In fact, a case could be made that sport as culture is the most encompassing of all Canadian cultural activities. In addition, daily physical activity is crucial to a balanced life.*

*2. High performance sport and broad based recreation programs are not mutually exclusive. In fact, they are reciprocally supportive. Our high performance programs need the maximum number of young Canadians to be active in sport at an early age to help identify those with the potential to pursue athletic excellence at its highest level.*

*Conversely, our elite athletes create role models for young Canadians and inspire many to become more involved in a broad range of physical activity. We need to increase our investment in both in Canada.*

*3. High performance sport is not asking for a handout from government but rather an investment with a very demonstrable return. Why invest in sport? Four reasons:*

*a. Numerous studies have shown that a more active society will place less demands on our health care system and dramatically reduce government spending on healthcare. Disproportionate dollars are currently spent on redressing the manifestations of an unhealthy lifestyle. Increased investment in sport can create lifestyle changes that subsequently save Canadian taxpayers money at a significant multiple of the original investment.*

*b. High performance sport activity in Canada generates significant economic activity and employment. Communities that attract major international sporting events know there is a net economic gain for their city that goes beyond the duration of the event itself.*

*c. Young Canadians who commit their lives to excellence in sport do so not only for their own personal accomplishment but that of their country. Their passion for excellence enhances all of our lives and their ongoing contribution to Canada is profound.*

*d. Nothing unites and excites Canadians more than the shared celebration of the success of our athletes on the international stage. An investment in their potential is an investment in the health of our national psyche.*

*4. High performance sport requires increased funding because preparing an athlete to compete at the highest level on the world stage takes more than raw talent and a dream. Progress occurs in small increments over a long period of time. Some of the factors that are key to that progress are:*

*a. Coaching We need to be able to attract, develop and retain the best coaches and high performance directors to provide the technical expertise and external motivation it takes to permit an athlete to achieve his/her maximum potential.*

*b. Technology Those sports with a technical or equipment component must be able to keep up with technical developments in their sport if they are going to compete and win when the point of differentiation between first and tenth can often be finite.*

*c. Travel To compete and train with the best. Whether fencers to central Europe or table tennis and badminton players to southeast Asia, our athletes need to be exposed to top level competition on a frequent basis if they are going to hone their skills to win consistently at this level.*

*d. Sport science and medical research We need to invest more in collaborating with institutes of higher learning on research related to sport physiology, bio-mechanics and other areas in order to provide our high performance programs with a broader knowledge base upon which to build their programs.*

*e. Athlete services Our sport centres need to expand their capacity to help more athletes with the broad range of services they need: performance enhancement teams, sport psychology, massage and physiotherapy, and career and educational counselling amongst others. In addition, they need to evolve in the direction of becoming true facilities based institutes that can bring all the elements of a culture of excellence together.*

*f. Facilities Our top athletes need to be able to train and compete in facilities that mirror those they experience at international competitions. In addition, it's important that Canada be able to attract major competitions. The inadequacy and scarcity of training and competitive facilities in many parts of Canada, particularly Ontario, has to be addressed if we are going to move our high performance program forward.*

*5. We need to bring about changes in our sport system that will result in enhanced performance at Olympic Games and major international events.*

*a. Get more money into the system to support athletes, coaches, NSFs and Canadian sport centres as discussed above.*

*b. Change the delivery and administrative mechanism that currently sees Sport Canada unable to circumvent the existing bureaucratic constraints that delay delivery of money into the system that has been already announced politically.*

*c. Create a series of facilities based sport institutes across*

*Canada that will facilitate a culture of excellence and provide the full range of support athletes need to focus on success while creating for them a holistic life environment. The closest we have to this now in Canada is in Calgary. We should work aggressively with CODA to further invest in and fine-tune this model and then roll it out to four or five other regions in the country.*

*d. We need to continue to aggressively evaluate our programs and focus on those that demonstrate the best current results as well as future potential for success. This means not only targeting resources such as those from the COC's Excellence Fund. It also means sharing what we know and learn with all sports and drawing on as broad a knowledge base as possible to enhance all programs. We should also integrate the sport and program review processes of the COC, CODA and Sport Canada to bring a clearer focus to our objective and reduce the administrative burden of NSFs.*

*e. We need to create clear and demonstrable targets! That which gets measured gets done. The Winter Sport focus on "Own the Podium" is a fine example. We need to establish measurable goals and build programs to achieve them.*

If I've gained any adherents to this point, they may have noticed that in this most admirable of mission statements; not once does the word university appear. Just sigh along. While it is difficult to criticize the CIS because even the bad guys are good people, the organization as a whole never tried to join the elite athletic achievement team.

That betrayal aside, how to attain, read pay, for this envisioned utopia? Not particularly business-oriented, I read business columnists to keep abreast in general terms, one of my favourites being Michael Campbell, brother of B.C. Premier Gordon. He writes for the Vancouver Sun and provides comment on local Global TV.

From, "Ours is not in any way a gold medal sort of country," subhead, "Excellence is elitist and un-Canadian," August 28, 2004, on the red-faced, 12-medal haul in Athens: "Mark me down as one who fears that the concepts of hard work and sacrifice so evidenced by our athletes put them in the minority in Canada. After all the lectures we've endured on "Canadian values" over the past couple of months, I challenge you to find a single incidence where competitive excellence was mentioned."

From, "Why not legislate a half-hour of exercise", Dec. 4, 2004, on the flourishing health care system: "Once you start thinking about the possibilities of ridding society of unsafe and unhealthy behaviour it becomes kind of fun. For those who believe we can legislate our way to nirvana there is no end to the possibilities of passing legislation in order to save people from themselves."

Susan Riley is an op-ed writer for the Ottawa Citizen, a capital city struggling to develop a sports identity. On August 4, 2004, she wrote, under the headline, "We're not a nation that values athletes":

*There is a curious distance between Canada's miserable performance at recent Olympic Games – a trend that appears to be holding in Athens – and ever-increasing participation by the population at large. Arguably, we have become the 60-year-old Swede. When I was a teen in the 1960s, most of my friends' parents limited their sporting activities to golf, curling, bowling, or in special cases, downhill skiing. By and large, these were things to do while drinking beer. Nobody's Mom jogged, no one rode a bicycle beyond the age of 15. Cross-country skiing was a niche interest, pursued by Nordic types wearing corduroy knickers and reindeer sweaters.*

*Nowadays, middle-aged boomers, and even seniors, are kayaking, mountain biking, snow-shoeing, rock-climbing and road cycling in record numbers – if crowds at Mountain Equipment Co-op are any guide. On a demanding recent cycle trip through Quebec – a tour that covered 658 kilometres in seven days – almost 50 percent of the 2,000 participants were between 45 and 54 years old.*

*This is not the demographic from which future Olympic champions are drawn, of course. Age aside, weekend athletes, who pursue their sport for pleasure and fitness rather than for glory, are a different species than the disciplined professionals who dedicate their lives to competition. Whether we are more healthy than our parents is also an open question. A 2002 survey by Statistics Canada says the proportion of people active in their leisure time grew by 21 per cent, to 41 percent, between 1994/95 and 2000/01. But over the same period, the number of obese adults increased by 24 percent to one in every seven.*

*Still, there is a contradiction between the increase in general activity among middle-class, middle-aged urban Canadians and the sorry image we present to the world every four years or so. We have established that we are good at sports. But we are not a serious threat, consistently, in any summer sport except, sometimes, rowing.*

*When we do win medals, it is often in obscure or emerging sports – synchronized diving, the triathlon or one of the wrestling sub-*

*categories. This is not an insult to our athletes, who are as dedicated and hard-working as any. Instead, it is another indictment of our neglect in developing athletes, our failure to support them and their families in their formative years, or to provide the venues and international competition that allow the best to flourish. Without reprising the familiar arguments that follow every disappointing Olympic performance, the simple truth remains: Canada doesn't value sporting excellence enough to provide serious financial support at every level. Until we do, smaller countries like Australia, which styles itself as a sporting nation, will continue to outspend and outperform us, and smaller, Nordic countries will beat us in winter sports. The rationale that our best athletes are drawn to pro hockey is outdated – and never applied to women.*

*Some argue against a focus on elite competition, and dismiss the Olympics as corrupt, drug-ridden and overtly commercial. They have a point: Watching the aggressive glee of the U.S. men's relay team after their swimming gold, you have to wonder, fairly or not, if it was fuelled by simple joy or something more sinister.*

*But individual events and performances can still inspire – among others, that large and growing cadre of Canadians who pursue their athletic goals at a more humble level. Anyone who has experienced the exhilaration of two hours on skis on a crisp winter day, bounced along a challenging bike trail, swum the lake or run a marathon can at least imagine exceptional performances.*

*We are not a nation of couch potatoes and the Miss Congeniality award is not enough. We need to support the arts, we need to spend more on sports. They aren't frills; they are essential to a balanced life and a growing number of ordinary voters understand this viscerally."*

Thanks, folks, one can never have enough corroboration when it's time for a revolution. All along the campaign trail but not at the watchtower it wasn't hard finding it — there are no end of qualified supporters, all one has to do is go searching.

Sometimes it's fun to let others do your thinking for you. Google Socrates and you get 15 million hits. Among the scourings:

"Socrates exercised his own body and recommended that others do so also. Xenophon records how he counselled Epigenes, who was out of shape, on the value of physical training. Epigenes rationalizes that he is not an athlete, but Socrates points out that in case of war it is those in bad condition who are killed or disgrace themselves, while the physically fit fight valiantly and can help their friends. Even though military training is not required by the state, he ought to consider the advantages of good health due to physical conditioning. Bad conditioning and bad health can even lead to loss of memory, depression, discontent, and insanity."

"In Plato's Republic we have Socrates' polished view of gymnastics and its relation to music. He suggests that training begin in early years and continue through life. Socrates reminds his listeners that it is the soul which improves the body, and not the reverse. Discipline of bodily habits is especially important for the guardians of the state. This would prohibit excessive sleep, fancy dinners, courtesans, and other luxuries. They should have no need of lawyers and doctors who invent names for diseases and prolong illnesses by pampering them."

"The traditional view was that gymnastics was for the body and music for the soul. However, Socrates here indicates that the purpose of exercise was not just to build muscles, but to stimulate the courageous spirit. Socrates describes the danger of too much gymnastics without music as a harsh and ferocious temper, while the opposite extreme leads to softness and effeminacy. By balancing the two together the philosopher will be gentle yet strong."

From a pair of research papers picked up from SIRC Sport Research, a Canadian sports best-kept secret.

*The Promotion of Health Through Physical Education and Athletics in Plato*

*At about 387 Plato returned to Athens and founded the Academy at a place of exercise in the outskirts of Athens. The Academy then was a major gymnasium, sacred to the hero Academus. Training in music and gymnastics was regarded by Plato as a complete education in virtue. Actually, he asks the question "what is education" and the answer is "music and gymnastics".*

*God, Plato believed, gave two arts to human beings music and gymnastics so that they might be harmonized with one another by being tuned to the proper degree of tension and relaxation. One should always exercise both his mind and body for the sake of health and harmony. Plato placed physical education among the goods of life that are hardships and yet are useful and advantageous to all of us.*

*The word "gymnasium" means a place where men exercised naked, since nudity was a common practice in Greek athletics. The influence of gymnasia was by no means confined to physical education only. They, as well made an enormous contribution to philosophy and the arts.*

*The Promotion of Health Through Physical Education and Athletics in Aristotle:*

*Aristotle believed that physical education and general activity is absolutely essential to the growth and health of children. Aristotle recommended light exercises till the age of puberty, followed by a period of three years spent in study, which should be followed in turn by a period of hard exercise and proper diet. This, according to Aristotle, is the best system.*

*Aristotle recommended that physical education should last for a longer period than the instruction of all other subjects, including literary and musical studies. In addition, he favoured physical exercises, because he believed that "a beautiful, strong and healthy body is conducive to a sound mind." The body should be trained before the mind, he contended, but the exercises should be of such a nature as not to prevent the proper growth of the children or cause problems to their health. He not only recommended the precedence of physical training to mental training but also pointed out that boys should not occupy both their minds and their bodies at the same time because these two kinds of labour are opposed to one another, the labour of the body impedes the mind, and the labour of mind the body.*

*Aristotle's emphasis on competitive games and victory is evident throughout his writings. The young, he says, are ambitious of honour but more so of victory. They desire superiority, and victory is a kind of superiority. Their desire for both superiority and victory is greater than their desire for money, to which they attach only the slightest value, because they have never yet experienced it. Victory, he argues, is pleasant; competitive games must be so too, for victories are often gained in them.*

*The intellectual abilities, Aristotle believed, are always influenced by the state of the body.*

In March of 2005, Canadian Olympian Rick Say spoke as part of an athlete's panel at PacSport's day-long "Business of Sport" seminar directed to the 2010 Winter Olympic Games. When asked why American support of its Olympians makes ours' look puny by comparison, his was a precise response, "Because it's not part of our culture."

Back to alpine skiing, and Ken Read. "The lessons learned from [the 2005 world championships in] Bormio demonstrate we are on track with the support of our elite athletes as they aim for the podium and in athletic development to nurture the next generation towards building that team of 22 athletes aiming for the top 12 or better every day.

"The results show how far we have come, yet how far Canada has to go in order to become a world leading racing country by 2010. We must and will find the resources required to gain a level playing field with the Austrians and Americans. There is still a lot of work to do. On the sport sciences technology front, we need to be exploring where we can gain the edge in equipment. In programming, the athletes need more support to physical conditioning and to push the envelope in year-round, on-snow training to prepare for tough courses.

"We must attract new sponsors and launch fundraising initiatives to find the $2-$3 million more annually that will level the playing field and allow Canada to deliver a program and team that will not only be competitive with the world's best, but be the world's best. Canadians were going for it, racing for gold and taking chances. Along the road to Torino [Olympics], there will be mistakes and hard lessons learned, but the will to go for number one is an essential element of delivering success in ski racing. Pushing the edge has become part of the culture of this Canadian team."

Bormio's world championships was Canadian podium-free, a few years removed from the 2002 Salt Lake City Olympics where the ski team performed dreadfully and the entire men's speed team coaching staff was canned. Sorry ski buffs, but Torino was another Canadian podium-free performance, alpine wise.

Jennifer Heil, Canada's ace mogul skier, Torino gold medalist, on it being OK to want to win gold. "As Canadians, we value the success of someone who makes it to the Olympics. But it's OK to want to win. We need to want to do more than just making it there. In the end, it's not necessarily about the gold medal; it's about doing everything you can do leading up to the Olympics and doing your best at the Olympics … There have been Canadians in the spotlight who came through and won — Jean-Luc Brassard, Catriona Lemay-Doan … it can be done and is done by us Canadians. But we have to continue to be focused on trying to reach the podium and not be afraid to say it."

Who is responsible for this mess, this crime of sport neglect? We are, all of us, so we must pay. I know, I know, that means another tax, and let's face it, what isn't taxed these days, even obliquely? Ask that question and you seldom get quick answers. It's like going for one on a Google.

So I say try government spending. It's all our money anyway, think of it as the ultimate tax refund. A one-time, one percent tax on federal, provincial, territorial and municipal government expenditures in 2005 dollars is roughly $5.5 billion, and there you have the endowment fund to tackle our previous shortcomings and help save the planet. Hyperbolic humour doesn't always work, exaggeration and repetition usually do. I'll still give it a go. At least save our country.

We start with our most renewable resource and our biggest asset, kids. On the campaign trail and representing a bandwagon of one I offer up the clumsy slogan "Sports Education Endowment Debate, the $5.5 Billion Question", which once passed into law by every level of government in the country nicely undergoes metamorphosis, one of nature's greatest achievements, into the $5.5 Billion Answer, "Sports Education Endowment Deal," SEED for our purposes from here on in. Those being the most complimentary part to life, you'd be amazed at how far you can make $5.5 billion in SEED-money go if you spend only spend $500 million of it the first year. Forever is the answer. Buckle up. Here we go.

The core of the disconnect in Canadian sport is the dearth of support in the form of athletic scholarships in our universities. This has distanced sport's greatest physical and mental resource from we, its people. In Canada, sports scholarships are a double hole in the doughnut, first within the university system, itself the hole in the doughnut of Team Canadas. It's the single-biggest problem in the elite sports delivery system. It shouldn't be that way. It hasn't always been that way. When it wasn't, and isn't to this day, great things occur in Canadian sport. This is where we plant the first seed, spend the first money. In 2004-05, $5 million in AFA was awarded to the 10,000 CIS varsity athletes, an average of $500 per, stop laughing, you've already read the numbers and they don't lie.

To be "fair," those self-same athletes received another $5 million in academic assistance, boosting the average per to a whopping $1,000 a year. Laughable. We make it $200 million annually, an average of $20,000 per, no varsity athlete left behind, in exchange for a first 2.5 million hours of community service from these very self-same scholarship students, one arena being pre-teen physical education, either in school or club. If every varsity sport in Canadian universities is covered, there goes "salary-cap" fears, recruiting fears, tiering fears, equity fears. Now what else was the CIS scared of? Oh, yes, Basket-weaving 101 grads.

Right.

But if the universities addressed this so-called problem themselves, as some do to the tune of exceptional, then what's to worry? Funnily enough, Ontario stands to gain the most, just to bury any lingering hard feelings. None of the invective I've hurled at the province or some of its people has been meant to provoke said hard feelings. In the words of Calgary's Dale Henwood, "I've said this to my colleagues and they don't necessarily like it. I'm interested in trying to get Canadian athletes on the podium, we're Canadian as opposed to anywhere or thing else. At the end of the day, I want Canada to do well. Do I want Calgary to do well? Sure I do. I want Canada to do well, I won't care if Calgary does well, per se. Now that's my job, is to make sure athletes in this area are doing well, but I want Canada to do well."

It's a bold step to break from a sorry past and of course there are other directions one could take, say baby-steps. You could, let's say, request presentations from CIS member institutions for new monies to develop their sports and make them offer original presentations, in other words, not a single guideline on what has to be in the presentation, no money limits, nothing, each one to be judged on its own merit, which of course runs counter to current day Canadiana, but which will force each university to aggressively market itself and its aims, goals and ambitions in order to be eligible.

Who's to judge? Whoever signs the cheques, but there's more of the Canadiana conundrum, in our politically correct world today, who is considered qualified? Everyone gets attacked. We need our universities bullish on sport, not bullying it. Who is the CIS responsible to? Certainly not the Feds, they've never been able to make them budge in this matter. When was the last time you heard our universities come under serious attack? Certainly not from the provinces, who merely handed over a collective few billion dollars to them last year. Let's compare the student egg-heads' athletic regimes to the mix, you know, the geeks, the sports is not my bag type, airily more concerned with the "loftier" pursuits of the mind. Their collective genius has certainly solved all the world's problems. I'd say those few types lower the humanities standards of any university, in whose libraries sports research is undertaken in the Social Sciences stacks.

Under Bruce Kidd's not-a-penny-more for elite sport thinking, we would have a state-subsidized basketball league for ambidextrous people under five foot five. Don't the unchallenged have the right to opportunity? We're talking a clash with way too many pasts, not of civilizations, here. To the element within the CIS sphere that to this day belittles by refusing to adequately support the education of Canadian athletes: Get out, get out, get out of the way. Anti-sports scholarships powers need to get with the picture, the national picture, instead of playing Raging Bull in their little pasture. A level field for every university in the country — each with the wherewithal to offer full rides to each and every one of its varsity athletes — means no more pussy-footing around, and settling once and for all this issue which has bedeviled university and consequently Canadian sport since Canadian time immemorial.

To the anti-sports scholarship pooh-bahs, when I enter the sports world I generally encounter hail fellow well met. It's as true of Special Olympians as it is of its academics. As for the past 100 years of CIAU/CIS, they did as well as could reasonably be expected given the constraints of fate. In order for them to be forgiven, changes must occur. Not only must we fund our elite athletes' university educations, not only must we encourage every last one of them to attend post-secondary education, we must simultaneously create a huge pool of them by presenting every first-day kindergarten student with the tools to do both. Consider it the most benevolent of brain-washings of vulnerable young minds as we help them improve their current grade of D for fitness and save a world's fortune in health-care costs.

Step Two requires another $200 million annually. The rationale comes courtesy of Nancy Greene-Raine and brings with it another 2.5 million hours of community service supporting the development of physical literacy in Canada's youth.

"If you need to be a university graduate to teach elementary school children to exercise then the chances of getting enough teachers to do that is not high. But why wouldn't you be able to take physical education, or take a different name for it, don't even call it physical education, as a one-year course, two-year course, three-year course, take summer programs and eventually get your degree," whatever subject matter that degree might be in. "I mean, the kids are suffering, kids need an hour [a day] because they're not getting anything, they're all fat."

But Nancy, what about the current emphasis on not damaging a kid's self-esteem by forcing the athletically-challenged into PE? "No, but if you start physical education at kindergarten …"

Theoretically you are more likely than not to have a fat kid at 14?

"Exactly."

Thank you so much Madamoiselle Female Athlete of the Century, now Chancellor of Thompson River University in Kamloops, B.C.

That first year, our universities scholar 10,000 of those inclined on the rudiments of the education process and the rudiments of exercise as play, the next year they flood into elementary schools on a daily basis, take their coffee, tea or fruit juice and bagged lunches in the staffroom, take note school teacher hiring practitioners. We instil mandatory hour-long PE, K-12. It has to be done. For every athlete we turn out we will turn out millions more healthy high school graduates. We will turn out 10,000 such teachers annually. Some will stay as such teachers, some won't, some will emerge as physics teachers. Some will emerge as coaches, some won't. It's young blood into the professions, all the professions.

Those two steps requires $400 million, and we casually add another $100 million to fund the management of SEED, which is much more than required but ensures every well-oiled link in the chain is secured to its partners, spare parts well stocked in reserve. The remainder, by far the bulk of that $100 million, is offered up to amateur sport, come one, come all, to get romantic here, applications for funding not only appreciated but requested. It would be a support fund extraordinaire for any aspect of sport: for communities, organizations, individuals, NSOs, SGBs that need just little bit of extra cash now and then on top of their annual budgets to do the job right. For pre-schools and day cares, minor sports associations, the burgeoning number of high school sports academies, the latter of which just about says it all. For each and every Canadian post-secondary institute, academic, vocational, artistic: Why can't an Olympic boxer be a university grad, why can't a cellist have a vocation for long-distance running or cross-country skiing, why can't a natural-born mason make a great weightlifter?

In a sardonic nod to those people who decry every increase in sports funding, you've already lost. Measured by per capita spending, Canada is one of the most generous in the world, as in most fields of human endeavour. It's just been poor shopping. In a sardonic slap atcha, SEED money is only a topping to every single last cent already being spent. Not only does it fill in the holes of the middle of two doughnuts, it catches the slips or blips in the system and assists their reintegration into the mainstream. Say a snowstorm like no other causes Superdome-esque damage to an arena in small town Canada. SEED money is there to help, one and all.

An extra $500 million dollars injected annually into our sports system is an admittedly rather extravagant figure given current spending levels, certain to be considered moronic by some at first glance, but please give a pause to do some math.

At the start of Year One, we have $5 billion remaining from our one-time one percent tax. Upon asking money-knowledgeable types about the process of managing and maintaining an endowment fund of that size, the first response I got was, boy, you've sure got to pick the right people to manage it. The second response was it is technically easy if you know what you're doing. Both elemental truths, mathematics is a field grounded in it. Informed that in today's economic environment one might reasonably expect to earn a return on investment of 6-7%, we'll take the higher guesstimate, on the basis of proposed sound management, which on $5 billion invested is a quick $350 million, leaving $150 million in fresh SEED money required annually to ensure perpetual motion.

It's not hard to think of a quick answer to that kind of money, not in a country in which the first lottery ever introduced came while Iona Campagnolo held court as Sports Minister to help defray the costs of the 1976 Montreal Olympics. At that time, the nay-sayers saw lotteries as a threat to society, today governments see the loss of them as threats to balanced (or surplus) budgets. Lotteries are among the most optional of all taxes on the social system, thus yet another one but a better one: all proceeds are SEED, not government, money. Sport by sport "athons" on Canada's new statutory sports holiday, the third Monday of February, puts the contribution process into our children's hands, too. It really isn't hard to think of ways to inject income into an endowment fund. Books have been written on the subject.

Big numbers need not be scary. To clarify, the afore totalled 5 million hours of "community service" derives from the conditions of 10,000 annual SEED sports scholarships and 10,000 annual SEED education scholarships, all of which provide $20,000 to a recipient, $15,000 towards academic costs, $5,000 towards their contributing 250 hours apiece of community service that doubles as the part-time job required by the vast majority of university students. They earn it, SEED pays it, the sports and education systems A-Z benefits, as we combine our best and brightest 18-22-year-olds athletes with the upcoming generation, loving those links, remembering that the average age of a Canadian Olympian in Athens was 27.

Oh yes, lest we forget, the CIS is already contributing $5 million of that $200 million. There's a nice 0.5% extra fat in the system right there. Sorry. Annually assisting 10,000 prospective athletes into the system will both expand and cement the width and breadth of SEED's mandate. Annually assisting 10,000 prospective teachers into the system will both expand and cement the width and breadth of SEED's mandate. In essentially every study of Canadian sport ever done, the need for improved coaching is the one constant. Only a miniscule number of those with Olympic aspirations ever get to inhale that sweet smell of ultimate success. Sport provides myriad opportunities to a myriad of types. You can bet your bottom dollar nearly all will emerge as our next generation of leaders coast to coast. Young blood into old professions.

In further defence of SEEDing, I'm going to run some fun facts and figures past you, campaign literature you might say.

*** The field of sports employment is booming, please take note educators.

*** In the 2006 Torino Winter Olympics, arguably Canada's best ever, our medal haul trailed only Germany and the United States. And we're already falling behind. A 2002 New York Times article examined the approach to sports taken by the now table-topping Germans, born of reunification. East Germany's incredibly successful but drug-maligned system has been adopted by the new Germany, minus the drugs. Four years ago, the country injected US$1 billion into elite sports academies for their youth, and don't you just love the reason: "With the opportunities and distractions of a wealthy market economy, officials fear that it will be increasingly difficult to attract and encourage athletic talent. We're losing them to the discos," said Armin Baumert, the German Sports Federation official in charge of developing the schools.

***A recent Senate review of the CBC proposed it drop "Hockey Night in Canada" as that is professional sport and thus the domain of private, not public broadcasters. Bruce Kidd you not. Because of under-funding the CBC has always struggled, so let's get rid of its biggest money maker. The Senate is appointed not elected, more's usually the pity in cases like this, but not for this SEED cause. Following Senate reasoning, amateur sport is the domain of public broadcasters, thus suddenly we have hundreds upon hundreds of hours of CBC broadcast time available for CIS and local sport, province by province. It would help sell the cause, because the private broadcasters aren't doing the job, which according to the Senate isn't theirs anyway.

***Two years ago the NCAA produced a TV commercial that ran like this: A short women's basketball player at a major university spoke of her career by mentioning she was a fourth-year philosophy student and that sometimes thinking too much isn't beneficial to just naturally playing the game. Cute. The kicker of that ad was that of the 365,000 NCAA grads every year, less than 1% turn professional in their sport.

*** In 1992, former CFL Commissioner Doug Mitchell, then managing partner of Calgary law firm Howard Mackie, founded the Howard Mackie Awards, which reward the country's top student-athletes with substantial post-graduate and athletic financial aid. Today, Howard Mackie is part of Borden Ladner Gervais LLP, the country's largest national law firm, which now sponsors the annual event each spring. "Our number one intent was to give a focus to university athletics in Canada. A part of that would be to say, yes, it can be big league, and you can be a part of it if you stay in Canada," said Mitchell, 15 years after the first BLG Awards were handed out. Since then, 17 nominees became Olympians, including 2003 winner Team Canada goalie Kim St-Pierre (McGill), while 2005 winner Jesse Lumsden (McMaster) is now starring for the CFL's Hamilton Tiger-Cats. "I think it has got identification beyond what we thought it would have in the universities, but in an indirect way. I don't think you could ever directly say how many people have been encouraged to stay in Canada because there is a major award they can aspire to," Mitchell forthrightly admits, "but where I have seen an impact is that it certainly has worked for us from a corporate standpoint." Any other blue chips out there listening?

***Thought through to its logical conclusion, SEED money could enable universities to generate the funds themselves, thus eventually taking them out of the financial grant equation altogether.

***One of the acknowledged goals of spending SEED money is more medals won in every Games we enter, perhaps, especially, improving our incredibly woeful results from Universiades.

\*\*\*SEED money recipients will earn their way, teaching and assisting our youth, en route to developing that resourcefulness as a source of national strength.

\*\*\*SEED money can assuage the fears of the intelligentsia. Although it will be awhile until that's fully achieved, it's up to the education system to figure out how to make use of millions of hours of labour from thousands upon thousands of eager beavers every year, scott free. I am no expert but I know the right attitude about sports can aid the education system, it's not really its fault we don't have it right now. This isn't about condemning current education policy. SEED money and efforts are but adjuncts, with the eventual aim of enshrining in one and all a sports-assists-life mentality.

\*\*\*Attention hockey fans and anti-Americans. SEED money presents a gift to the NCAA and American hockey moms and dads by repatriating all our players ASAP. Here you go, our American cousins-in-pucks, more openings for you. Then we challenge 'em in one-off series every year, men's and women's. Hmm, sounds like hockey worth watching by millions to me.

\*\*\*No athlete can train all the time, nor should any scholar only study. The fact the former is true demands the latter. The elements of discipline in each endeavour mesh perfectly. The community service required of SEED scholarship recipients is a smooth a fit to either. SEED graduates are Canada's future backbone.

\*\*\*If nothing else, SEED money can assist in the resurrection of the University of Toronto Blues football team, which hasn't won a game in years and years. SEED money can restore the imbalance between West and East in today's CIS: universities east of the wall building up along the border with Manitoba have long won less than their proportional share of CIS national championships. Ontario, our biggest and most populated province, benefits the most, but at no other's expense.

\*\*\*"I had one scholarship offer, and I didn't have any NBA players in my neighbourhood. I don't even think I dreamed about this," said Steve Nash after winning his first NBA MVP award. Said Jay Triano, former Canadian national team coach, "I think it is one of the greatest achievements in the history of Canadian sports." Is he referring to the scholarship offer?

\*\*\*SEED money is nothing but an adjunct to every existing municipal, provincial, federal, organizational initiative, repeat, SEED money is nothing but an adjunct to every existing municipal, provincial, federal, organizational initiative on the athletic side. Everything else, really, is already established or appears to be falling into place under Podium Canada, which the federal government announced to trumpeting silence in 2006: "Podium Canada is a partnership between the major national funding partners for high-performance sport in Canada: Sport Canada, the COC, the CPC, and VANOC. Podium Canada's role, as an advisory body, will be to make funding recommendations to the national funding partners based on expert analysis and to help NSOs implement their technical programs. Finally, Podium Canada will monitor NSOs' implementation of their high-performance programs to ensure maximum performance results."

***VANOC is facing heat these days over the cost of staging the 2010 Winter Games. Studies during the bid process predicted $10 billion in direct economic activity, twice as much as the SEED fund, the creation of 228,000 direct and indirect jobs in the province, and up to $2.5 billion in incremental tax revenue in the run-up to 2010, half the entire SEED fund. And still there are vociferous, indignant nay-sayers of the Games, more dandelions seeds come to roost.

***SEED doesn't disparage professional sport. One need only look at the number of Canadians playing Major League Baseball today compared to the pre-Expos and pre-Jays days to see an example of what, if given the opportunity, a program with excellence as its peak can produce. Behind every one of those Canadian baseball success stories is an army of individuals, in this case mostly ball fans, imbued with the values of sport. Can you say Trail's Jason Bay, whose sister Lauren is an ace pitcher for the women's national fastball squad, Trail, originator of Minor Hockey Week in Canada and which was the first Canadian Little League champion to feature a girl on its squad, ace pitcher Stephanie Davidson no less.

***SEED money is available to the burgeoning number of high school sports academies across the country. These are far, far more than just jock factories. At one of British Columbia's most respected high schools, Sentinel High School in West Vancouver, District Principal Diane Nelson has brought one to fruition that purposely shies away from the elite athlete. Her multi-sport academy is based on the value of a heavy dose of sports every school day to create better students, academically, better citizens socially. Imagine then the smile on her face when one of those mediocre athletes "graduated" from her academy as a Western Hockey League draftee.

***SEED money funds Dr. Roger Jackson and Mark Lowry's

Business Plan for Excellence, which the government failed to move forward, as was expected, in its 2007 budget.

Try turning full circle. Ask any gymnast, figure skater, synchronized swimmer, diver or trampolinist and it's no problem. Ask a downhill skier, it's not so easy.

But here we go, full circle from the formation of the national ski team at Notre Dame to $5.5 billion in SEED money. In 2005, this was part of an e-mail received from a COC staffer with sympathetic ears.

*David Skinner*
*Former Executive Director of Alpine Canada*
*Letter sent to AIH - CBC Radio - As It Happens.*
*Dear Sir:*

*I listened with interest to your articles concerning Canadian Swimming aired on Tuesday night on AIH. Writing from the (now retired) perspective of over 25 years as a professional leader in Canadian sport (including the 80's decade as a senior executive for Canada's Alpine Ski Team), I submit that the problems in swimming are symptomatic of more global issues within Canadian sport, which were forecast by many over a decade ago.*

*Of all the overriding issues, misunderstood by the media, the public and our political and corporate leaders, is the critical fact that high performance athlete development must be a long term investment. With some exceptions, it generally takes between 10 and 15 years for an athlete to reach the levels of physical, technical and emotional maturity required to compete at world levels.*

*The evidence supporting this is most clear from our recent Olympic results. In the wake of the 1988 doping scandal, the two year hiatus of the Dubin inquiry followed by the Chrétien/Martin cuts and freezes of the early 90's, the sport funding tap (both public and private) was reduced to a trickle during most of the 90's. Many predicted then that the inevitable performance consequences would be evident 10 years later ... and they were correct.*

*One only has to look at the names of successful Canadian athletes during the Olympics of the 90's to see that those athletes almost all entered the Canadian sport development system a decade earlier when it was relatively well funded under the impetus of the Calgary Olympics.*

*While there has been much talk about the need for more money, I believe it is much more important that future sport funding*

*policy address some broader principles, that might be encapsulated in*
*an acronym I propose called S.L.A.P.;*

> *\* Funding must be SUSTAINED*
> *\* Funding must be LONG TERM*
> *\* Funding must be ASSURED*
> *\* Funding must be (mostly) PUBLIC*

*Unfortunately, with the short lifespan and turnover of our*
*elected governments, such long term, sustained and assured funding*
*never happens. The Canadian sport system arguably boasts more*
*dusty, shelved and unactioned pages of study and more Ministers of*
*State (try naming them all) over the past 25 years than any other*
*Public/NGO partnership in the country, rendering a sad reflection of*
*the priority of sport in our society.*

*Unless steps are taken to build these funding principles into the*
*fabric of the Canadian sport system, we will continue to oscillate*
*between boom and bust. In short the Canadian sport system needs a*
*good SLAP!*

*Regards*

*David J Skinner*

Never met the man, but slap on, sir.

I could have suggested spending 10 times —$5 billion! — as
much annually on Canadian sport through the education system and it
wouldn't have mattered. This little one-time one percent idea has
about as much chance of taking root and coming to fruition as the CIS
has of turning over a new Maple Leaf any time soon and embracing
scholarship types. My take on things, though, is that until my preferred
slap is a fait accompli Canadian sport won't be taking many major
steps but will just continue perfecting its stutter step.

## The End